SOUNDERS FC:
AUTHENTIC MASTERPIECE
THE INSIDE STORY OF THE BEST FRANCHISE LAUNCH IN AMERICAN SPORTS HISTORY

BY

MIKE GASTINEAU

ISBN: 1491068345
ISBN 13: 9781491068342

Library of Congress Control Number: 2013913312
CreateSpace Independent Publishing Platform
North Charleston, South Carolina

This book is dedicated to the life of Molly Conley (1998-2013).

At the start of the 2012 school year Molly was selling coupon booklets to raise money for her soccer team at Blanchet High School in Seattle. I asked her if the team was going to be any good and jokingly told her I wouldn't buy one unless they were. "I'm pretty sure," she said with the beautiful optimism and conviction of youth, "that we're not going to lose a game."

You were a winner Molly.

FOREWORD
by Grant Wahl
August 19, 2013

I n the final analysis, I was the victim of bad luck. When I lived in Seattle, from 2000 to '04, pro soccer wasn't a very big deal there. Oh, the sport was thriving as a participation activity, with youth and adult leagues all over the city, and I have fond memories of watching games from distant locales at the George & Dragon Pub in Fremont. But in those days the hometown soccer team was hardly a phenomenon. The Sounders USL minor league outfit had some loyal followers, but the memories of gigantic Kingdome crowds and visits from Pelé in the 1970s NASL salad days were long gone.

It's worth pointing out now, in 2013, with the MLS Sounders now five seasons old, averaging more than 40,000 fans a game and creating one of the most festive atmospheres in soccer, anywhere, that none of Seattle's runaway success was inevitable. A number of factors had to come together: a first-class ownership group; a smart start-up strategy; the right people in the right positions, on and off the field; the timing to coincide with the departure of the SuperSonics; and, not least, a supporters culture that is organized and passionate, yet welcoming to new members who've caught the bug themselves.

There will always be some precincts of the U.S. soccer community that shun so-called "outsiders," in the same way that fans of an underground band get all cranky when their guys actually hit it big and go mainstream. Thank God this hasn't happened with Seattle soccer. For the sport to keep growing in America, we need a big tent and fans quick to share a ready smile and a cold pint with anyone who wants to join the flock. That's what I've always seen in Seattle, whether it's at an Emerald City Supporters party at Fuel or at an American Outlaws U.S. fans pregame fest at the

Golazo headquarters in Capitol Hill or at the games themselves. There's a feeling of togetherness that you just don't get in other sports cultures. Why, in 2011 famed Sounder Roger Levesque even stopped by the Fuel pregame party to pay his respects. How often would a Seahawk or Mariner do that?

This is where Mike Gastineau comes in. I've known Gas long enough to be well aware that he wasn't exactly a hardcore soccer fan during most of his years in the radio business. And the fact is, Gas could have dug in his heels and resisted the soccer bug, using the tired old crutches that still plague certain quarters of the established U.S. sports media. There's a safety in sticking with what you know best, in refusing to take on something new and perhaps end up looking foolish in the process. Instead, Gas did the opposite. He learned the sport—no small task, when you think about it—and got just as swept up in the Sounders as so many other Seattleites. Yes, he questioned some soccer verities on occasion, but you know what? They were good questions. His effort to learn *"fútbolese"* has paid off, not just for Gas but for all of us with the release of the book you're about to read. Just about all of us started off not being "soccer guys," but if you stick with it long enough, eventually you become a "soccer guy" without even knowing when it happened. Gas is now a soccer guy.

A good journalist recognizes a dynamite story, and that's exactly what Gas has done with the Sounders. Combining his extensive list of contacts with his innate curiosity and natural interview skills, Gas has asked the right questions and told the tale of the team Seattle fell in love in with. American soccer has so many riveting stories, and they're made even more compelling by the feeling as a writer that you're telling them more or less for the first time. MLS is still at the point in its development that it feels, I imagine, like it did for a writer covering the Super Bowl in the late-1960s, when you could sit next to Joe Namath at the swimming pool in Miami during the days before the Big Game and ask Broadway Joe just about anything.

In the book you're about to read, Gas introduces you to all the major players in the Sounders story, putting you on the ground with Kasey Keller and Adrian Hanauer, Joe Roth and Chris

Henderson, Sigi Schmid and all the rest. He explains how this team not only got off the ground but did so in a way that would become the benchmark for expansion teams in any sport, including soccer. Transitioning from radio-hosting to book-writing is no easy thing, and not many people would be capable of pulling it off. But Mike Gastineau has done so here, leaving us all a historical record of soccer's remarkable Seattle success story.

KICKOFF

March 19, 2009
St. Louis, Missouri

Peter McLoughlin settled into his favorite chair and flipped on the TV. The CEO of the St. Louis Blues needed to do a little late night TV duty tonight. The Blues were in Vancouver to play the Canucks, and the game wouldn't start until after 9 o'clock St. Louis time, which was still an hour away.

There were a handful of East Coast NHL games underway, and it was the opening night of the NCAA basketball tournament so there was plenty of good college basketball to watch. McLoughlin is a fan of all sports, so he naturally began channel surfing. It is physically impossible for a man with a remote to not change channels — even if he's watching something he likes. The reason for this, of course, is that there might be something better on another channel.

Bouncing between hockey and the NCAA tournament, he eventually landed on ESPN2. What he saw there caused him to put the remote down, mesmerized by "the energy coming from the screen."

As an NHL executive, McLoughlin truthfully had little reason to pay close attention to a soccer game across the country. But as a sports executive, he knew a good show when he saw one. As he watched he realized that this was the debut of the new Major League Soccer franchise in Seattle. He was surprised to see they were playing at the Seahawks' stadium and even more surprised by the size, sound, and sight of the crowd.

He stared at the screen in amazement at this spectacle, this stadium packed with fans singing, chanting, waving their scarves, giving off palpable energy for an *EXPANSION* team playing its very first game.

"Tod Leiweke," McLoughlin said out loud to himself. "He did it again."

McLoughlin was referring to the CEO and President of the Seattle Seahawks of the NFL. In his career Leiweke had built a reputation as one of the bright minds in sports management. His latest accomplishment had called for him to forge relationships among several unique parties that resulted in the city finally obtaining an MLS team.

Pulling it off took the faith and cooperation of one of the richest men in the world, one of the most powerful movie executives in Hollywood, and a minor league sports owner who would have to take a big leap into the world of big league sports.

Along the way they'd get help from a former NFL executive who spent much of his NFL days ridiculing anyone who watched soccer. They'd find a coach who had almost become an accountant. They'd build the on-field product around that trickiest of sports stars: the local hero attempting to come home to finish his career on a high.

They'd do their primary customer research not at youth soccer fields in the suburbs, but at dark, beer drenched soccer bars tucked away in various Seattle neighborhoods. They'd form a union with the most dedicated group of sports fans any of them had ever encountered. Then they held their collective breath hoping that union would work. They'd get radical ideas from a comedian/TV star on how to set up the most unique team/fan interaction in American sports.

By the time they opened for business in March of 2009 they had the whole thing wired for success, as evidenced by the scene McLoughlin was watching on TV. The Blues CEO couldn't have known then that 18 months later he'd replace Leiweke in Seattle, taking charge of this stunning sports franchise. When he arrived in 2010 to get a close-up look at how the success had been achieved, he knew for sure that what he watched that night in St. Louis was no mirage.

"I think there was a confluence of a variety of events and a very smart approach to engage the fan base as part of the creation and development of the franchise," he says today. "I think it all came together beautiful with the marketing, the branding, and the authenticity of how the game is played here. I think it was masterfully done."

Call it an Authentic Masterpiece.

**Later that same night
Seattle, Washington**

The engine and the stereo system in Kasey Keller's Porsche roared to life within seconds of each other. As Keller let the engine warm up on the typically chilly last night of winter he let his senses warm up with the full aural assault of the American rock band Tool.

Keller loves music that is fast, hard, and loud. He says he typically listens before and after games to "Tool or even something a little harder." Tool is a terrific band, but on the list of things "a little harder" would be stuff like a derailing locomotive or a succession of bulldozers smashing into a steel wall. Nevertheless this is how Keller chooses to relax after games; a ritual he conducted for years in various exotic and far-flung ports of call.

But tonight was different. In any athlete's career, games become like mileposts on a highway. They fly by and stack up quickly, and before you know it you're where you were going. But some mileposts are bigger than others and tonight's was one such marker. After nearly two decades in England, Spain, and Germany, Keller was home and he couldn't get over how good he felt, nearly overcome with two harmonious emotions: Joy and relief.

He had been the starting goalkeeper in the very first MLS game in Seattle Sounders FC history and he had delivered the best a keeper can do, a sparkling white clean sheet in a 3-nil Sounders victory over New York. The game had been witnessed by a preposterously large crowd of over 32,000 fans and watched by many more on TV. The night had been an unqualified success.

Keller had signed with the Sounders seven months earlier and spent that time helping the new team set a certain tone in everything they did. This game, the opening night in franchise history, was their only chance to make a first impression and Keller wanted everything to go right. He felt the first game was crucial for the franchise to help establish the success they all craved both on the pitch and in the Seattle sports and business community.

Keller also couldn't escape his roots. He was still the kid raised on a farm outside Olympia, Washington. He had gone on to glory in Europe and with the US Men's National Team. But now he was home and it was expected (more by him than anyone) that he would get the job done. That job started unequivocally on opening night.

Like most involved in the sport, Keller spent a lot of time battling the unending tide of American soccer naysayers. Every day from August to March he had pondered what it would sound like if he and the Sounders face-planted in their first game. It's not as if the whole thing was some flimsy house of cards that would come tumbling down with one defeat, but after all the work that had gone into the launch of the team a loss would have been a setback. A blowout loss after the huge buildup would have been devastating.

"There was all the hype for the first game and the last thing I wanted was for people and the media to say 'THAT was what we were excited about? This team getting their asses handed to them 4-nil?' I didn't want people to look at me like 'Oh, yeah… THIS guy is going to help us out.' I felt the first game was crucial. You get off to a good start both personally and team-wise and everything then falls into place."

On March 19, 2009, everything did fall into place for the Sounders. The indefatigable Emerald City Supporters set the tone of the evening early for the sellout crowd. The pageantry of the night went off without a hitch. Fredy Montero wrote himself into legend with his goal in the 11th minute, the only goal the

Sounders would need thanks to great backline play and Keller's work as the final line of that defense.

His journey home would take less than 15 minutes. But the journey he and many others had taken to get to this night was a long winding road and it was only now as the road appeared in the rearview mirror that the decisions made along the way came clearer into view: Some good, some bad, some full of wisdom, others that benefited from the serendipity that seemed to always kiss this project.

What else came into view on this night was a city with a sports community desperate to feel good about itself. "Soccer's really tribal," says Emerald City Supporters member Aaron Reed. "That's the best word you can use for it. It was really the first organized sport historically that was all about the pride of your city."

And by the end of 2008 Seattle's sports pride had been severely beaten down. That year, Seattle fans watched the once-mighty University of Washington football team stagger like a drunken hobo crossing a railroad trestle to an 0-and-12 season. The Seattle Mariners had achieved the dubious distinction of being the first team in baseball history to lose 100 games while spending over $100 million on salary. The NBA Seattle Supersonics no longer existed, pirated off to Oklahoma City after a game of chicken between former owner Howard Schultz and the city's political and business community went disastrously wrong.

In this toxic atmosphere the thought that Seattle, of all places, could be the home of the most successful sports franchise launch in American history was beyond rational belief.

Here's the story of how it happened.

CHAPTER ONE

C

"My goodness, is it loud in here."

He stood near the top of the stadium that he and the Seattle community had agreed (barely) to build together almost a decade earlier, but Paul Allen might as well have been on the top of the world. A private man by nature it wasn't his plan to be the focus of 67,837 fans and national television cameras, but nevertheless there he was standing on a platform on the upper deck of the Seattle Seahawks beautiful home. He had been given the honor of raising the 12th man flag before the NFC Championship game between the Seahawks and Carolina Panthers. A crowd already primed by the magnitude of a championship game was now pushed even louder as they roared their thanks and approval to Allen.

On the national broadcast of the game, fans around the country got a taste of what visiting teams had come to dread at games played in Seattle as the sheer volume of the crowd elicited a memorable opening line from FOX TV's Joe Buck who introduced himself, paused, and then said in voice bordering on yelling: "My goodness, is it loud in here!"

Fans of the Seahawks had waited 30 years for this game and the day played out perfectly in its entirety. The Seahawks scored the game's first 17 points and rolled to a rousing 34-14 triumph. In a city long on sports passion but woefully short on championship moments, this day would be seared into the collective sports soul.

And yet, all of it: Allen's emotional pre game moment, Buck's one-line homage to the loudest fans in football, the team's dominant one-sided win sending the Hawks to the Super Bowl ... all of it might not have happened if it weren't for soccer.

Nestled in between the Cascade and Olympic Mountain ranges, with the Puget Sound carving a sideways "J" shaped waterway out of the surrounding land, and featuring a skyline that on clear days is dominated by Mount Rainier, the city of Seattle is the beautiful equal of any in the world.

The city has thrived as a home to creators and innovators. It is home to world-class restaurants, museums, theaters, and concert halls. But for some reason Seattle has almost always had a stormy, ashtrays-flying-across-the-living room relationship with its professional sports teams.

The city lost a baseball team (the Pilots) to Milwaukee in 1970, nearly lost a second baseball team (the Mariners) to Tampa in 1992, and lost the NBA's Supersonics to Oklahoma City in 2008. All of these stories involved facility disputes between the owners and the city and it was another of those disputes that led to the near departure of the Seahawks.

In terms of high comedy, nothing exceeded the clumsy and ultimately unsuccessful attempted escape masterminded by Seattle Seahawks owner Ken Behring in 1996. A native of California who was a land developer by trade with a big game hunting habit, Behring had never seemed a good fit for the Seattle sports scene. He didn't like the team's stadium (the Kingdome), and after a halfhearted attempt to raise interest in building a new stadium, he decided to take his team to the warmer climes of Los Angeles.

He ordered moving vans to take the team's equipment to Southern California and made plans to play his team's games in Anaheim Stadium. He floated the idea of building a new stadium in partnership with the Angels and even talked of trying to build an NBA arena. But he found no willing takers.

He attempted to explain himself to fellow NFL owners by claiming that the Kingdome would be dangerous in an earthquake. Owners laughed in Behring's face at the idea that a fear of earthquakes could be assuaged by a move to Southern California. They then threatened to fine him heavily if he didn't move the team back to Seattle. That came after Seattle government officials pointed out that Behring's team had a lease requiring them to play games in Seattle, a fact he had apparently overlooked in his haste to flee south.

Foiled in his "California Here I Come" dream, and having thoroughly fouled his own nest in Seattle, Behring wanted out. And in April of 1996 Paul Allen agreed to take the team off his hands, with one contingency: Allen didn't like the Kingdome either, and made striking a deal for a new football stadium a condition of his purchase.

Allen set a deadline of July 1, 1997. If no deal were reached, his option to purchase the team would expire. The team would then revert back to Behring, whose plan might include putting them into bankruptcy, which would make it easier for him to move the team. Regardless, the longer Behring owned the Seahawks, the more precarious their perch in Seattle.

Allen studied his stadium options, which included a remodeling of the Kingdome, a remodeling of Husky Stadium (with the finished product being home to both the University of Washington's football team and the Seahawks), or building a new stadium. He eventually settled on building a new stadium, but he wanted the public's help in paying for it. He offered to buy the team for $200 million and pay an additional $100 million in stadium costs. The public would pick up the remaining $300 million cost for the stadium. The public's contribution could only be made after what was going to be a very difficult two-stage fight. The second stage would be a statewide election in which voters would be asked to tax themselves. But there was an even trickier challenge before that could happen.

First, Allen had to get his proposal through the legislature and onto the ballot. This would not be easy. Angry voters were still regularly blistering state lawmakers over the deal that built a new baseball stadium in Seattle in 1995. The Mariners owners said without a new home they'd be forced to sell the team to out-of-town interests who would no doubt move it away. The original plan for that stadium was to put it on the backs of Seattle taxpayers. That proposal was narrowly defeated at the ballot box, but in a Hollywood style twist the Mariners (for the first time in their history) were actually playing great baseball. In the 1995 season's final weeks improbable victories piled up like lumber at a sawmill and on the final day of the season they caught the Angels and made the playoffs for the first time in their history.

No doubt caught up in the fervor, state legislators put together a new tax package for the stadium that spread the burden among the region. This package wasn't voted on, it was simply approved by the legislature. Voters, predictably, howled, and were still howling two years later when Allen made his offer to purchase the Seahawks contingent upon taxpayer help for a new home. Nervous legislators still being pilloried for their baseball stadium decision would need to be convinced the football stadium was worth risking additional political capital.

LIFELONG SPORTS FAN and Seattle attorney Fred Mendoza read the news of Allen's proposed deal with interest. He was in favor of doing what was necessary to save the city's NFL team, but he also recognized the huge political mountain Allen had to climb. He had some ideas that could help make the stadium a reality.

Mendoza had been working for a few years with other interested parties to put together a plan to obtain a soccer team for Seattle in America's latest try at a national soccer league, Major League Soccer. He had worked primarily with Michael Campbell, who was at the time the chairman of the Seattle Sports and Events Council. Over the course of three years they kept running into the same problem: With no facility deemed worthy of playing host to MLS in Seattle, there was no ownership interest for a team.

Mendoza's idea was simple and obvious: Build the new stadium for a potential soccer team as well as for the Seahawks. He and Campbell set up a meeting to discuss their proposal with Allen and Bert Kolde, who had been named vice president of Football Northwest, the company that had been formed to purchase the Seahawks.

Mendoza and Campbell were just a few minutes into their pitch when Kolde interrupted them. "Gentlemen," Mendoza remembers him saying, "That is a great idea."

Kolde recognized that adding soccer to the mix would add the political clout of an estimated 300,000 Washingtonians who played the game. This would make it easier to get the proposed plan through the legislature, and presumably would make it more likely to pass at the ballot box, too.

"We had found on our own research that the public wanted to know that the stadium was going to have a wider use than just 10 football games a year," Kolde says. "We knew soccer resonated in a special way in Seattle, particularly in the suburbs. We felt that could become a really important base for us."

There were only a few weeks left in the 1997 Washington State legislative session so Mendoza's plan was quickly put into action. With a required sense of urgency he suddenly found himself spending time at the state capitol in Olympia.

"They said 'thank you, you're on board now,' and within a matter of days I was working with a team of consultants, lobbyists, and political advisors. We had to convince the legislature that it was a good thing to do, but I'm just a volunteer. I'm still trying to practice law and my partners kept asking if I was ever coming back to work."

Their efforts to get the bill passed and onto the ballot were successful, but the election would be in June, just two months off. That meant Mendoza would continue dividing his time between his law practice and his new job as a soccer stadium evangelist.

"We had April until June to go pound the grass and that's when we really went to work. Every Monday morning I'm

getting a schedule of events I'm supposed to be at as a representative of soccer. I drove all over the state speaking to soccer
leagues. They had a portable PA system and they'd set up a
little stage. I'd get up on this soapbox and preach the gospel."

As he spent time crisscrossing the state with Kolde and other
Allen representatives, Mendoza came to an obvious conclusion.
"They had decided 'we can't win this without soccer.' They
knew it."

They were right. Fifty-one percent of those eligible voted in
the election and the decision to build the stadium passed by less
than two percentage points. Mendoza's response when asked if
the vote would have been yes without adding soccer to the mix is
doubtless and declarative.

"Oh, God no. No way. It doesn't even come close. If it had not
been for the soccer moms and dads this thing would have died."

"It was a squeaker," Kolde agrees. "We needed soccer. It
powered this thing through. We wouldn't have won it without
that. Not at all."

At a party near where the Kingdome would be replaced by
the new stadium, hundreds of volunteers celebrated on the night
of June 17 when news of the victory came in. Guests were treated
to music by the band "Grown Men," which happened to feature
Paul Allen on guitar. Mendoza was among those at the party,
and if he had any notion that his work was done it would be
short lived.

The new stadium would need a governing body and in July of
1997 Mendoza was appointed as an original member of the board
of directors for the new Public Stadium Authority (PSA). As such
he would work together with the designers, architects, and build-
ers of the new stadium to make sure the public's interest was being served. It was in that capacity that he ended up in a fight that
made the stadium election look like a recess playground spat.

ONE COMPLICATION involving the new football/soccer
stadium was the fact that while the vote happened in June of
1997, construction couldn't begin for another two years. The

stadium would be built where the Kingdome presently stood and the giant concrete structure was also home to the Seattle Mariners who needed to play in it until their new stadium was done in 1999.

While the Mariners could play in the Kingdome as their new stadium was being built across the street, the Seahawks would need a temporary home to play their games for two seasons since to build their new home they would first have to tear down the old one. As luck would have it, there was a suitable place available about four miles from where their new stadium would be built: Husky Stadium at the University of Washington.

Among the upgrades the Seahawks wanted to make at Husky Stadium while they played there for two years was a new field. An emerging French company with an office in Georgia had created a new style of artificial turf called FieldTurf. The latest version of fake grass, FieldTurf was marketed as being the closest artificial turf had come to replicating real grass.

FieldTurf had first been installed in an American stadium in 1999 at the University of Nebraska and received enthusiastic reviews. Interestingly enough, the first professional installation of the product came two years prior to that when English soccer team Middlesbrough FC installed it on a training field.

In 2000 two more schools would join Nebraska (and Middlesbrough) as early customers: Washington State University and the University of Washington. Washington's new field was paid for by the Seahawks, and by the time they had finished one season on the new field they had reached a decision: they wanted their new stadium to have the same surface.

This alarmed Mendoza, who had campaigned for the stadium with the understanding that it would be built with a natural grass playing surface. Up to that point Mendoza had found the Seahawks extremely cooperative on design ideas.

"My board from day one was absolutely all over the Seahawks to keep their promise to soccer. When the designs came out early in 1998, the corners looked too tight for soccer. They had an oval design, which would make it difficult for fans to see the corners of a soccer pitch. I kept saying in meetings 'what about soccer?'"

In an effort to address Mendoza's concerns, Ellerbe Becket (the firm designing the building) sought advice from Salt Lake City-based architect Jim Anderson. Anderson had worked with FIFA officials to help set up the American stadiums used to stage the 1994 World Cup. Mendoza was part of a group that presented the proposed design of the new stadium and asked Anderson for suggestions to make sure the building would be a first-class soccer facility.

Anderson returned the plans with about a half page of suggested changes, including changing the design of the corners from oval to square to better accommodate a soccer pitch. He also made suggestions on camera locations and angles, sightlines, and lighting for the new stadium. Mendoza was thrilled with the reaction in Seattle.

"Ellerbe Becket went back and made all the changes," he says. "Paul and his guys did everything we asked to make this a world-class soccer venue."

For most soccer fans the phrase "world-class soccer venue" would mean a building with a natural grass field. The Seahawks actually preferred grass, too, but had decided FieldTurf made more sense and their argument was not altogether unreasonable.

Seattle sits far enough north that direct sunlight is nothing more than a rumor from Halloween until Easter. Factor in the area's legendary rain and the fact that much of the time when it's not raining it's moist and damp, it became clear that growing and maintaining grass in a stadium used for both football and soccer would be a challenge.

The soccer constituency countered with one small but not insignificant detail. They had voted to tax themselves to build an outdoor stadium with *natural grass*.

"Every piece of literature I have says this was going to be an open air, grass field, football and soccer stadium," Mendoza says, "but the Seahawks wanted Field Turf and pitched the idea to us. It's our building so we have to approve all the design decisions."

Mendoza and the PSA's first response to the Seahawks request for turf was a direct "no." But when asked to keep an open mind on the issue they agreed. The Seahawks had been great partners to soccer and had compromised on issues regarding the stadium to this point and Mendoza felt the least he could do was be considerate of their request. As the playing surface discussion slowly evolved over what was eventually a period of four months he began to see the wisdom of the Hawks request.

"I had seen all the sun studies. It was going to be difficult to grow grass in the stadium due to sun angles. We knew that with two teams you'd end up playing on mud and you'd be replacing the field twice a year."

Mendoza began getting positive feedback from people in the soccer community regarding turf. Legendary Seattle Pacific soccer coach Cliff McCrath and University of Washington coach Dean Wurzburger both agreed turf would work. World soccer governing body FIFA began loosening its strict "no turf" policy and actually began certifying some turf fields for play. FIFA officials told Mendoza that it was likely the new turf field in Seattle would be approved for every kind of match up to but not including the World Cup final.

Mendoza weighed both sides of the debate. The Hawks' request had common sense on its side and a growing willingness within the soccer community. Still, a larger part of that soccer community had voted for a natural grass field and would be happy with nothing else.

His fellow board members told him they'd protect his back, but that as the board's soccer guy the ultimate decision had to be his. Mendoza felt he could justify a vote for turf if he could extract some concessions from the Seahawks.

He demanded that the turf not have stitched-in permanent football lines. "When we played soccer," he said, "I wanted it to look like a soccer field."

He also wanted the ability to put a temporary grass field down if necessary to host an international match, and a compromise was reached. If an international match required a grass field, one would be installed. If more than 40,000 fans attended the match, the Seahawks would have to pay for the temporary installation. If fewer than 40,000 fans attended, the international teams or the promoter would pay for the field.

The deadline arrived when the stadium board had to vote on the field. To wait any longer would make it unlikely either grass or turf could be ordered and installed in time to open the building.

Mendoza worked with Bob Collier who was the project manager on behalf of Paul Allen's interests. The two discussed Mendoza's proposal until 11:30 p.m. the night before the vote before finally striking the deal. Mendoza would get his concessions for soccer, and in return he would recommend that the board vote to install FieldTurf as the Hawks wished.

The next day Mendoza gave a long speech to a room he recalls was "packed with soccer people." He voted in favor of FieldTurf so the Seahawks got their wish, but he had negotiated a compromise that he felt still protected soccer with the concessions he insisted be built into the deal. Not everyone saw his compromise as a good thing.

"You should see the hundreds of emails I got from soccer people calling me a traitor. I lost a lot of credibility and it took a long time to get it back."

In the murky world of American stadium politics in the 21st century changing the playing surface of a new stadium, while an affront to some, barely moves the anger meter in the general population. In this case at least the decision had been made in the open and after much consideration. Nevertheless, to this day in Seattle the topic is still debated and some soccer fans bristle at the "bait-and-switch," that they were promised one thing in a vote and given something else.

Fans upset over the playing surface at least got a nice consolation a few weeks later. In a thoughtful nod to Seattle's sports history it was the Sounders who opened the new stadium just as they had opened Seattle's new Kingdome in 1976 in a legendary match against Pele and the New York Cosmos.

On July 28, 2002 the USL A-League Sounders played their rivals the Vancouver Whitecaps. The home team won 4-1 in front of a league-record crowd of 25,515 people. Standing there that night it was easy to envision Seattle quickly making the leap to the big league of American soccer, Major League Soccer.

Five years earlier (yes, all the way back in 1997) when the frantic campaign was on to build a new stadium in Seattle, MLS commissioner Doug Logan came to town to lobby for the stadium. At a meeting of business leaders at Seattle's Harbor Club Logan famously said of MLS expanding to Seattle "if you build a new stadium, MLS will come."

The new stadium was now a reality so surely the phone would ring with news of an impending MLS arrival soon, right? Somehow, that arrival would take nearly seven *more* years.

CHAPTER TWO

∽

"You forgot the 12th Man! You forgot about us!"

T hey had everything conventional wisdom dictates you need for success in the National Football League, but something was inexplicably wrong with the Seattle Seahawks.

They had a wealthy local owner in Paul Allen, a brand new stadium the equal of any in America, and a Super Bowl champion head coach in Mike Holmgren. Yet they weren't successful on the field or in the stands.

After he bought the team in 1997, Allen had installed Bob Whitsitt as team president. Whitsitt, after all, was the president of Allen's other sports team — the Portland Trailblazers, and previously had been general manager of the Seattle SuperSonics — so Allen didn't have to look far for someone to run his growing sports empire. Whitsitt took over a damaged product, and had some big challenges to overcome.

The Seahawks franchise had originally been owned by the Nordstrom family, which carried its legendary customer service philosophy to its football fan base. But after 15 years of owning the Hawks, the Nordstroms decided to concentrate on the real family business, and sold the team to Ken Behring. That was an unmitigated disaster: For starters, fan interest in the team had severely eroded during Behring's disastrous reign and his attempt to move the team to Los Angeles. After Allen bought the team, the Seahawks stadium campaign (as all such requests for public money tend to do) further irritated some fans.

While their new stadium was being built the Hawks had to play two seasons at the University of Washington which didn't make anyone's job easier. Husky Stadium was great for college games but it was not close to an adequate NFL facility. Among other things, the team couldn't serve beer at games, and let's face it: The NFL without beer is like breathing without air.

They weren't very compelling on the field, either, managing a mediocre 31-33 record during Holmgren's first four seasons as head coach. Empty seats pockmarked every home game. In their first year in the new stadium (2002), three games were not even televised in Seattle, victims of the NFL's blackout policy for games when not enough tickets are sold.

It added up to very challenging situation, which wasn't helped by Whitsitt's sometimes abrasive demeanor within his own office. According to insiders who worked for the Seahawks at the time many changes in office personnel were made and not all of them were handled gracefully. Whitsitt also had historic photos taken down. He marginalized team executives whom he felt challenged by. He and Holmgren were in the early days of a not-so-subtle power struggle that further served to exacerbate tensions in the office.

People whose jobs were to prompt the public to believe in this organization were reduced to worrying about their jobs. The organization was not healing from the Behring regime; it was continuing to hemorrhage — exactly the last thing Allen had in mind when he bought the team.

Into this boiling soup in 2003 came new CEO Tod Leiweke, who would play a prominent role in getting the Hawks back on track. Soon after his arrival, he got to know Gary Wright, a veteran executive who Whitsitt had pushed to the backburner. Leiweke recognized in Wright a like-minded attitude in what it took for a franchise to be successful. His decision to reemphasize Wright and his role within the organization would help to reenergize the Seahawks. Along the way, almost by accident, Wright would become a key person in the Sounders story.

LEIWEKE KNEW THE Seahawks were partially broken when he arrived in Seattle. During his 20-year career as a sports executive he had come to specialize in connecting teams with their fans. Accomplishing that feat in Seattle would be a tough task because many fans felt the team had deserted them. There was no better example of this than a decision the Seahawks made when their new stadium opened.

In the 1980s when the Seahawks played at the Kingdome, crowds were legendarily loud to the point that the team retired the number 12 in honor of the fans. It was a fan base that the Nordstroms had nurtured for more than a decade, and included 117 consecutive sellouts in the Kingdome. A banner was hung in the rafters of the Dome, and fans boasted that no other team had honored fans in this way.

Inexplicably, when the team moved into the new stadium in 2002, management neglected to hang the banner. It was one of a series of decisions that left fans feeling isolated and led to the empty seats Leiweke was now trying to fill. In an effort to do a little market research Leiweke reached out to several former season-ticket holders and invited them to an exhibition game with the understanding that they would meet before the game to help the organization answer a simple question: "What can we do better?"

John Rizzardini had been hired to direct the team's marketing efforts, and the pregame meeting with fans took place two days before he officially started with the team. He remembers the night clearly.

"Tod asked these fans what we were doing wrong ... and he just got *ripped*," Rizzardini says. "I remember one guy standing on his chair and screaming at him: *'You forgot the 12th Man! You didn't even bring the jersey over and hang it in the new stadium. You forgot about us!'*"

That was an answer right in Leiweke's wheelhouse. He patiently took note, and within a week he outlined a simple plan to salute the fans: The team would install a flagpole in the third deck behind an end zone. Just before opening kickoff, a former Seahawk or another local celebrity would raise a huge "12" flag. The brief ceremony has become a source of pride and is always accompanied by a raucous stadium-wide ovation for the honoree that helps launch every game.

In addition to reconnecting the team with fans Leiweke had to rebuild morale and reignite passion among a staff that felt underappreciated. Poor attendance, poor play on the field, poor management of the office had left the staff feeling somewhat beaten down. "There were good people, but they had just lost their way," Rizzardini says. "We were able to quickly put things in place and establish a culture of cooperation and partnership."

They were aided in this part of the venture by Wright, who had been part of the collateral damage in the power struggle between Holmgren and Whitsitt. Holmgren had originally been given near total control of the Seahawks when he was hired in 1999, but by the end of the 2002 season the team had made just one playoff appearance and Whitsitt subsequently took away Holmgren's general manager title. The message was clear: Whitsitt was now the most powerful man in the Seahawks office.

Along the way Whitsitt had marginalized Wright's role with the team. Wright was told he would no longer travel with the team on road trips and his voice in company meetings and decisions was deemphasized. "I think he (Whitsitt) respected me and I don't think it was personal," Wright says. "He knew I was very close to Holmgren and I don't think he wanted that closeness." That decision was a mistake.

At first glance you might not necessarily jump to the conclusion that Wright is one of the most respected sports executives in America. His small physical stature and his unwillingness to draw attention to himself belied the influential and powerful voice of a man who worked quietly behind the scenes in a variety of ways. Indeed, he was so good at getting things done without attracting attention that longtime Seattle radio talk show host Dave Grosby accurately nicknamed him the "stealth executive."

He had joined the Seahawks for their first season in 1976 and served as publicity director. By 1987 he became a vice president. His pro football experience and knowledge wasn't limited to Seattle. He assisted the NFL with media relations help (among other things running the press box for 23 Super Bowls) and became a trusted advisor at the league level of the most successful league in the world.

When Steve Largent became the first Seahawks player to be inducted into the Pro Football Hall of Fame, he gave Wright the honor of introducing him. The move surprised fans, many of whom had never heard of Wright. But to people who knew the Seahawks organization, and knew Wright as a steady, guiding hand through coaching changes, management changes, ownership changes, and seasons good and bad, the move made complete sense.

Leiweke recognized almost immediately that he had found a key ally in repairing this once-great franchise. The man Leiweke dubbed "the cultural barometer of the organization" suddenly found himself back in key meetings and back in the loop on key decisions.

Similar in personality and demeanor Leiweke and Wright complimented each other nicely in contrasting terms of management style. Leiweke is not a loud, brash man but his enthusiasm is a bottomless well. He's able to easily communicate with everyone he works with and maintains an ability to always see a team's operations in big picture terms. He also, more so than Wright, doesn't mind getting a little attention. If Wright is the "stealth executive" Leiweke is more like the flyover at the Daytona 500.

"He manages from 20,000 feet" is how Seahawks radio producer Matt Johnson puts it; Wright he says, "was more of a manager on the ground."

Despite different styles they shared several important characteristics, notably they're good at building a team-style camaraderie within a professional sports franchise's office, and they understand the importance of bonding sports teams (both the business side and the team itself) with the community. They are good listeners (an underappreciated art in our shrinking-attention-span world) and share the skill of empowering those around them by counting on them to carry out daily duties that always come back to improving how the team is interacting with the fans and community.

Leiweke and Wright had something else in common, too: Soccer. Leiweke hadn't really thought about the sport that much for 15 years. Wright thought about it a lot since a somewhat fateful trip to Spain in 1998.

GARY AND ANN WRIGHT CONCLUDED their long journey from Seattle to Spain on June 12, 1998, certain of just one thing: They were both sick. Somewhere between crossing the US and the Atlantic Ocean, spending three days in Portugal, then flying and driving across Spain they had both caught a bug, and were in no mood for tourist activities. They were so sick that the first thing they did was seek out an English-speaking doctor. (Improbably, the one they found was named Dr. Ann Wright.)

So on their first night in Spain on the Mediterranean coast in the beautiful town of Calpe, the Wrights would stay in and watch TV. Speaking little Spanish, they sought out the only English program on their TV, which happened to be highlights of the opening ceremonies of the 1998 World Cup in France.

That Wright would spend time on vacation watching soccer owed much more to the fact that he was waylaid by sickness than to any desire to see the sport. "I wouldn't have given you anything for soccer," Wright says. "I wouldn't have walked across the street to see a soccer match. When Pelé came to Seattle in

1976 I knew who he was but I had no interest in seeing him play. I knew the NASL Sounders were popular and drew upwards of 20,000 per game. I thought that was kind of neat. I knew it existed and I knew people here enjoyed it. I didn't."

Wright wasn't always content to keep his feelings to himself. Dave Neubert, who assisted Wright in the Seahawks media relations department in the '90s and is a big soccer fan, was the victim of Wright's disdain particularly during the 1994 World Cup. "He's watching games and I'm going, 'What are you doing watching that? Why would you even *care* about that sport?' I didn't give a rip about soccer. Not one bit."

Still, Wright was always interested in the staging and promotion of big events, if for no other reason than to see how they compared to the NFL. "I told Ann, 'I don't want to watch this game, but I want to see the opening ceremonies and see what they do.' So I'm watching and it's pretty good. It's not as good as the Super Bowl in my mind but it's still pretty good."

As the highlights wrapped up, the broadcast shifted to live coverage of that night's game, and Wright immediately was caught by what he calls the "buzz" he felt from the crowd.

"It really captivated me. There's dancing and balloons and the crowd is going nuts. I'm thinking 'maybe we'll watch the beginning of the game and see what this is about.'"

The excitement was due to the fact that the French team was set to play their opening game of the World Cup versus South Africa. When the game began Wright surprisingly found himself captivated by one guy on Les Bleus.

"This guy in the middle, he's got the ball velcroed to his foot and I can't believe the things this guy is doing. I don't know the first thing about soccer, but I do know athleticism. He's making one move after another, these nice graceful passes. Everything was so easy. What should have been difficult looked so easy for this guy. The guy has this cool name, too: Zinedine Zidane."

Zidane led France to a 3-nil win over South Africa. His interest piqued, Wright wanted to see more games. He watched Brazil destroy Morocco and was blown away by the team fans lovingly call *Canarinhos* (little Canaries). "Oh, wow. It was Roberto Carlos up one side and Cafu up the other side and Ronaldo in the middle ... and I'm going 'this is different.'"

It was during France's second game of the tournament against Saudi Arabia that Wright decides he was all in on soccer and the people who play it.

"Having been a high school football coach, I had always thought if you weren't on our football team and you were playing soccer, you weren't a good enough athlete and you weren't very tough ... typical American way of looking at it. The more I'm watching the World Cup, the more impressed I am with their athleticism. But I still *know* they're not tough. I just *know* that."

That changed when Wright sees Zidane take a shot from Saudi player Fuad Anwar Amin. Zidane retaliates by knocking Anwar to the ground *and* stomping on his chest. "He just nails this guy, flattens him, and stomps on his chest, and I said to myself, 'whoa!'" Later, Zidane claimed Anwar directed a racial slur at him.

Two things came out of the incident: First, Zidane was suspended for two games. Second, Wright was now convinced soccer players are athletic *and* tough. He was hooked.

A lifetime spent compiling and interpreting stats in the NFL helped fuel Wright's new addiction. He couldn't read Spanish, but he could figure out numbers. So he walked up the hill from his villa each day to buy Spanish newspapers and get the latest lineups, stats, and player ratings.

Eventually Howard Mudd, Ralph Hawkins, and their wives joined the Wrights on their vacation. Mudd and Hawkins were both veteran NFL assistant coaches, and they were somewhat shocked to find out that their daily routine now included soccer, as Wright insisted that before they leave for dinner each night they watch the World Cup.

Perhaps just to keep peace in the villa, Mudd and Hawkins developed an interest in the games. Hawkins — who was the Seahawks secondary coach for Chuck Knox's teams in the '80s, and then became a longtime NFL scout was particularly taken with Brazilian Roberto Carlos. He claimed in rising enthusiasm that Carlos could be a cornerback for the Seahawks, a starter in the NFL ... and actually, a Pro Bowl-caliber player!

For their three-week stay in Spain, Wright immersed himself in soccer. Upon his return to the U.S., he was surprised to find the semifinals of the tournament were not being shown on regular American TV. He found a bar that showed the semis on satellite TV ... a place in Seattle's Fremont neighborhood called The George and Dragon. So off to the bar he went with his two sons to watch Brazil and France advance to the finals. He watched the title game at home as France won the championship 3-nil behind Wright's favorite player, Zidane, who twice found the back of the net.

One month after he arrived in Spain as a soccer hater too sick to do anything but watch TV, this NFL executive had watched dozens of World Cup games and couldn't get enough soccer. But he thought the ride was over. It was 1998, after all, and little soccer was available on TV for the average American fan. The next day he opened up USA Today and saw a full-page ad that read, *"If You Liked Watching The World Cup Then You Have to Have Fox Sports World."*

Wright signed up for the channel that day and hasn't stopped watching soccer since.

SOCCER WAS A DIFFERENT THING altogether for Leiweke, who had worked as an entry-level employee for the Kansas City Comets of the Major Indoor Soccer League (MISL) in 1981. It was not only his first taste of soccer, but also the start of his career in sports management.

The MISL could in some ways be dubbed the Leiweke Family Business. Tod's older brothers (Tracey, Terry, and Tim) were all involved in the league. Terry had helped found the league in 1978 when he managed the Houston Summit arena. Tracey Leiweke was involved in the St. Louis team's management. By 1981, Tim was general manager of the Comets, with Tracey and Terry working alongside. The three big brothers ganged up on young Tod and convinced him to join them to help with the Comets. Although the MISL was a long way from the bright lights and big leagues in which Tod would eventually operate, the experience served as graduate school in pro sports management.

"I did everything from PA, to selling stuff," Tod says. "We all just jumped in. It was a fun time. We were outdrawing the (NBA) Kings by a substantial number. We played half as many games but drew twice as many people."

Part of the reason the Comets trounced the Kings so thoroughly at the box office might have been game presentation. In the early 1980s game presentations involved none of the histrionics that accompany pro and college sports today. It was basically, announce the lineups and start the game. The Leiweke brothers (and in particular Tim) are credited with being the first group to decide to dim the lights of the arena and put on a show for introductions.

"Tim was the godfather of game presentation," Tod says. "He invented a lot of the pregame stuff. We'd turn out the lights and blow stuff up. We had lasers and smoke and strobe lights." The show they put on before each MISL game became legendary and was eventually adopted by just about every team in every league in every sport. NBA commissioner David Stern dubbed the Leiwekes the "kings of promotion" in an article in the *New Yorker*.

Fueled by the success of the franchise and his role in that success, Leiweke found a new passion. "I learned to love the game of soccer and met some interesting people. It was a great game."

STILL, SOCCER as a new passion for Wright and a former one for Leiweke did not mean it was at the top of their minds in the summer of 2003. They were NFL executives, and their only concern was getting the Seahawks back on track.

As part of that effort Rizzardini remembers Leiweke making an eyebrow-raising statement the Monday after the team's first regular season game in 2003. The game had not sold out which was the fourth such occurrence in the nine regular season games played in their new stadium. Leiweke assembled his staff to discuss the attendance situation.

"We only had 31,000 season tickets," Rizzardini says, "And we didn't sell out our first game. Tod stood up in a staff meeting the next day and said 'We're going to sell out every game the rest of the year.' And we did. He said we had to, he led the way, and from there everyone followed him."

The team not only sold out every game the rest of that season but every game since. Some of the credit goes to Leiweke for rekindling the fire in a staff that had felt smothered. But a lot of it also had to do with oldest marketing trick in the sports book: Winning.

The Hawks won a total of 32 games in 2003, 2004, and 2005 and made the playoffs each of those years after they had managed *ONE* playoff appearance in the previous 15 years. The 2005 team won 13 games and the NFC championship.

In the middle of all this, Whitsitt lost his power struggle with Holmgren when the coach delivered a "one of us has got to go" ultimatum to Paul Allen after the 2004 season. The owner chose to keep his coach.

Wright had been ready to retire before Leiweke arrived, due at least in part to his reduced role. He instead enjoyed a front row seat to the team's only Super Bowl appearance following the 2005 season. The team made playoff appearances again in 2006 and 2007. As the 2007 season wound down Wright again considered retirement. This time, his decision wasn't based on frustration but satisfaction.

The franchise he had been with since the start had survived a decade of stumbling around in the dark. Just like the '80s, the SRO sign was a permanent fixture at the ticket window. The Seahawks ruled the Seattle sports community and he had played a huge role in making that happen. It was time, he felt, to sit back and enjoy himself.

He was going to enjoy himself, all right. But he wasn't going to be sitting back. Or retiring.

CHAPTER THREE

JANUARY 2002
MINNEAPOLIS, MINNESOTA

⌒

"I have no idea what I'm doing."

innesota Thunder general manager Jim Froslid reached across his desk to answer the phone. Just 33 years old, Froslid had already put together quite a resume in soccer and was in his second year as the GM of his hometown soccer club.

After a successful high school and college career as a player, he spent eight years working for the United States national soccer program, and in 2000 he returned to the Twin Cities to run the United States League (USL) Thunder. It didn't take long for Froslid to make his mark as a solid, savvy operator.

The voice on the other end of the phone belonged to a fellow young soccer executive from a rival USL franchise in Seattle, a guy he had met at the recent league meetings.

Unlike Froslid, Adrian Hanauer didn't have a lot of soccer experience. He had played the game as a kid, and like so many kids in Seattle in the 1970s spent lots of time at Sounders games when the team played in the North American Soccer League (NASL).

By the mid 1980s, the Sounders and the NASL had collapsed and Hanauer had grown up. He went to the University of Washington, and on to what would become a successful business career. When the Sounders reformed as an A League team in 1994 Hanauer occasionally attended matches, but that was the extent of his involvement with the sport until a plane flight from Los Angeles to Seattle in 2001.

On that flight, the guy sitting next to Hanauer happened to pull out a laptop, "And I saw out of the corner of my eye that he was working on something Sounders related," Hanauer says, "so I struck up a conversation with him." Hanauer and then-Sounders general manager Brad Kimura spent the entire flight discussing the Sounders. Among the topics that came up was the fact that owners Neil Farnsworth and Scott Oki were looking for other investors.

"That's what they called them. But it turned out you weren't really an investor; you were more of a philanthropist. So I ended up sitting down with Neil Farnsworth and becoming friends with him."

Hanauer decided he wanted to invest in (or donate to) the Sounders. He met with his family to discuss the situation. Hanauer's father Jerry ran Pacific Coast Feather Company and over three decades had taken it from a million-dollar company to the largest bedding company in the United States, with hundreds of millions of dollars in annual sales. Along the way Jerry Hanauer and his family gained a reputation as philanthropists particularly in Seattle's arts and education communities. Adrian Hanauer knew his father was passionate about soccer and therefore might be interested in the Sounders.

"The USL team in Seattle was a good little community asset with a couple thousand fans attending games, it was good for kids and families, so we decided to put a few dollars into the Sounders," he says.

The family committed $100,000 a year to the team without any expectation that they would actually make money. This was an investment in the Seattle soccer community. No different in the family's opinion than giving money to arts and education.

Except there was a difference: Unlike donations to arts and education, which can take an abstract form, this donation was to a living, breathing thing. The Sounders were a business that had daily operating expenses along with the opportunity to raise revenue through ticket sales, advertising, media partnerships, and other avenues. Adrian Hanauer knew about running businesses, and as an investor in many tech ventures during Seattle's booming '90s he was used to keeping an eye on his money after investing.

"We put the $100,000 in, and it was a time in my business career when I had time to go into the office. Because I put money in, I wanted to understand the business a little bit. So I started going to the office and asking a lot of questions. The business was losing about a million dollars a year."

The business was about to lose two other things: a head coach and a general manager. On November 8, 2001 Sounders interim coach Bernie James was fired. James and Farnsworth exchanged nasty barbs in the *Seattle Times* regarding the dismissal. James maintained he was booted because he wouldn't play Farnsworth's son Chris, who was a 22-year-old forward with the club. Farnsworth countered that James was fired because of a refusal to play young players in general (including his son) and that by doing so was preventing long-term development of the team.

Perhaps it was just collateral damage, or maybe Brad Kimura saw the writing on the wall, but the same day James was fired Kimura announced his resignation as the team's GM. The team was suddenly leaderless. Having put millions of dollars into the Sounders, Farnsworth and Oki had grown weary of the day-to-day operation of such a money hole, so they were only too glad to leave the rebuild up to Hanauer.

"Neil and Scott looked at me," Hanauer remembers, "and said, 'you broke it. You fix it.'"

They added the title "General Manager" to the "Managing Partner" moniker Hanauer already had, which at least partially explains why Jim Froslid's phone was ringing in Minnesota.

Hanauer didn't know Froslid well, but this was the only USL team exec he knew well enough to reach on the phone.

"Jim? It's Adrian Hanauer. I have no idea what I'm doing. Can you help me?"

"I had zero qualifications for the job other than running businesses in the past, which as it turns out added value," Hanauer relates. "I understood business and I understood the game, but the middle 90 percent wasn't there in terms of my capabilities. We were 90 days away from kicking off. I didn't know who the players were. I didn't know how they got paid. I didn't know how we got our uniforms. I didn't know how referees showed up. I didn't know how we sold tickets. I didn't know what a sponsor really was, or if there were broadcast issues to deal with or stadium negotiations. Do we have a lease with Memorial Stadium? I had no idea what I was getting myself into."

Froslid calmed Hanauer down and played on his strength as a businessman. He reminded Hanauer of a basic business axiom: Things are seldom as complicated as they seem and certainly weren't as complicated as the overwhelmed Hanauer was making them. He advised Hanauer to prioritize and sort through his long list of projects one by one.

In addition to Froslid's levelheaded advice, Hanauer had the benefit of a good right-hand man during this period. Bart Wiley had joined the Sounders organization about the same time Hanauer did and together they worked through the long list of things they didn't know about running a soccer franchise, rapidly turning each one from an unknown into a known.

"Bart is a scrappy entrepreneurial guy and he didn't like the fact that we were losing all this money. In terms of job security, the longer you work for a company that's bleeding cash the sooner the chances are that you'll be one of the guys to go. Bart ended up being a fantastic Swiss Army knife. He was able to take on a ton of different pieces of the business." (It makes sense that Wiley eventually became the Sounders' VP for business operations.)

That was valuable because Hanauer had to trim the organization's losses. To do that he had to trim costs. That meant dismissing some people and not replacing others who left. Soon enough the office had become a two man operation.

He eventually got the business side working again. Ticket sales gradually picked up and Hanauer was able to convince some of his business friends to purchase team sponsorships, although he admits that in this case "sponsorship" was more of a code word for "donating money."

As the spring of 2002 approached, Hanauer was as lean as he could be on costs and still wasn't close to the number he and Farnsworth and Oki had targeted as an acceptable loss for the business in 2002. That's when he realized he would have to trim the salaries of his players.

"There was also a horrible week as I started to understand the salary structure of our players. Our overall salary for players was $500,000 and I needed to drive it down to $250,000. I had meeting after meeting with players where I would say 'I know you've been a great member of this team and a contributor but I need to cut your salary in half for this business to survive,' The players were fantastic. They weren't happy and there may have been one or two who wanted to move on, but to a man they understood. Our salary structure was a little bloated relative to other teams in the league."

Hanauer also tried to soften the blow by making each player who stayed with him a promise. "I said to them 'if we lose less than half a million dollars I'm going to take a third of the amount under a half million and give it back to you guys.'"

Buoyed by the leaner, more effective front office, the lower payroll, a better team, and the game with Vancouver in July that served as the first-ever event at the new Seahawks Stadium (and drew over 25,000 fans), the Sounders cut their losses for the year to $350,000.

"So we gave $50,000 back to the players," Hanauer says. "It was only a couple thousand per guy, but it showed we were true to our word." It was a small but apt reward for a group of players who produced a division title for the fans after a fifth place finish in 2001.

In his first year as general manager Hanauer had trimmed losses by 65 percent, giving him confidence that this thing could work. He still had more to learn, but at least he had experienced one successful year running a sports franchise. The year also rekindled his passion for soccer — a passion that would soon eclipse everything in his professional life and truly present him with his calling.

HANAUER WAS IMMERSED in soccer at an age so young he doesn't even remember it. "My mom has these stories of when I was two years old I'd make her go to the backyard and stand on the deck and watch me and cheer for me as I dribbled back and forth," he says.

His father was a first generation German-American who brought a love of soccer to his family. Jerry Hanauer was born in Stuttgart, Germany in 1927. A decade later he and his family fled Germany to escape the Nazis, spending two years in Lichtenstein before traveling to the south of France and boarding a boat that took them to Portugal and eventually to the United States, where they settled in Seattle with family members who had started a furniture building business.

In 1974, when Adrian was 8, the NASL expanded into Seattle, and Hanauer remembers attending games with his family at Memorial Stadium at the foot of the Space Needle. They had sixth-row tickets and Jerry Hanauer would teach his children about the game, often pointing out that the subtle beauty in this sport came not so often in the scoring but in how the game itself was being played. After games the Hanauers would join other families at team-sponsored parties in the Center House next to the stadium. There, Adrian would jostle with other kids to get player autographs.

They weren't alone. The team was an instant hit in Seattle and drew more than 13,000 fans per game, twice the league average. It was during these years that the first seeds were planted of what would become the wild popularity the Sounders FC would enjoy.

The Seattle sports landscape wasn't exactly teeming with success in 1974. It wasn't exactly teeming with anything. The NFL didn't arrive until 1976. Major League Baseball returned to town the following year. The Sonics existed but had yet to make an appearance in the NBA playoffs. Don James wouldn't arrive for another year to revive the football program at the University of Washington.

The Sounders did everything they could to connect with Seattle, hosting those post-game autograph sessions as well as school assemblies and after-school and summer soccer camps. They were everywhere. Back then, Hanauer only knew that it was all pretty cool. Today he realizes how important those days were to what he and the Sounders would become.

"All those guys were my heroes," he says. "They were a real fabric of the community. It left this really strong impression on me and got the Sounders brand in my blood."

On April 9, 1976 the Sounders hosted the New York Cosmos in the first event ever held in the Kingdome. Of the half million or so people who lived in Seattle at the time approximately all of them (including Hanauer) claim to have been there. It's easier to find someone eating Atlantic salmon for lunch in downtown Seattle than it is to find someone who will admit they weren't at that game. In reality 58,128 fans attended the match, and while it was an undeniably awesome way to open the then-state-of-the-art stadium it also brought an end to the exciting atmosphere that existed for Sounders games the first two years at Memorial Stadium. Attendance increased, but the intimate mood disappeared. In the cavernous Kingdome, 24,000 fans didn't have the same effect as when 16,000 crammed into Memorial Stadium.

There are a myriad of reasons the NASL and the Sounders didn't make it. The league was mismanaged and over expanded. Too many of the original owners were infatuated with soccer, but not dedicated to the long-term success of the league. In Seattle the Sounders of 1974 enjoyed little or no competition, but by 1980 the NFL and MLB had arrived, the Sonics had won an NBA championship, and the Washington Huskies had begun a long string of college football success.

But Hanauer emphasizes that move from the cozy confines of Memorial Stadium to the Kingdome. Attending a game where empty seats outnumbered tickets sold couldn't help but undermine the fan experience. All of these things combined to sap the life out of the Sounders' fan interest in less than a decade.

"It dwindled to a place where there wasn't this massive excitement for the team anymore," Hanauer remembers. He says he doesn't recall being devastated by the demise of the team. No longer a wide-eyed child asking for an autograph, he was instead preparing for college. But he's grateful the timeline wasn't shorter.

"The Sounders lasted until I was 17, which was my full childhood. Upon reflection, if it had been from when I was 5 to when I was 8 maybe it doesn't leave such an indelible a mark on me. But 8 to 17 was all my formative years as a child."

HANAUER LOOKED FORWARD to the upcoming 2003 soccer season. Buying a share of the Sounders had been a straightforward deal. Running the team as the general manager? That had been much more daunting, but the success enjoyed both on the pitch and in exceeding revenue goals in 2002 made him anxious to see what was next.

Two important things happened in 2003. The first offered a short-term boost, the other offered dramatic long-term implications for Hanauer and professional soccer in Seattle.

First, he came up with a couple of ideas to increase the USL Sounders season ticket base. Soccer giants Manchester United and Celtic were playing a game in Seattle on July 22, and 66,722 fans would jam Seahawks Stadium to see them. Months earlier Hanauer had purchased 4,000 of the best seats from the game's promoter. He used those as an incentive to potential Sounders season ticket buyers. Any new season ticket purchase came with the opportunity to buy tickets to the Man U/Celtic game.

Hanauer admits he was nervous about the deal. Who, in their right mind, wants to hold 4,000 tickets to anything? But 1,500 new Sounders season-ticket holders quickly snapped up the

4,000 premium seats for the match, making his risk pay off. The added capital would help the Sounders bottom line in 2003 and further convince him that perhaps he could figure out this soccer business, after all.

"This was a risk that having an owner-operator involved allowed us to take where the previous regime would not have done that," he says.

Hanauer and his partners also had decided to make the US Open Cup, a tournament involving teams from all American soccer leagues, a much bigger priority. They not only pointed to those games on the pitch but they were as aggressive in bidding to host the games. It wasn't lost on Sounders fans that the team was attempting in Hanauer's words to bring a "big league attitude to the game, even though we were a minor league team."

They did these things because it hadn't taken Hanauer long to realize that owning a minor league sports team in a major league sports town was going to be an unending uphill battle survivable only by as he puts it "the good graces of people willing to write checks to support it."

The ManU/Celtic ticket deal and the US Open Cup games added to the team's bottom line, but Hanauer knew there was no guarantee the team could make money by relying on special events. He set his sights on America's top league and began pondering the best way to make the jump into MLS.

The other important thing that happened to Hanauer in July of 2003, the one with potential long-term ramifications, began with news delivered to him from his friend and advisor Jim Froslid. He called Hanauer to give him background on Tod Leiweke, the new CEO of the Seahawks. Leiweke had been hired away from the NHL Minnesota Wild after a successful run as their CEO. Froslid had gotten to know him during his stay in the Twin Cities and admired Leiweke's enthusiasm and willingness to work with a minor-league soccer executive. He suggested to Hanauer that he seek out Leiweke.

Leiweke had only been in Seattle a few weeks when Hanauer set up a meeting where he wasted no time getting to his point, blurting out that he wanted to partner with the Seahawks to obtain an MLS team. Hanauer laughs now as he remembers Leiweke's reaction.

"He said 'Whoa! Whoa! Whoa! Slow down partner. I just got to town and my first priority is to get the Seahawks going. Give me a couple years to get this thing sorted out and then we'll talk.' There was something about him that told me he meant what he said, that he wasn't just giving me a brush off. From early on Tod and I hit it off personally and professionally. We like to do business in similar ways. We both believed good guys sometimes finish first. So I stayed in contact."

They began meeting regularly and those meetings paid off early for Leiweke, who had joined an organization that had been unsuccessful selling suites in their brand new stadium. Hanauer knew this and at one of their first meetings offered to buy a suite. "I knew suites were a challenge and I knew Paul Allen had put suite sales high on Tod's to-do list. I agreed to do a suite to help Tod out and to be a good community partner." The move made sense for Hanauer since his soccer team would now play all home games in Seahawks Stadium. Still, the willingness to help out was not lost on the new CEO.

"We were working very hard to sell our suites because we hadn't had the success that was hoped for when the stadium opened," Leiweke says. "So this guy steps up and buys this suite and it really struck me that I'm dealing with a good and honorable guy here."

Leiweke also reached out to Fred Mendoza in his early days in Seattle. "He called me in the first few weeks he was in Seattle," Mendoza says. "He told me 'I know about the promise that was made to bring an MLS team to Seattle and I want to keep it. But I want to be candid with you. Paul says I can't even talk about soccer until I straighten out the Seahawks situation. I'm with you, I'll support you, and I'll do what I can.'"

Undaunted, Mendoza made it a point to get in Leiweke's ear about soccer whenever he could. John Rizzardini says Leiweke would return from almost every Public Stadium Authority board meeting with another tale of Mendoza promoting soccer and reminding Leiweke that the original stadium deal contained language regarding a soccer team for Seattle. "Fred was gracious, but persistent," Rizzardini says.

Mendoza appreciated Leiweke's honesty and willingness to listen, but as the guy who had campaigned so vigorously for a new stadium within the soccer community, he wasn't ready to put all his eggs in one basket. For that matter, neither was Hanauer. He and Mendoza had actually been working together on, of all things, building a new soccer-specific stadium somewhere in Seattle's suburbs.

This left turn came courtesy of a shift in ideology within MLS when the league changed commissioners. The league forced out original commissioner Doug Logan after reported losses in excess of $30 million dollars in 1999. Logan gave one of the great departure quotes of all time when he told reporters at a news conference, "Yesterday I was an 'is.' Today I am a 'was.' There's no elegant way to say I was fired."

Frustrated with growth they considered too slow, league owners turned toward an NFL executive named Don Garber. Told by interested Seattle parties that Logan had promised the city a team if they voted to build the Seahawks new stadium (which they had) Garber quickly pointed out that he hadn't made the promise, a guarantee he said that never should have been made in the first place. In addition he didn't think it was best for the league's interest to play games in NFL stadiums.

Among the things he believed would help the game grow was the building of soccer-specific stadiums. The year Garber started with MLS (1999) just such a stadium was opened in Columbus. In the next decade similar stadiums would be built in Los Angeles, Dallas, Denver, Chicago, Salt Lake City, and New York City.

After Seattle taxpayers had agreed to build a stadium for both pro football and soccer, the league was looking favorably on cities that had their own soccer stadiums. And with MLS planning to add two expansion teams in 2004, Hanauer and Mendoza began working in earnest to land one in Seattle.

"We believed we needed a stadium so we spent a decent amount of time in several communities trying to kick the tires and drum up interest for a stadium," Hanauer says. "The plan was to launch in the Seahawks Stadium and see how things go from there."

According to Mendoza several options were discussed. They looked at locations in various suburbs located between Seattle and Tacoma. One company pitched them on a plan to build the stadium half way between the two cities in the aptly named town of Midway. They even looked at remodeling Memorial Stadium, the original home of the Sounders. But Mendoza says "there was no group that ever came forward, and no land we were ever offered was ideal."

Hanauer continued working with other partners and MLS on a bid to acquire an expansion team but admits he drove a tough bargain with the league which was not yet in great financial shape. David Beckham to Los Angeles hadn't happened yet. The league's TV deals weren't great. Hanauer had his doubts.

"We dove pretty deep into what a profit and loss statement would look like, because although I wanted to do it yesterday, I didn't want to get creamed financially for myself, my family and any partners. I didn't want it to be a black eye for soccer in the community. We were enthusiastic, but we had our trepidations. It was a buyer's market. At that point there weren't many people willing to put money in MLS."

Mendoza had been desirous of a team in MLS since the day he met Paul Allen and Bert Kolde. He was frustrated with Hanauer's hesitancy, but admired his business sense. "Adrian is a passionate soccer guy, but God bless him, he's an astute businessman. I could never convince him to put his passion in front of his business sense. I tried but I couldn't do it."

The league ultimately settled the new teams in Los Angeles and Salt Lake City. The decision to go to Los Angeles was preordained. The Galaxy had just opened the Home Depot Center and the league wanted a second team for the stadium, one that would be geared towards the huge Mexican/American population in Southern California (it became Chivas USA).

Hanauer was hardly devastated. "Given how many teams in MLS were struggling at the time and given the fact that we thought we'd be struggling — we'd lose more money in MLS than USL — it wasn't a huge blow. It was more like 'we tried. We didn't get it. We'll move on.'"

Part of moving on was the continued ownership and operation of the Sounders in the USL. As he continued in that capacity Hanauer was always looking for ways to increase his team's bottom line and one such opportunity popped up in early 2006.

Leiweke called to tell him that Real Madrid was interested in playing a match in Seattle as part of a US tour before their season began. They had signed a deal to play DC United of MLS but needed a location for the game. Leiweke told Hanauer he didn't want to risk his time and money on promoting the game. Hanauer told him he would take both risks. He formed a company with a business friend (Rick Cantu) and the duo put up $1.5 million to promote and run the game.

Real Madrid at the time featured among other players the legendary David Beckham who wasn't necessarily the best soccer player in the world but was certainly the best known and most charismatic. Would that be enough to sell tickets to a game in Seattle between a team from Spain and a team from as Seattleites sometimes referred to the nation's capitol "the *other* Washington?"

Hanauer admits he was nervous, but he didn't need to be. A crowd of 66,830 packed the stadium on a beautiful August night. The fans hummed with energy all night long, that hum rising noticeably every time Beckham touched the ball. At the end of the night Hanauer had made money and had increased his business credibility with Leiweke. Significant, too, the night was "another indication that soccer in Seattle had some legs to it," Hanauer points out.

The calendar turned from 2006 to 2007 and Hanauer continued running the Sounders, but he was starting to get restless. The team had won the USL championship in 2005 (and would again in 2007). Hanauer had proven he could help pull off huge international soccer events in Seattle. But at the end of the day, his team was still minor league in a major league town. To boot, he was still the minority owner.

"I've been busting my ass on this USL thing for 4 years. And because of the way the equity was structured, I still only own 10 percent even though I'm running the thing, I'm writing checks, I'm lowering the losses…" Hanauer decided to approach his partners (Farnsworth and Oki) and proposed a restructuring of the team allowing him to become the majority owner.

"There was really no reason to do it," he says laughing, "besides ego." Indeed, the Sounders were still a money-losing operation. And once Farnsworth and Oki agreed to allow Hanauer become the majority owner, the majority of the money lost belonged to him (and his family). They went from "contributing" about $100,000 to $250,000 per year. Hanauer had his control, but it had come at a price. He recognized he couldn't make money or be happy running a minor league team indefinitely, so he continued working on plans to get Seattle into MLS.

"About once a quarter I'd have a conversation with Mark Abbott (president of MLS). But nothing was breaking through. Then one day in 2007, out of the blue, I got a call from Don Garber."

The commissioner told Hanauer "Joe Roth is really interested in owning an MLS team in Seattle. You should meet with him."

Hanauer had one question for the commissioner: "Who is Joe Roth?"

CHAPTER FOUR

DECEMBER, 2007
EL DORADO GOLF CLUB, CABO SAN LUCAS, MEXICO

❧

"You're going to lose your ass."

L es Moonves walked toward the tee box alongside Joe Roth and listened to Roth explain his next big project.

As Hollywood power golfing duos go, these old friends would sit near the top of any list. They were similar in many ways. They had been born a little over a year apart in the late '40s in New York City. They had built successful careers in the entertainment business and routinely dealt in the world of eight, nine, and 10-figure deals. They had on occasion done business together.

Moonves was President and CEO of CBS and had been a major player in television for decades. Roth accumulated his power and fortune in the movies and had been the chairman first of 20th Century Fox, then Walt Disney Studios before forming his own company, Revolution Studios in 2000.

Roth had been involved in hundreds of movies in his career and as he approached his 60th birthday he had decided to slow down a bit in that area. Instead of making six or seven movies a year, he wanted to be a little choosier and make just one or two.

That didn't mean he was ready to retire. He just wanted to try something different. "I knew," he says, "I was going to have excess energy, and the answer wasn't make another movie or two. The answer was, 'I've got to find something else to do.'"

That something else would involve another lifelong passion: soccer. He had played the game at the Division 1 collegiate level at Bowling Green and Hofstra. He had coached his kids for years and had attended World Cup and MLS matches. In a city where buzz is everything, he had watched the excitement generated in Los Angeles in 2007 when the Galaxy had signed David Beckham. He wanted in on that action. He met with MLS commissioner Don Garber, who suggested he explore markets in the Pacific Northwest, where the league was eyeing expansion.

Now, a year later, he enthusiastically told Moonves about the partners he was working with in Seattle and the potential he saw for success in the Emerald City. Moonves listened, patient but skeptical. As Roth wound down, Moonves pulled a golf ball and tee from his pocket and leaned over to set up his shot. Finally, he turned back to Roth and offered the kind of blunt assessment you get from close friends.

"What in the world are you doing investing in *soccer*? You're gonna lose your ass."

Roth smiled. He had to learn toughness at an early age and that had served him well over the years in a business where successes and failures are played out in the most public of ways possible. He certainly wasn't going to back down from a statement like that ... and responded with a two-word retort often heard on golf courses.

"Wanna bet?"

Moonves stepped away from his shot.

"I'll betcha I don't lose money," Roth said. "We'll do better than break even in the first year."

Moonves smiled and eagerly accepted the offer. The golf partners shook hands on a wager taken right from the book of Mortimer and Randolph Duke in the movie *"Trading Places."* If Roth could defy Moonves' prediction and finish his first season as a professional soccer owner in the black, Moonves would owe his friend *one dollar.*

ROTH WAS BORN in July of 1948 in New York City and grew up on Long Island. What was a typical childhood was altered somewhat in 1959 when his father joined a group of parents who filed a lawsuit against the New York Commissioner of Education regarding prayer in public schools. In 1951 the New York State Board of Regents had approved daily recitation of a prayer in schools asking for God's blessing on the school, teachers, students, and country. The parents wanted that practice to be stopped.

Originally over 50 parents agreed to join the fight, but by the time the suit was filed many of them had been intimidated into bailing out. Lawrence Roth was ultimately one of just five plaintiffs. Susan Dudley Gold in her book *Engel v Vitale: Prayer in Schools,* quotes Lawrence Roth thusly: "My basic feeling was that if the State could tell us what to pray and when to pray, there was no stopping."

Joe Roth was just a kid at the time and admits he wasn't all that gung ho on the idea. "Dad was pushing it. As it got further along and I got a little older I could see what it was. I couldn't see the politics in it, but I could see the right and wrong of it."

Losing unanimously at every stop along the way, the case ultimately went to the Supreme Court. It took four years, and during that time Roth and his family were the subjects of occasional intimidation. A 25-foot tall cross was set on fire in the family's yard. The FBI kept them under close watch.

Along the way Joe Roth was simply trying to be a kid, albeit one who was often the object of hushed conversations and furtive finger pointing by other kids and their parents. What helped him the most during this time was sports. Roth says his skill at athletics helped him maintain some sense of normalcy, particularly in the eyes of his peers. "How's this kid involved in this thing, but he's out here playing ball with us?" For kids, that was ultimately good enough. Let the adults have their boring arguments. Kids just want to play ball. "The fact that I played three sports and was a leader on my teams saved me. If I was a bookish kid afraid of his own shadow, I would have really had a hard time."

Roth says he wasn't even aware the case was being argued at the Supreme Court until the day he rode his bicycle home from school and found his house surrounded by TV trucks. The Court had ruled 6 to 1 in favor of the plaintiffs. A half-century later he says the entire experience is a huge influence on his life.

"It colored my life significantly. It gave me a view of the world that most people don't get to see when they're 12 years old. I think it gave me courage. You've got to stand up for what you believe in, and sometimes that's painful."

ROTH MOVED TO SAN FRANCISCO, CALIFORNIA in 1970 and began a career in show business by accident, he says. A woman he knew was living with a guy in the movie business. Roth says he got to know the guy, found the business interesting, and accepted an offer to work as his assistant. The guy did business with a company called American Zoetrope which was a new studio founded by a pair of young film makers named Francis Ford Coppola and George Lucas.

In 1976 Roth produced his first film, *"Tunnel Vision,"* a comedy about an uncensored TV network that featured then-unknown future stars Chevy Chase, John Candy, Laraine Newman, Howard Hesseman, and Al Franken, among others. The movie cost $33,000 to produce and grossed $20 million. Roth was on his way.

By 1987 he was part of a partnership that formed the studio Morgan Creek Productions. Two years later after a string of hits that included *"Young Guns"* and *"Major League,"* Roth became the chairman of 20th Century Fox. One of his first projects there was a small budget movie about a kid accidentally left behind by his parents when they leave on a vacation. *"Home Alone"* became one of the movie businesses' all-time success stories, grossing nearly half a billion dollars at the box office.

"I was proud of it," Roth says. "That was a tiny little movie and we could see it played so well. You could so easily consider it a third-tier offering, and we put it out as a first-tier offering and it went through the roof."

Roth oversaw several other hits (and typically of Hollywood film makers a few misses) while at Fox. Some were blockbusters like *"Die Hard 2"* and *"Sleeping with the Enemy."* Others were sleepers, small movies that became wildly popular, like *"My Cousin Vinny"* and *"White Men Can't Jump."*

Roth left Fox in 1992 to join Walt Disney Studios, where he eventually became chairman in 1996. He enjoyed tremendous success there, overseeing dozens of hits.

In 2000 he struck a partnership with among other entities Sony Pictures and formed his own production company called Revolution Studios. Over the next seven years the company produced hits like *"Black Hawk Down"* and *"XXX,"* and misses like *"Gigli."* In 2004 Roth also produced the Academy Awards TV broadcast.

Running Revolution Studios grew increasingly complex, as the challenges of bankrolling and making up to eight movies a year were exacerbated by the emergence of technology that was changing how people could be entertained. When his deal with Sony expired in 2007 he shuttered the film division of Revolution, a move that coincided with his desire to make fewer movies and tackle a new challenge.

"I love soccer. I played as a kid, I played in college, and I was a little frustrated the sport hadn't achieved the popularity in America that it deserved. I woke up one morning, came downstairs and said to my wife 'You know what? I think I'm going to start a soccer team.'"

He says his wife Irene "shrugged her shoulders in a positive way" and off he went. He sought out Tim Leiweke and Dan Beckerman, who (among other things) were executives with the Los Angeles Galaxy. Leiweke and Beckerman took Roth through the mechanics of what getting involved with MLS would mean. They suggested he go to New York City and meet with league commissioner Don Garber.

At the meeting Roth stressed his love for soccer and his ability to market. He had marketed the movies he had made over the years and felt his marketing acumen could help the league — that marketing a sports team or league was really no different than marketing a movie.

"They're exactly the same," he says. "My job in both businesses is to appeal to people who are at home with an awful lot of things that they can do, including not go out, and I'm trying to get their entertainment dollar. I've got to market to them and deliver product to them that makes them say 'instead of staying home tonight I'm going to go out.'"

Garber liked what he heard and gave Roth one piece of geographical advice. "He said to go look in the Northwest, because that's where they were looking to expand."

Roth explored Portland, Vancouver, and Seattle. He liked all three markets, but saw Seattle as having the most potential. Part of that stemmed from the timing of his arrival in town, which coincided with yet another of the seemingly unending battles over facilities between the city and its pro sports teams.

WHEN STARBUCKS CHAIRMAN Howard Schultz had purchased the NBA's Seattle Supersonics from Barry Ackerley in 2001, his arrival was greeted with great anticipation. The Sonics had been largely successful under Ackerley and the belief was that Schultz would build upon that success with the same golden touch he had shown at Starbucks.

But Schultz was behind the 8-ball almost immediately. He had the misfortune of buying into pro basketball after the disastrous lockout of 1999. The changing economics of the NBA made it harder to make money, and the glaring hole in the Sonics game was Key Arena, which opened in 1995.

The building had been known as the Seattle Center Coliseum and was originally built in 1962 for the World's Fair before being completely remodeled. The good news was Seattle had a new arena. The bad news was the remodel had been done on the cheap. Seattle fans need only drive three hours south to Portland or three hours north to Vancouver to see new arenas that were opened in the same year that made Key Arena feel comparatively small and unimpressive. The arena's club seat sections were so poorly designed that they were eventually taken out, denying the team a lucrative money stream available in most other NBA arenas. Key Arena's suites paled in comparison to the suites in new stadiums built for the Seahawks and Mariners. And, unlike those stadiums, the Sonics didn't control any of the parking around their arena.

Citing those new stadiums and the fact that he was losing money, Schultz tried to stir up interest in a new arena in 2005 for his basketball team. His pleas for help were greeted with a look that would remind you of Uncle Pennybags on the Monopoly *Chance* card that demands payment of a "Poor Tax." Palms up and empty pockets pulled out made clear the message from government officials and taxpayers weary of stadium politics: Key Arena had been remodeled just nine years earlier ... you'll have to make do.

If it had just been Schultz on the losing end, maybe he would have chosen to hang in there. But he had over 50 partners in his Sonics ownership group and many of them were tired of capital calls. Those with check-writing fatigue wanted out, and the sooner the better.

Speaking of Sooners, enter Clay Bennett. The Oklahoma businessman had put a group of his own together and offered Schultz the outrageous sum of $350 million for the team in the summer of 2006. Schultz had paid just $200 million only five years earlier, and he reacted like an auctioneer who's chiseled an extra few bucks out of a drunk at a charity fundraiser: *"SOLD!!!"*

The original spin on the deal from the Seattle side was that Bennett would have the wherewithal to get a new arena deal done. The frightening thing is how many people in the Seattle community bought that load of crap, particularly considering Bennett's stated intention regarding the new building. He and his wealthy group of Oklahomans would pony up exactly zero dollars. Bennett's plan from day one was clear to anyone dealing with even a modicum of common sense. That included Roth, who by 2007 was beginning to explore the Seattle business scene with thoughts of purchasing an MLS expansion team for the area.

"When I got to Seattle, Bennett was playing with a couple of aces," Roth relates. "He was saying to the city 'either build me a $500-million-dollar stadium or I'm leaving.' I talked to all the guys around me up here and they said 'well, you know, maybe it will work out.'"

Maybe it will work out? Roth was flabbergasted. "I said, 'you guys are nuts. This guy is from Oklahoma City, his money is from Oklahoma City, and you're never going to get the money to build the arena. He is on his way out.'"

Sadly for Seattle basketball fans, Roth was right. Bennett's "build me a $500 million dollar arena" request went over like a fart in a space suit. He eventually reached a deal to pay the city $40 million dollars to buy his way out of the final two years of his lease and moved the team to where he, his partners, and his money lived: OKC.

Roth took no particular joy in being right, but the Sonics departure was one factor that made Seattle attractive to him as a potential soccer market. "It's a sports crazy town," he says, "and there's only two pro sports teams. It was also a city that had a great history in soccer."

Roth was already convinced he wanted to own a soccer team. Now he was convinced he wanted to own a soccer team in Seattle. All he needed were business partners who knew Seattle, soccer, and how to run a sports franchise.

He reconnected with Tim Leiweke, who offered to set up a dinner meeting in Seattle with his younger brother Tod. Roth didn't know it yet, but his latest show business project was about to get green lighted.

LIKE HIS BROTHER, Tim Leiweke had worked in professional sports since the days the duo were turning out the lights and "blowing stuff up" before MISL games in Kansas City. His path had taken him to Los Angeles where he was president of Anschutz Entertainment Group (AEG), the massive sports, arena, and entertainment company. Leiweke helped owner Phil Anschutz build a juggernaut that included ownership of the Los Angeles Kings of the NHL, the MLS Galaxy, the Staples Center and its adjoining entertainment complex LA Live, the O2 Arena in London, and part of the NBA's Los Angeles Lakers. He has since moved on to a similar position with Maple Leaf Sports and Entertainment in Toronto. "My brother," Tod says of his older sibling, "makes me look like I've got a hobby."

But on this night it was the younger brother who held sway. Roth wanted into the Seattle sports scene, and as the CEO of the Seahawks Tod Leiweke was in a position to help make that happen. The trio dined at Skycity, the revolving restaurant atop the Space Needle, and as he listened to Roth discuss his goals of establishing an MLS team in Seattle, Leiweke saw the possibilities. He thought of his friend and occasional soccer business partner Adrian Hanauer, who had long wanted to own a team in MLS, but felt such a venture was too risky to go it alone. He told Roth about the success Hanauer had achieved with the minor league Sounders. "He'd be good in this partnership," Leiweke concluded, "You should meet him."

Shortly after the dinner meeting with Roth, Leiweke contacted MLS commissioner Don Garber, who called Hanauer and suggested he and Roth get together.

"I call Joe," Hanauer says (presumably after finding out who he was), "and we have a very brief conversation and agree to meet at the MLS All-Star game in Denver in July of 2007."

The duo had at least two things in common. They were both successful businessmen and they both liked soccer. They quickly found out that they had another thing in common, and that interest served as an icebreaker at their first meeting.

"We got introduced and spent about 20 minutes talking poker," says Hanauer who had established himself as a good player, once winning $120,000 in a Las Vegas tournament. Roth also played the game and while he was happy to have a conversation starter, another positive about Hanauer's card-playing skill immediately struck him.

"I thought it was a good thing," Roth says, "for a general manager to be a good poker player." Their mutual interest in cards allowed them to briefly get to know each other before discussing the future of soccer in Seattle.

Once the conversation turned to business, one of the first things Roth told Hanauer was that he had to be the majority owner of the new team. "I wasn't going to do this and not be the majority owner," he says. "I have never worked well where someone has legal power over me. If it's going to fail, I'd rather let it fail on my shoulders. I'm the guy who likes to take the last shot. I'm comfortable with it."

With another person in another situation that might have been a non-starter, or at least a point of debate. But as an astute poker player, Hanauer understood the cards he'd been dealt. "I'm a pretty easy going and accommodating guy. Joe made it clear he wanted to be the majority owner and I was fine with that. I deferred to him and told him that however this comes about, I'm in. Joe was high profile and MLS wanted a high-profile owner. If they could have their pick, they'd want Joe as majority owner instead of me. I know my place in the world and I'm very comfortable with it."

Recalling that decision later Leiweke still admires Hanauer's willingness to work with Roth. "It was a real act of faith because he was putting up substantial dollars, but wasn't going to be the majority owner."

So Roth became the top owner (35 percent), delivering the high national profile that MLS wanted. But Hanauer had more than just money to bring to the partnership. "It felt like a movie studio, where I would be the chief executive," Roth says, "But I needed a guy in Adrian who lived and breathed soccer."

Hanauer's commitment to the Seattle soccer community had been well established by then and his family roots sank deep into the Puget Sound community, so in that regard he was the perfect complement to Roth, and would be in for 32.5 percent of the team.

While Roth and Hanauer were discussing pocket aces and partnerships in Denver, Leiweke considered ways the Seahawks organization could participate in the deal. He knew that his boss, Paul Allen, was interested in fulfilling the promise made to soccer fans — that if they voted "yes" in the 1997 stadium election an MLS team would come to Seattle. But he also knew Allen already had plenty of exposure and financial investment in pro sports, so getting him involved would take a little creativity.

The idea Leiweke hit on was not only creative, but would give the new franchise a foundation upon which unimaginable success would be built.

CHAPTER FIVE

SUMMER 2007
SEATTLE, WASHINGTON

⌀

"You've got some nice momentum right now,
but you're going to be like the Thunderbirds..."

Like many great ideas, in hindsight Leiweke's plan to get Paul Allen involved in the partnership with Roth and Hanauer to bring MLS to Seattle looks like a no-brainer. But at first glance it might have sounded a little one sided to Roth and Hanauer.

Leiweke proposed that Allen would own 25 percent of the team, but instead of putting up money he would provide business infrastructure in the form of the Seahawks marketing, sales, promotion, and media staff, as well as use of the team's stadium rent-free for home games.

Leiweke had convincing to do on both sides. On the one hand he had to convince Allen that his staff and management could handle the extra responsibility of a new soccer team. Allen's only concern was whether or not his top executives would get distracted from their duties with the Seahawks, but Leiweke assured him that wouldn't happen.

Meanwhile, Leiweke convinced Roth and Hanauer that what they really needed from Allen was the Seahawks organization's expertise. Roth and Hanauer wouldn't get any capital in the deal, but they instantly had an office staff trained in how to run a professional sports team.

"What they got," Leiweke says, "couldn't have been bought with dollars."

Roth's pragmatic side helped him instantly see the wisdom of the deal. "Paul Allen came on as a minority partner mostly for the staff. Because what do I know? I don't know how to run a team and I don't have any people here and I don't live here. I needed someone who could run the team, who had the people to sell the tickets and run the stadium."

Leiweke knew he had the right soccer guy in Hanauer because he'd known him and done business with him. He quickly began to feel the same way about Roth. "Joe brought a swagger to the whole thing. He was a very good guy to collaborate with because he had an opinion on everything but he didn't have to always be right. He always wanted to think bigger and press the frontier. He liberated, pushed, cajoled and expected everyone to think big. And he was dealing with guys who had had some success so the combination was really potent. As he pushed we were capable of the climb."

One of Roth's opinions actually turned into more of a mantra for the new team. He had been a fan of soccer for years and grown frustrated with the lack of respect the sport received in the USA. It frustrated him because among other things it set Americans apart as the one nation that doesn't "get" soccer. It also frustrated him because he thought part of the problem stemmed from soccer itself.

"One of the things I felt all along about MLS and soccer in America was they accepted their role as a secondary sport. So the first thing I felt was that we have to come out like we are a first-tier sport, like we are baseball, basketball, or football. I kept saying that everything we do we've got to do first tier. Our enemy was the 50-year-old white male sportswriters who thought of soccer as something their daughters played."

Roth brought more than his own cash and swagger, he brought another partner as well. As the deal was being put together he got a call from actor and comedian Drew Carey who told Roth he wanted to be a part of the ownership group. Carey's success in the TV business as an actor afforded him the kind of money it took to get into the group.

Roth was hesitant at first since the deal was almost done but the more he listened to Carey's passionate plea the more he liked the idea. "I put my head in a Seattle space. If it were a certain kind of Hollywood actor I wouldn't do it. Because then they would say it's a Hollywood thing or something like that. But that's not Drew. Drew's a regular guy, kind of America's guy. So he came in as a partner."

The group had no idea what Carey's partnership would actually lead to.

WITH THE DEAL IN PLACE Leiweke began the task of convincing the Seahawks office staff that they should be enthusiastic about the added workload: Managing the daily business of an expansion franchise playing a sport many of them didn't know much about.

He first had several meetings with the Seahawks executive team to discuss implementation of a strategy that would make the deal work. At these meetings Leiweke noticed that he had one executive more than any other who was consistently able to speak fluently and authoritatively on the subject of soccer.

Since his trip to Spain in 1998 when he made his 180-degree turn on soccer, Gary Wright had immersed himself in becoming an educated soccer fan. Subsequent European trips had been built around major matches and afforded Wright the opportunity to experience the game at the highest level in legendary locations. But for the most part, he kept these stories to himself. After all, discussing passion for soccer sometimes invited the kind of teasing that Wright himself once dished out to co-workers who loved the sport.

He often found himself on the end of pointed barbs from his close friend Holmgren, who didn't get Wright's new obsession.

Wright took the digs good-naturedly. But as 2007 unfolded and the Seahawks executive team began discussing the eventual arrival of an MLS team, his expertise allowed him to take a larger role in soccer discussions. No one was more surprised by this than Leiweke, who had never imagined him to be such a knowledgeable (and suddenly valuable) resource on the topic.

"Tod was shocked," Wright says. "He likes to say I came out of the closet. I know I'm on my way out, retirement-wise, but I'm participating in the meetings and I'm giving my opinion on what we should do and how we should do it. There weren't a lot of people in that room that knew anything about soccer."

While Wright knew a lot about the sport and was happy to be a source of information in meetings, he harbored no thoughts about working for the MLS team and spent part of his days pondering life after retirement. "Soccer was on my radar to the degree that I'm going to retire and I'm going to go watch soccer games in Europe."

But Leiweke realized he'd struck gold. For the first time he noticed that Wright's office contained an amazing array of soccer art, books, and memorabilia. The cultural barometer of the Seahawks organization wasn't going anywhere. He would play a critical part in establishing the culture of MLS in Seattle.

"He was ready to retire," Leiweke says, "but this was such a unique and interesting opportunity that intrigued him. He became fundamental to the whole thing." His partner Roth concurred. "I spent some time with Gary," he says, "And I said 'oh, no, you're not retiring. If I'm coming up here you're going to be there.'"

Wright first would take on the challenge of convincing the Seahawks staff to buy into the organization's new commitment to soccer. Preaching with the kind of zeal found only in the newly converted, Wright began working desk to desk to build enthusiasm for the project.

The benefit of hindsight makes it appear as an easy sell, but in fact it was anything but easy. The bulk of the organization, marketing, ticketing, sales, media relations, and office staff had to somehow be sold that doubling their workload (without a corresponding doubling of their pay) would end up being a positive. Wright's longevity with the organization gave him well-earned credibility with everyone in the office. When he talked, people listened.

Among those listening early on and eager to help was Matt Johnson. Johnson worked for the Seahawks media relations department and produced their games on radio. He was also a lifelong soccer player and fan and an enthusiastic backer of the idea Wright was pitching.

"Gary's delivery to the hands-on people convinced them," Johnson says. "He was saying 'you just wait and see; this is going to work. You'll love it. You'll get it. If it happened to me it can happen to anyone.' And it worked for about 98 percent of the people. People trusted him because he already commanded your respect. People would follow Gary over a cliff."

Wright says he felt his role was "to help influence where we were going and to help paint the broad picture. The big stuff Tod was going to do. When it came down to putting the details in there, that's where I had some expertise."

The job the Seahawks did convincing people to commit to soccer was not lost on Hanauer. "Friday afternoon, everyone in the Seahawks office left and they were just focusing on football. Monday morning they came in and they had another job piled on their desk. People could have taken that as, 'Now I have more work and more events to go to and I'm not getting paid any more money … this is total bullshit. And by the way I don't even like soccer.'"

Reaction was the exact opposite Hanauer says because of Leiweke and Wright. "Tod set the tone, and Gary carried the torch."

"On the ground," Wright says, "the troops have to buy into it too. Some of the things we did kind of helped that. We put together a group to work on our mission statement and our brand wheel. When we did that we made sure we had contrarians in the room. We didn't want people that just bought into this. We needed some who didn't buy in or didn't know anything about it."

The brand wheel is a tool by which a company (or team) tries to define itself using a series of words and phrases. It's an internal piece of literature designed to let people who work for a company know exactly what that company stands for in short, simple terms. It's easy to dismiss as a gimmick, but Wright says it was an important tool.

"When Tod arrived in 2003 the Seahawks were struggling as a business. He brought in a consulting company and they created a brand wheel for the team. It essentially answers the questions: 'Who are we? How are we perceived? What's our franchise DNA?'"

By the time the soccer team was emerging, the culture within the Seahawks had changed to the point that no consulting company was needed for the Sounders. The people who worked there created the brand wheel that would be used for soccer. "That as much as anything allowed us to continue on the same path," Wright says. "Not every franchise knows who they are, but we did. It's pretty important."

They not only knew who they were, but they also knew where they wanted to play and to whom they wanted to primarily market the team. Both of those decisions ran counter to MLS philosophy. The accepted wisdom within MLS in 2007 was that a new team's fan base would best be built with a stadium located in the suburbs and the pursuit of fans centered around soccer moms, dads, and kids. Seattle's emerging soccer team early on had ditched the suburban stadium plan — directly against the advice of the league and commissioner Don Garber.

"Some felt using a big stadium was a potential franchise killer," Leiweke says. "The league wanted us to build a specific stadium as part of the team launch because they weren't convinced it would work. And it did defy all logic within the league at that point."

Leiweke's motivation in the argument was twofold. He reported directly to Paul Allen, and as such didn't want to try to explain how a potential revenue stream had been diverted away from Seattle's new stadium to an even newer (and smaller) soccer stadium.

He also was sincere in fulfilling the promise that the Seahawks had made years ago to soccer fans: Help us get our stadium built and we'll use it for MLS games. So he took the argument back to what he calls a patriotic place. "The plaque on the side of the stadium says it is a 'football/soccer stadium' and if we build a new stadium just for soccer, people are going to be mad. That's not what they voted for."

There was one other reason Leiweke had for not wanting to even think about a stadium in the suburbs, and it came as a result of confidence with perhaps a slight dash of bravado. "I remember telling Don (Garber) that if we build a 20,000 seat stadium it won't be big enough."

So it was settled. Their games would be played on the south edge of downtown Seattle in the heart of the city. As for the primary marketing effort, the entire group felt the "market to the youth soccer organizations" model favored by many MLS teams was simply the incorrect way to go.

"I never want to do something because it's the way it's always been done," Hanauer says. "I can't stand that kind of thinking." He had studied and liked the way the MLS expansion team in Toronto had integrated into the community by marketing to soccer *fans*.

"Toronto illustrated to us that this business didn't need to be and shouldn't be built on the backs of the youth soccer market," Hanauer says. "In the history of MLS prior to that it had always been built on youth soccer, but trying to get people to come to a game after they spent eight hours at tournaments on a Saturday was a difficult sell." So while soccer moms, dads, and kids would be enthusiastically welcomed, they would not be the focus of the new team's marketing effort.

"We decided we didn't want this to be a team where kids were dropped off while the parents go to dinner," Leiweke says. "The kids go to the game and we run Sponge Bob videos on the board. That was my trite characterization as to how soccer was presented in many places. We wanted to start with those people I saw at The George and Dragon."

The George and Dragon is a bar that had a well-earned reputation as a place where soccer fans gather to watch games from
around the globe. Wright had learned that back in 1998 when
he watched the World Cup semifinals there. The George and
Dragon was the type of place where if you arrived at 6:45 for a
game that started at 7:00 you were often out of luck in terms of
finding a seat. That's 7:00 a.m., by the way.

The new Seattle team would be marketed to and built primarily for that type of soccer fan. Indeed it was at The George
and Dragon on a Monday morning in November of 2007 that
the announcement was made that an MLS expansion franchise
had been granted to Seattle. The announcement was made by
a guy comfortable working a bar crowd. The guy Roth called
"America's guy." Drew Carey.

Sometime during all these discussions, the idea of what to
call this new team came up, leading to long internal debate influenced (unsuccessfully) by MLS. That debate resulted in another
good decision in the spring of 2008.

The name Sounders was not only the name of Seattle's current USL team but had been synonymous with soccer in Seattle
going back to the NASL days of 1974, and as far as MLS was
concerned that was reason enough to *NOT* hang that sobriquet
on the new team. It was a name MLS felt that was associated first
with a league that didn't exist anymore, and then with a minor
league team.

The debate within the office presented reasonable arguments
on both sides. There was a strong lean to keep the name as a nod
to history, but there was the argument that something new was
being started and deserved its own identity.

"We went back and forth internally," Wright says. "We'd
have a meeting and decide we don't want to be the Sounders because that's a minor league team. Yeah there's a history there, but
we can't have anyone thinking we're a minor league team. Then
we'd meet again and decide maybe we should be the Sounders
because of the tradition and things like that."

Hanauer believed that the new team should be called the
Sounders and carry the weight of the colorful history of Seattle's

past, but he was willing to consider the other side of the argument. Perhaps a new team should have a new name and a fresh start. While on a business trip in France, he checked in on a USL Sounders chat room on the Internet ... and he was strongly swayed back to his original point of view.

The announcement of a plan to allow fans to vote on a name for the team was just days away, and Hanauer noticed several heated on-line discussions from fans who were convinced that the name Sounders wouldn't be a part of the vote. Their reaction? *Outrage*. Hanauer contacted Leiweke and told him the team was making a big mistake if they didn't somehow, someway, give fans the chance to vote for the name "Sounders." The league was still against using a minor league name but a nice compromise was reached.

Fans who wanted to vote could choose from three MLS approved (cringe-worthy) names: Seattle Alliance, Seattle Republic, or Seattle FC. But they'd also be given the fourth option of a write in vote.

"The naming of the team was the first issue where the fan passion really came forward," Leiweke says. "We put this thing out there and thousands of people voted. And if you combined the other three options, they didn't add up to the number of votes for the Sounders. That heartened all of us. We were thrilled. The fans stepped up and did the right thing. Their voice was heard and it was the first ember that sparked the bigger flame."

John Rizzardini says there was a more tangible effect that materialized after the vote. "All of a sudden our season ticket base started climbing. The supporters groups started recruiting their friends to buy tickets. They told their friends 'we won. The authority figures wanted this other name and they were going to disrespect us. They didn't think we were important.'"

As the momentum continued to build Rizzardini still occasionally questioned whether it was all going to work. "I had a media sales guy pitching me on a big advertising package and I didn't bite on it because we weren't going to do as much mainstream advertising. We wanted to go a different direction. He said to me 'You've got some nice momentum right now, but you're going to be like the Thunderbirds (Seattle's junior league hockey team). You won't get much media coverage. You'll have a nice crowd the first year.'

"At the time he said it, that was very reasonable. No one knew. All we had was this great vision on a bunch of flip charts."

THEY HAD CONVINCED the rank and file within the Seahawks organization to embrace the idea of soccer. They had convinced MLS that they should (and would) play in an NFL stadium. They had decided to forego traditional MLS marketing ideas and forged one of their own: to reach out to what they believed to be a huge part of the Seattle sports scene that was underserved. And when the league pushed them to avoid a traditional nickname, they pushed back and allowed their growing fan base to make the right call.

They now had a name: officially it was Sounders FC. But for many fans they were simply the Sounders.

The next big decision made during this critical time was one that most fans weren't aware of, but it was the final piece to connect the new soccer team to the Seahawks culture. Phones would now be answered "thank you for calling the Seattle Seahawks AND Sounders FC." Business cards were updated to include the Sounders logo. Email addresses were changed to @seahawks-soundersfc.com.

A small detail at first glance, that decision went a long way towards establishing the Sounders credibility. They would not be an afterthought. They would be a part of an already established and successful organization. The regular meetings on the team began expanding to include more than just executives, which allowed workers to begin to feel ownership of the new team.

"What they (Leiweke and Wright) did from day one," Hanauer says, "was position this thing within the Seahawks business offices as something new and exciting. Something you not only could be proud of, but that was also was good for your career. They treated it like a top-level professional team."

Roth's mantra, everything must be first tier, was taking root deep within the team's emerging internal culture. "We never accepted the idea that we were anything but the main attraction. You kind of will that after a while. You believe it and the people around you start believing it."

Wright helped establish that attitude by remembering the lessons from two stops during his early days in pro sports. In the mid-1970s he was the VP of operations for the Phoenix Racquets of World Team Tennis, and then the director of publicity for the Southern California Sun of the World Football League.

Both of the franchises (for that matter both leagues) suffered from a severe lack of capital, which led to constantly cutting corners. Teams in both leagues were sometimes dishonest with the media in business matters, which called the credibility of the entire operation into question. Wright saw firsthand the damage done by such actions.

He vowed that the Sounders would not succumb to shortsighted thinking or attitudes. "Being first class was absolutely essential. We had to be seen as major league like the Seahawks, the Mariners, or the Sonics. To be any different we were setting the bar too low. I think too many times new franchises will do that. We didn't."

To that end, Wright insisted that major team announcements be made in grand style at places like the Space Needle or the Columbia Tower. Press conferences were presented in the same manner and style as those done by the Mariners or Seahawks. That was the kind of thing Wright had specialized in for years: a small detail that made a big statement.

Wright also began arranging for important international games to be shown in the Seahawks auditorium and invited the entire Seahawks (and now Sounders FC) staff to watch. He would send interested staffers home with a soccer book or video and encourage them to write up a report on what they saw. Soccer photos from old Sounders games were hung throughout the office and Hanauer was allowed to sit in with coaches and player personnel people the day of the NFL Draft to see how the Seahawks went about building a team.

That last move was more than just a courtesy; it came about after another important decision the emerging organization made. Hanauer had been the general manager of the Sounders in the USL for several years by now and had impressed Leiweke and Wright with how well he ran the team.

"He learned the ins and outs by running a minor league team and he was able to get an education that no one could have given him," says Wright who also liked the teams Hanauer put on the field. "They always had chemistry. You could tell they liked playing together and they worked hard for each other. He knew how to put that piece together."

The Sounders had won two USL championships on Hanauer's watch and in the department of if "it ain't broke don't fix it," a decision was made to use his talent to not just co-own the new team, but help put it together.

The idea at first surprised Hanauer who recalls that "at our first strategic meeting Tod said 'I think Adrian should be the General Manager. Owner and GM, how cool would that be?' I said 'well...I don't know. Maybe it's cool. Let me think about it.' So I sort of got volunteered to be general manager and began to focus on the sporting side."

Roth had participated in and observed all of these events and regularly made trips to Seattle from Hollywood. He was in an interesting position in that he was the majority owner, but he didn't have much history with any of the other key players making decisions. Wright, Hanauer, and Leiweke had known each other for years and had built up a level of trust and comfort. Roth was attempting to do the same on the fly and occasionally brought allies with him from Los Angeles for meetings.

"He would show up with these guys with Creative Artists who were coming up for the early meetings," Leiweke says. "At first he was a bit dubious about whether or not an NFL team would take this on and pay enough attention to it."

Creative Artists Agency is a huge Los Angeles entertainment and sports firm, and Roth had hired them to observe and advise him on his new sports investment. The more he watched what was happening and how it was happening the more he knew, Leiweke says, that he'd made a good investment.

"He realized the depth of the passion and how much fun we were having. We loved it. It was so much fun and it was the right thing for our city. It was making good on an unfulfilled promise of bringing a team. So there was no downside at all."

Roth and Hanauer were touching base daily on the phone and Hanauer got a good indication of the gravitas Roth carried when on one occasion he was too busy to take his call. "Joe's a big deal in Hollywood, but I didn't know he was *that* big of a deal. To me he was just my soccer partner. His assistant called me and said 'I have Joe Roth on the line.' I said 'I'm sorry I'm in the middle of something, can I call him back?' She was stunned. As if no one had ever said that to him. I was like 'is that bad? Did I screw up?'"

Another time, he called and Roth wasn't there. "I started to leave my number and his assistant said 'no, no, no! You're the only phone number in the whole world he knows by heart.'"

IT HAD BEEN A LITTLE OVER a year since Leiweke had met Roth for dinner at the Space Needle. In that time a creative ownership group and business structure plan was put together. The Seahawks staff had enthusiastically embraced soccer and had already been engaged by a fan base that had put down 10,000 season ticket deposits in less than a month. Everyone had been overwhelmed with fan response to the team name vote.

Leiweke and Wright knew enough about how the business end of sports worked to know that what they had witnessed over the past year was a special, once-in-a-lifetime thing. By the time Wright's "retirement" from the Seahawks was announced in 2008 he had long ago accepted a job to help run the business side of the Sounders. Nonetheless the Seahawks wanted to honor him for three-plus decades of service, so a retirement party was held at the stadium. At the party it was announced that the press box where the Seahawks and Sounders played would be forever known as the Gary Wright Press Box.

"I remember telling him," says Leiweke, "you don't have to be dead to get things like this to happen; you just have to be really good."

Wright says Leiweke told him something else that night. As the two reflected on Wright's NFL career, they also excitedly looked ahead to the arrival of the MLS to Seattle.

"With everything we've got in place," Leiweke said, "we could paint a masterpiece here."

CHAPTER SIX

♪

"These kids know what a beer's for!"

Ever since pro sports arrived in earnest in Seattle — which is to say when the Kingdome opened in 1976 — Pioneer Square eating and drinking establishments have been within a Kasey Keller goal kick of the action.

Consider that the NASL Sounders opened the Kingdome with the legendary Pele game, the Seahawks and Mariners soon took up residence in the building, and the NBA Supersonics played the majority of their home games there from 1978 to 1985. The Dome hosted the NFL Pro Bowl in 1977, the MLB All Star game in 1979, and the NBA All Star game in 1987. The NCAA Final Four was played in the building three times (1984, 1989, and 1995).

And when the Dome was imploded in spectacular fashion in 2000, it took two new stadiums to take its place ... and of course they both went in the same area at the south edge of the Pioneer Square neighborhood. Right there, waiting to greet them across King Street from the Kingdome then and Century Link Field now has been Mick McHugh, the original, longtime, and only proprietor of legendary Seattle watering hole F.X. McRory's.

McRORY'S HAS BEEN SERVING Seattle sports fans food and drink since it opened in 1977, and McHugh enthusiastically embraced the idea of the Sounders moving to MLS; a reaction based more on being a business owner than a soccer fan. He knew that adding 20 major events a year to the neighborhood would mean more customers on more nights. He just didn't realize how many more.

Like much of Seattle he was pleasantly surprised by how big the crowds were, and he immediately ramped up his staff on game nights to take care of the before and after crowd of hungry and thirsty fans. In the midst of the Great Recession, the increase in economic activity in the area made all the difference to McRory's and lots of other establishments.

Amid the din of a bar packed with Sounders fans following a 2-nil win over San Jose in 2009 a friend shouted to McHugh, "How's business?" He glanced over the crowd with a smile on his face and maybe the slightest glint of dollar signs in his eyes, and thundered: "Let me tell you something about soccer fans.... These kids know what a beer's for!"

McHugh refers to everyone younger than him (a significant portion of the population in his bar) as kids. And he has come to love the "kids" who support the Sounders. After all, they saved his business.

"Those 20 soccer days saved us," he says. "We're married to the Mariners for 81 days, and that's a huge chunk of why we're here from April 1 to October 1. We'd plan everything around Mariners home stands."

That was a plan that worked well between 1995 and 2003 when the Mariners were good enough to set attendance records. But as the club became stuck in a decade-long slump, attendance dropped significantly, and along with it, revenue for bars and restaurants in the area.

Cue the cavalry, here came the Sounders!

"To have those games with 40,000 people," McHugh says, "It's been huge for the whole neighborhood. These guys were the saviors. They put some life back in the city."

On game nights, McHugh's joint is packed to the point he sets up a small bar in the lobby to help handle the crush of thirsty fans. He quickly noticed something interesting about the soccer crowd that was different than a football crowd. At the request of some Sounders fans he started stocking the British beer Boddington's Pub Ale in his lobby bar.

"There's a tremendous British influence on this crowd," McHugh says. So tremendous that before long Boddington's was outselling Budweiser on Sounders game nights. "That," he says, "never happens."

JOHN BAYLISS or GARETH ETCHELLS could have given McHugh a scouting report on the British influence on soccer fans and how passionate these fans were going to be. Bayliss (from Hereford, England) owns The George and Dragon Pub, which has become known as *the* soccer pub in Seattle. It's the bar where Sounders executives first began to formulate the idea of marketing the team to soccer fans, rather than soccer moms.

Bayliss laughs when his pub is referred to as a "soccer bar," saying "You can go anywhere around the world, go into the smallest bar and restaurant, and if there's a game on, there's going to be a TV with people glued to it. In Europe you can walk into a place that dates from the 1500s and there's a TV in there somewhere and soccer is on. So the term 'soccer bar' is kind of funny."

The George and Dragon has become legendary for hosting big matches. The legend dates to the pub's opening in 1995 when it was one of the few (if not only) places that showed European league games. Bayliss invested significant money in satellite TV technology that allowed him to show games that no one else could get. "We were the only place where you could watch the

English league. When we opened in 1995 we'd have big crowds coming in to watch games at ungodly hours. It was all closed circuit and it was only us carrying it."

Soccer fans from as far away as eastern Washington and even Vancouver, B.C., went to The George and Dragon to watch Premier League games. Kasey Keller's mom occasionally watched her son play there. So, funny or not, Bayliss's pub became known as a soccer bar.

Etchells (from Cambridge, England) was a bartender at The George and Dragon before opening up his own English-style pub called the Atlantic Crossing, in the Roosevelt neighborhood on Seattle's north side. The Atlantic Crossing has become known as the primary drinking home of the Emerald City Supporters since hosting the first ECS viewing party for a USL playoff game in 2008.

When Seattle-based Red Hook Brewery collaborated with ECS to brew a beer specifically for the group, the concoction (*ECS No Equal Amber Lager*) was first poured at the Atlantic Crossing. It is even the home of the Cascadia Cup; the supporters trophy awarded each year to whichever team has the best record in games between Seattle, Portland, and Vancouver.

So, Bayliss and Etchells could have told McHugh that soccer fans would be ready to party. Bayliss remembers a time when the police were called to The George and Dragon on a noise complaint. This is not an unheard of phenomenon for a neighborhood pub, but on this occasion the cops showed up to investigate a party raging at 7:30 ... on a Thursday *morning*.

The US Men's national team was playing Ghana in the 2006 World Cup. "I think it was a 7 a.m. kickoff," Bayliss says. "We opened the parking lot as a beer garden. We had 200 inside and 200 outside. We've also got some pretty good-sized speakers for the commentary. So the police came by and said, 'someone's complained about the noise, all these people out here chanting and cheering.'"

Bayliss explained to the officer that it was the World Cup and it was team USA, after all. "I told him 'if you want to ask the people who complained to come down and ask us to turn it down, you can.' The policeman, perhaps infused with a sudden dose of patriotism, elected to let the party rage on.

"These kids know what a beer's for!"

ETCHELLS REMEMBERS EARLY morning duties at games like that as a bartender at The George and Dragon. Later, when he owned his own place, there was another World Cup game involving the US team set to kick off at just after 4 a.m. Etchells announced that, of course, the Atlantic Crossing would show the match, and when he arrived at 3:45 a.m. to open, he actually had to elbow his way into his own place since the line to get in stretched from his front door to the end of the block. *At three forty-five in the morning!*

Etchells had to serve the crowd coffee and soft drinks because even with a temporary license that allowed for his bar to be open at one of the thin hours between "last night" and "tomorrow morning," he still wasn't allowed to serve the good stuff until 6 a.m. "People were looking at their watches counting the minutes until 6 o'clock," he laughs. "They're staring at their watches and saying 'one more minute! God I need a beer!' We went through several big pots of coffee waiting for 6 a.m."

Asked about the typical atmosphere during games at the Atlantic Crossing, Etchells jerks a thumb skyward toward a ceiling with several stains. "That's beer all over the ceiling. That's a good sign of how crowds get in here during games. That's from goals. We sometimes have beer dripping on your head after a goal."

Like McHugh and Bayliss, Etchells says his bar is so crowded for Sounders games (both home and away) that he doubles his staff to handle the extra demand. Bayliss went further than that to handle the demand of a growing soccer fan base. He doubled his bars. In 2010 he opened The Market Arms Pub in Seattle's Ballard neighborhood (about 10 minutes from The George and Dragon). The bar opened at 7 a.m. on the first day of the 2010 World Cup and in a refrain that should be familiar by now, it was filled with 200 customers by 7:05.

"These kids know what a beer's for."

The Seattle soccer pub scene was about more than just raising hell and drinking beer with your scrambled eggs (or nervously counting down the seconds until you *could* drink a beer with your scrambled eggs.) Places like The George and Dragon and the Atlantic Crossing were where Seattle's soccer culture was developing. At these bars you were more likely to hear someone discussing the recent Arsenal-Tottenham match than last night's Mariners game. They became places where soccer fans, often marginalized by mainstream sports fans, got to know one another.

"It was kind of like, 'oh ... you're into soccer, too!'" says Etchells. "It was how you met people. You'd be cheering together, and a goal would be scored, and you'd hug the guy next to you. Then you'd introduce yourself and say 'you know, typically, I wouldn't be hugging you.'"

Aaron Reed joined the ECS in 2009 and eventually became the group's travel coordinator. "A lot of places you go people will give you shit for being a soccer fan. Atlantic Crossing gave soccer fans a regular place to go where they could be themselves." It also became an incubator for the fledgling support group.

The ECS of those days was a much smaller group following a minor-league team. Games drew less than 4,000 fans, but the Sounders were usually good. They won the league in 2005 and 2007 and they made the playoffs in 2008, when they were assigned a first-round match at Montreal.

There wasn't any traditional over-the-air or cable TV broadcasts of the game, but the USL did make an online feed available on the league website. The ECS planned a viewing party at the Atlantic Crossing. ECS co-president Greg Mockos recalls that the viewing portion of the viewing party was less than stellar.

"We put in a shitty, grainy feed from a laptop on a wifi that was shitty into the TV," he says. The broadcast quality? You can figure out the one-word answer to that question.

But it was the crowd at the event that impressed Mockos. "That was the first time the Sounders organization had acknowledged ECS. We had 200 people come out to that event and that was the first time we kind of realized how big it could be."

THE AWAY GAME VIEWING party became a valuable recruiting tool for ECS during the Sounders early days in MLS. The parties were held at the Atlantic Crossing or other soccer friendly pubs where the group was allowed, in Reed's words, to "sing, chant, and be dumb asses for as long as we wanted." This behavior naturally attracted attention and led to people wanting to join in on the fun. Reed gives a lot of credit for the group's growth during this time to Zach Crisman, an ECS member who died in 2011 at the age of 29.

"He was our outreach guy, this big guy wearing a scarf who would walk up to and engage anyone. He was the evangelical supporter of the Sounders. If someone was standing over in the corner and didn't know what was going on or didn't know the words to the song, he'd put his arm around him and explain what was going on. He made sure everyone felt included."

The Seattle soccer community continued to grow, and as it did, Bayliss says, "There was a feeling that with all these guys in here watching it at 7 a.m. live on the TV, wouldn't it be great to go to a nice, big stadium and see it week in and week out?"

In what became yet another happy accident on the road to the launch of the Sounders into MLS, two of the team's key officials already knew about The George and Dragon and knew about the passion on display there from fans seemingly all day every day. Gary Wright had discovered it after his sudden plunge into soccer in 1998 when he needed a place to watch the semifinals of the World Cup. He had since become, if not quite a regular, a frequent visitor ("He was in here all the time watching Champions League games," Bayliss remembers.)

"It was part of what convinced me that soccer could work so well here," Wright says. "I'd go to watch games there and it was packed ... 7 a.m. for a Liverpool game, packed ... 4 p.m. for an Arsenal game, packed."

Adrian Hanauer also was a frequent visitor to the pub to watch games. When the Sounders executive team and ownership group was being assembled in the fall of 2007 and decisions were being made on how best to market the team, both Wright and Hanauer told Tod Leiweke that he should visit The George and Dragon. Leiweke had never heard of the place, but he began dropping by the bar to learn about soccer fan culture.

"I was in there one night with my nephew," he says. "They were showing a replay of a Champions League match and it was just crazy. I was lucky enough to find a stool. My nephew was standing. I don't know if that was the moment that it occurred to me, but it was an incredible reinforcement that there was this population that loves soccer that *absolutely* understood the phenomenon of global soccer, and they were right here in Seattle just looking for an organization."

Neighborhood pubs like the Atlantic Crossing and The George and Dragon were where soccer fans watched big games, but with an MLS team coming to Seattle, those same fans would need a gathering place closer to the stadium on game nights. The fact that many of them assemble at the Pioneer Square bar Fuel is as much about luck, timing, and loyalty as it is some grand plan.

MIKE MORRIS HAD A LONGTIME dream to own a sports bar near the football and baseball stadiums in Seattle, and in March of 2006 that dream became a reality when he opened Fuel, a classic shot-and-a-beer spot three blocks from the stadiums. Morris grew up in Spokane, Washington, played high school soccer and was the kicker on his school's football team. So while he had a little background in soccer, he was mostly a sports fan, and had no inkling of Fuel becoming a gathering place for soccer fans. "When I chose this location soccer wasn't even on my mind. Now, it's the biggest thing that ever happened to us."

Morris remembers noticing "maybe one or two fans" wearing Sounders jerseys in his bar in the spring of 2006 on nights the USL team played. He asked them about the team and says it dawned on him that in addition to marketing his new bar to Mariners and Seahawks fans, he should try soccer fans, too. A regular patron kept telling him soccer was going to be the future of his bar, and Morris decided to become proactive.

He reached out through the social media site of the day: "I got on Myspace and found this group called the Emerald City

Supporters. I sent them a message inviting them to Fuel and offering to buy them some appetizers and maybe a drink or two. They hit me up on that."

Morris found a small-but-dedicated group of Sounders fans. They had been meeting before games at Fado, an Irish pub a few blocks away, but had worn out their welcome there. Fado had told them they couldn't sing their songs or do their chants because they were disturbing other customers.

Morris had a brand new bar, loved sports and the accompanying fans (after all he was one of them) ... and needed the customers. "I said 'you can chant all you want here.' And that's where the relationship started. I opened my doors to them when they were in the USL and had 30 members. I had no idea MLS was coming. Then, when it did ... that's when it exploded."

When it "exploded," Morris found himself feeling like a guy who worked three jobs to put his better half through medical school only to get jilted when the goal was achieved.

"They (the ECS) had lots of bars try to take them away with this deal or that special," he says, "but the one thing their leadership group always says is, I welcomed them when they were a nobody and allowed them to chant and sing. So when they went to MLS and the group changed from 30 to 2,000 people overnight, they remembered that I had opened the doors. So they made this their home bar."

Morris has reciprocated that loyalty: ECS members always get 10% off their bill at Fuel and never have to pay a cover on nights when the bar hosts a band. Reed points out that Morris also, "didn't bat an eye" when the group broke a table in the bar during a celebration when the Sounders won the 2009 US Open Cup tournament.

Game days at Fuel are like a gigantic, chaotic family reunion. Hugs and high fives are exchanged, beers are quaffed, and nachos demolished by giant crowds dressed in rave green and wearing ECS scarves. For big games, Morris clears out the parking lot next door and creates a beer garden effectively doubling the space of his bar.

And those lucky enough to be in Fuel on the right day or night, might even get their drinks paid for.

"We call it the Drew Carey Power Hour," Morris says. Carey contacts Morris about once a year on the day of a game and tells him he is coming by. Carey then tweets out the word, and a few minutes later, in he walks ready to cover the entire bar's beverages for an hour.

"Craziness ensues," says Morris who has noticed his customers tend to up their game when Carey is paying. "People who are drinking a Bud Light suddenly say 'can I have a pitcher of Bud Light and a Long Island Iced Tea and a shot of Patron, some nachos and a hamburger, and maybe a shot of Grey Goose.'"

Morris says Carey is monster tipper and says one of the added benefits is that despite the fact he only does it once a year, fans come by before every game to see if it's the Drew Carey Power Hour. He echoes McHugh's thoughts about what the Sounders and their fans have done for places like his in Pioneer Square.

"It's been so huge for the entire neighborhood. Pioneer Square was really hurting in 2008, but soccer kept it alive. Soccer was its saving grace. In 2008 bars were going under left and right. Everyone's numbers were down. Then the Sounders came around and it changed. Everything started going back up hill."

Along the way to their leap from the USL into MLS the Sounders were smart enough to recognize a huge community of people who didn't just play soccer on weekends or watch their kids play. The team embraced people who lived the sport, built their days around it, and made plans to be at their favorite pub to watch their favorite team, no matter the time.

Leiweke felt too many MLS teams in the past had discounted the existence of such a market in their communities, but he knew it existed in Seattle from first-hand experience, and it was those fans who become primary targets of the Sounders' original marketing efforts. "Those trips to The George and Dragon served as the inspiration for the core fan base we were going to build around. It was the epicenter."

McHUGH INSISTS HE WASN'T all that surprised when the MLS Sounders made such a big wave. He'd opened F.X. McRory's in the NASL glory days in Seattle and remembers some wild times, particularly when Vancouver came to town. "We had a great rivalry with them. They'd come down here with their big flags and they'd be marching around in here half looped and the pole would knock out one of our chandeliers. There'd be glass everywhere. I'm saying 'Damn it you guys! Get the hell out of here.'"

McHugh laughs and then corrects himself. "Actually, I told them to take the guy with pole out of here, but the rest of them could stay and keep drinking. It was all great fun."

He also experienced the great fun of having Carey in his bar after a Sounders win. Carey wasn't looking to buy the house a round, and in fact on this occasion it was the other way around. McHugh made sure Carey's group of four was taken care of and before they left he presented Carey with a copy of the famous Leroy Neiman painting of the bar.

When Carey asked for his tab the bartender told him McHugh had taken care of it. "So," McHugh remembers, "he ordered a soft drink, paid for it with a card, and added a huge tip for the staff."

The Sounders didn't just hit on the idea of selling the team to the pub crowd; they've cultivated the relationship over the years. Their website has a list of MLS Pubs in Seattle and players, coaches, and management make regular appearances to visit with fans. Bayliss says his customers are always pleasantly surprised at how accessible the Sounders are at these appearances: "They are happy to sit down and chat with anybody."

By the time they were ready to make the official announcement about an MLS team coming to Seattle, the Sounders had built up such a respect for the pub culture of soccer fans that they decided not to hold a press conference at a fancy hotel or the Space Needle or the stadium. No, Carey delivered the first official word of the team's impending arrival in November of 2007 to a packed house at The George and Dragon.

"We were allowed to release a snippet on our website," Bayliss recalls, "that there was going to be a special announcement regarding soccer locally, and of course that word spread pretty quick. By 11 that morning there's 250 people there with Sounders scarves of old."

John Rizzardini recalls that shortly after they arrived for the announcement, Carey became somewhat of a loose cannon. Carey had proposed several radical ideas in meetings with team officials regarding how the team should interact with fans. Borrowing from European clubs, Carey wanted fans to be able to vote the general manager out of office. He wanted fans to have a true voice in how the team was run.

"We had been talking privately, in meetings, about the idea of democracy in sports and having a vote on the GM," Rizzardini says. "Drew had proposed that we have a marching band. We were considering his ideas, but maybe not doing all of it for the first season. We were supposed to meet after the announcement to discuss how and when we were going to do these things."

The timetable for implementation of Carey's plans changed the second the red light of the TV news cameras came on.

"He gets out of the limo," Rizzardini says with a laugh, "and grabs the mic and starts announcing all these things we were going to do. I remember writing all of them down. 'OK ... he just said *this* so we're doing *this*. He said *that* so we're doing *that*.' It was all things we should have done anyway."

The fans obviously ate it all up. "There were cheers and a big celebration," Bayliss says. "It was a pretty good day for us."

It may have only been lunchtime on Monday but Carey's announcement triggered a rush at the bar, because after all, these kids know what a beer's for.

CHAPTER SEVEN

SUMMER 1983
LOS ANGELES, CALIFORNIA

♪

*"That was a soccer call, wasn't it?
It's time we had a talk."*

Sigi Schmid was living a double life. He was an accountant specializing in real estate accounting from January until July. He was good at his job at (then Big Eight firm) Peat Marwick Mitchell, and was well liked by his superiors and his clients.

He spent August to December as the head soccer coach at UCLA, where he had also enjoyed great success. But the economic limitations of being a college soccer coach in the early 1980s made it necessary that he held a "real job" to pay the real bills.

Schmid arrived at UCLA in 1973 as a soccer player who wanted to be a writer, so he was planning to major in English. That plan was rejected by his father who pointed out (accurately) "writing isn't a profession." He settled on accounting and when he graduated with that business degree in 1976, he was confronted with a choice: Soccer or the real world?

The Los Angeles Aztecs of the NASL offered him a tryout. Terry Fisher, who had coached Schmid at UCLA, coached the Aztecs.

"He was the only coach I ever had problems with, and it was the only time in my career I didn't start," Schmid says, explaining why he turned down the Aztecs. (Fisher's career eventually brought him to Seattle, where he runs the Washington State Youth Soccer organization.)

Schmid's other offer came from the Los Angeles Sky Hawks of the American Soccer League. The ASL was a league with a long history (dating to 1921) but limited national exposure with franchises primarily located on the East Coast. But in 1976 the league hired NBA Hall of Famer Bob Cousy to be commissioner, and added five western US teams including the Sky Hawks, who offered Schmid $400 a month. He could make $300 playing semipro soccer in Los Angeles, and without travel demands, he could attend grad school ... so he stayed in school and turned down the Sky Hawks.

By turning down teams in the NASL and the ASL, it might appear that Schmid was casting his lot with accounting. But there was more to it than that: Even while a student at UCLA Schmid began dabbling in coaching, first with his younger brother's youth league team. By his senior year, he was coaching a club team he had formed from various youth leagues around Los Angeles. That team won the state championship and the coaching bug now had sunk its teeth into him.

He began plotting life as an accountant, with some soccer coaching (and playing) on the side. As his accounting career took off, the demands of trying to crunch numbers, coach kids, and play semiprofessionally became unrealistic. Schmid backed off playing, realizing that any long-term prospects in soccer would come from coaching. That dedication led to UCLA offering him an assistant coaching job in 1979.

UNLIKE YOUTH LEAGUES, where training could be scheduled around his accounting career, the UCLA job would demand more time, but wouldn't generate much money, so he'd still need the accounting job. As luck would have it, Schmid's boss (Howard Bland), had previously seen a circumstance like this work in the firm's New Orleans office, where a young accountant named Ike Harris also happened to be a wide receiver for the NFL's New Orleans Saints. The NFL in the 1970s wasn't yet the big-time business it is today, and players often moonlighted with second jobs during the off-season.

Bland saw no reason a similar deal couldn't work in Los Angeles. He gave Schmid his blessing to be an accountant for the first seven months of the year and a soccer coach for the last five. Schmid's primary client was also the firm's largest, and they not only liked Schmid but soccer, too. So things worked out.

Things also worked out on the Bruins' pitch. After a year as an assistant, Schmid was promoted when head coach Steve Gay took a sabbatical. What was to be an interim gig became permanent after Schmid led the Bruins to an 18-2-2 record and an NCAA tournament berth. The success led to an inevitable encroachment of soccer into his number-crunching time.

In the summer of 1983 Schmid was having a meeting in his office with Cal Wallace, a partner in the accounting firm, when the phone rang. Schmid had been meticulous about not allowing his two careers to interfere with one another, but on the line was a parent whose son was being recruited to play soccer at UCLA. The father had several questions and Schmid began mumbling answers into the phone.

"I'm looking at Cal and I'm trying to disguise that it's a soccer call," he says, laughing. "But this guy is talking to me about his son leaning towards San Diego State. I'm trying to answer his questions without being soccer specific. Eventually I hang up the phone and Cal goes 'that was a soccer call wasn't it? It's time we had a talk.'"

Schmid was making just $10,000 for his work at UCLA, so he gave the Bruins an ultimatum: Either turn the position into a full-time job with commensurate pay, or he had to leave. By then Schmid had a gaudy 46-11-5 record in his three years as coach. The Bruins came through, and even though he ultimately took an overall pay cut he would be making enough from UCLA to make soccer his real job. Sigi Schmid was now a full-time soccer coach.

BY THE TIME HE ARRIVED in Seattle as the Sounders first coach, Schmid's entire career could be summed up in one word: Winner. He dominated college soccer for almost 20 years at UCLA. He won the MLS Cup in both Los Angeles and Columbus. He made his mark as a successful coach in the international game with several stints involving US national teams.

His first vivid memory of soccer came from being awestruck due to access he was granted thanks to his mom. As a young boy he remembers attending Los Angeles Kickers matches with his father Fritz. The Kickers were the German club in the Greater Los Angeles Soccer League (GLASL), a group of teams typically divided by the ethnicity of the first generation immigrants who populated them.

In the post World War II era hundreds of thousands of immigrants drawn by a desire to start a new life in the warm California sun were responsible for a huge growth spurt in Los Angeles. Among the traditions they brought with them was soccer, and as the population grew so too did the popularity of the sport. GLASL games drew crowds of up to 10,000 fans to watch teams like the Kickers take on rivals from other neighborhoods.

After games the team would return to its clubhouse for a postgame meal prepared by, among others, Schmid's mom Doris. "My mother was a cook by trade and cooked for the Kickers. So from the time I was five years old I remember Sundays going with my dad to watch them play and then sitting in the kitchen of the clubhouse and watching all these players who were becoming my idols come in and eat, and it was a big thing. It wasn't as if my Dad played or was a good player and got me into it that way. It was my mom cooking for the club."

The Kickers provided another important feature of Schmid's life. Although born in Germany he had moved to America with his parents at the age of three. German was the language of choice in his house, but his schooling was all done in English. So as a kid he was still learning German while also trying to figure out English. One thing that helped the German side of the equation was the monthly magazine published (in German) by the Kickers.

"I never had formal German schooling or German language in school so I taught myself to read German through the Kickers soccer magazine. I knew then that soccer was something I loved and enjoyed."

Schmid began playing the game in the streets of his neighborhood, which was a mixture of people of German and Hispanic descent in South Central Los Angeles. But then his parents moved about 15 miles southwest — to the other side of the San Diego Freeway — to the city of Torrance. It was more of a typical American suburb of the early '60s, which meant baseball, football, and basketball, but little or no soccer. Removed from the ethnic influences of his former neighborhood, Schmid didn't play soccer for two years.

But fate intervened for Schmid in the person of Hans Stierle; a friend of his father was tired of driving into Los Angeles, where he organized youth games primarily among German-American kids for the Los Angeles Soccer Club. Instead, he decided to start a youth club right there in Torrance.

Thus the American Youth Soccer Organization (AYSO) was born. Sigi Schmid was one of 54 players who comprised the four teams from Torrance in AYSO's first year. The organization also had 71 players from Culver City on five more teams. Nearly 50 years later the organization Stierle founded in part to beat the LA traffic blues has 50,000 teams and 600,000 players spread across America.

So, at the age of 11 Schmid rekindled his love of the game. He ended up being selected to an all-star team that competed around the region, called the Los Angeles Toros. Through his involvement in AYSO Schmid began receiving instruction from men who had played the game on very big stages. His coaches included Helmet Bicek, a member of the US Men's National Team who had scored a goal in Team USA's then-famous 3-3 draw with Mexico in 1960.

As he got older Schmid knew he was good at soccer, but he never dreamed he could make a living from the game, and certainly hadn't connected the dots that the game might pave the way for him to go to college. But one of AYSO's founders, Joe Bonchansky, became aware that Schmid had good grades at Bishop Montgomery High School and that, combined with Schmid's soccer skills, might be enough to get him into UCLA. For Schmid, whose parents had not attended college, the concept of going to college (let alone to UCLA) wasn't something he'd thought about. But Bonchansky took him to Westwood, introduced him to the soccer staff and suddenly he had a path to a college education.

In 2011 when Bonchansky was inducted into the AYSO Hall of Fame, Schmid recorded a video thanking him for taking an interest in him as a kid. Schmid choked up near the end of the video when he credited Bonchansky with being a primary reason for the success of his career.

Soccer might get him into UCLA but he'd still need money to pay for school and expenses. That money came from a talent he had acquired combined with a little help from his mom. Schmid was playing in a men's soccer league while he was in high school. The team liked to get together to play poker, and Schmid, who had grown up playing cards, saw an opportunity. He got himself invited to games and, "I found it was good for my financial well-being because they drank when they played and I didn't. It worked out fairly well."

Fairly well?

"This is the late '60s and early '70s and I was making 200 to 300 bucks a night playing poker with these guys," he said. "My dad was working a graveyard shift at the brewery. I told my mom I was just playing cards. I promised her I wasn't drinking and asked her to not tell Dad. I would be out until three or four in the morning and she would cover me."

He earned enough money at these all-night poker parties to pay his tuition at UCLA and had enough cash left over to buy a new Mercury Capri.

His playing career at UCLA was a success as well, including two appearances in the NCAA title game. It was during his time at UCLA that Schmid first started thinking about coaching and what went into it. To that end he found himself occasionally wandering into Pauley Pavilion after soccer practice to watch UCLA's basketball team practice. A friend of Schmid's was a student trainer for the team and introduced him to Coach John Wooden. "Tony Spino introduced me to Coach Wooden. I got to know him a little bit. Not well. But the main thing for me was just to watch him work at practice and learn from him."

As UCLA's head coach Schmid may not have been quite the equal of the Wizard of Westwood (10 national championships in 12 years) but his teams were quite successful, racking up 322 wins and making the NCAA tournament in 16 consecutive seasons. Three times Schmid's Bruins won the NCAA championship.

AS HIS REPUTATION AT UCLA grew he caught the attention of the US National soccer organization and became an assistant coach for US national teams during the 1991 World University Games, the 1994 World Cup, and the 1995 Pan American Games. He also was the head coach for the US under-20 team in the 1999 World Youth Championship.

Perhaps if Schmid had been a football or basketball coach he would have stayed at UCLA forever. He certainly would have been more richly compensated in those two sports, but soccer coaches don't approach the multi-million dollar contracts routinely given to even moderately successful coaches in the two revenue-generating sports. So when the Los Angeles Galaxy contacted him in 1999 they quickly got his attention. Schmid admits there was another motivator as important to him as money.

"The other side of it was ego. College soccer was the epitome of soccer in the states for a while and I had been involved with the national team, so I felt like I was in an elite group. All of a sudden there's this pro league and all these guys are coaching there, and I'm thinking 'I'm as good as those guys there. I want a chance to prove it.'"

It would have been understandable if Schmid's first foray into professional sports as a coach had been his last, because he saw everything the pros had to offer in fairly quick order.

He rocket-shipped right to the top of MLS, taking over a sputtering Galaxy team early in the 1999 season and leading them to the MLS Cup final, where they lost to DC United. His team won the CONCACAF Champions Cup in 2000 (only the second American side to do so), as well as a Supporters Shield and the MLS Cup in 2002.

Also in 2002 Doug Hamilton joined the Galaxy as general manager. Hamilton was a rising executive in the sport and certainly deserved some credit for the success of 2002. Perhaps inevitably he and Schmid became another in the long line of coach/GM duos in pro sports to clash over control of player acquisition.

In 2003 the Galaxy had their first losing season under Schmid and he was convinced he was going to be fired. A friend had informed him that on several occasions he had noticed Hamilton and Galaxy CEO Tim Leiweke visiting with Costa Rica national team coach Steve Sampson, who had played and coached with Schmid at UCLA. Schmid suspected his end-of-season meeting with Hamilton and Leiweke would be his last as head coach of the Galaxy.

Instead Hamilton told him that he had convinced Leiweke to keep him for another year. Schmid agreed to stay, but wanted more control, which he was given. The Galaxy started hot and by July had the best record in MLS. Schmid coached the Western Conference in the league all-star game.

Meanwhile Sampson was fired by Costa Rica after a loss to Cuba in the World Cup qualifying tournament, so suddenly the guy Hamilton and Leiweke appeared to want was available. When the Galaxy stumbled through a five-match winless streak in August, they pulled the plug on Schmid.

Among other things Hamilton said was that he was uncomfortable with Schmid's staff, pointing to their "uncommon loyalty" to the head coach. In the end it was a classic professional sports power struggle: the GM wants his own coach.

While Schmid went on to success elsewhere, Hamilton was on three occasions named the top MLS executive and was GM when the Galaxy won the MLS Cup again in 2005. He died suddenly of a heart attack in 2006. The MLS Executive of the Year award is named in his honor.

Kurt Schmid was a senior playing at UCLA when his father called to tell him he'd been fired. "I'd never known him to face any adversity in coaching," he says. "I knew he'd land on his feet, but I was stunned." He remembers something else that happened shortly after Sigi was fired.

"Right away when he got fired by the Galaxy he started talking about how much he liked Seattle and how he wished they would get a team so he could coach there."

Schmid returned to the national stage as coach of the US under-20 team and led them into the 2005 World Youth Championship (WYC), when for the first time the US was able to win its group stage. To do so they shocked Argentina 1-nil picking up a win over a team that featured among others a 17-year-old kid named Lionel Messi. That Argentina would eventually capture the championship, and Messi the Golden Ball and Golden Shoe awards only underscores the US team's accomplishment.

After the 2005 WYC, Schmid took a trip to Seattle to visit his son Kyle, who had enrolled at the University of Washington. While there, he called on Adrian Hanauer. With the Galaxy, Schmid had done business with Hanauer, loaning young players Brian Ching and Herculez Gomez to the USL Sounders.

He met Hanauer at a Seahawks preseason game and they hit it off. It was early September and Hanauer's first bid to join MLS had been unsuccessful, but he believed there would eventually be another opportunity for Seattle. He and Schmid couldn't help but discuss it.

"At the end of the night," Schmid recalls, "I said to Adrian 'when your dream comes true and you get an MLS team in Seattle, don't forget about me.'"

A month later Schmid signed a three-year contract with the Columbus Crew. He was ready for another bite at the MLS apple. Schmid had heard the typical chorus of cynics who chirp at successful people. "Anyone could win at UCLA," went the thinking. "The Galaxy was already good when he got there and had gone on to win after he left."

So he took an offer from Columbus, an inconsistent and average MLS team. "I wanted to take a team that was struggling and show people I could turn them around."

Schmid accomplished his goal, but it took him the length of his contract. In his first two seasons with the Crew they finished sixth and missed the playoffs. But the third year, the Crew rolled all the way to the title, defeating New York 3-1 and delivering the MLS Cup to Ohio.

Just 23 days after his team won that match Schmid was named the first head coach in Sounders history. Some of the details of how the Sounders pulled off getting Schmid so quickly remain a bit murky. The Crew accused the Sounders of tampering. Specifically they claimed the Sounders had talked to Schmid while he was still under contract to the Crew, thus violating the noncompete clause in Schmid's contract.

Even years later, the Sounders' stance on the matter is something akin to Ralph Kramden's "hamana hamana hamana" routine on the old *"Honeymooners"* TV show. Everyone involved is a little vague on the specificities of exactly when and where they first crossed paths with Schmid in regard to taking the Sounders job. But they clearly targeted him as the top candidate.

"Sigi was someone in whom we had expressed interest in as early as 2005," Hanauer points out as he recalls the evening he spent with Schmid at the Seahawks game. "Once we announced that we were bringing MLS to Seattle, we discussed internally that Sigi would be very high on our list. We knew he was under contract, but we also knew that the contract expired at the end of the 2008 season. I think he was aware that there could be an opportunity in Seattle in 2009, which is probably why he didn't extend his contract."

Probably.

While Hanauer had known him for a few years, his right-hand man, Sounders sporting director Chris Henderson, had known Schmid for over half his life. Schmid had recruited Henderson to play at UCLA and had coached him there and on the US Men's National Team. Henderson laughs when he remembers playing for Schmid at UCLA.

"There'd be times at UCLA where we'd say 'Sigi's going to blow a brain,' which meant he was going to make us run or kick balls against the fence. His emotions would get to him and you could see it was coming. He's mellowed out a bit since those days."

Henderson spent 11 seasons playing in MLS and had been briefly reunited with Schmid when Colorado traded him to Columbus in 2005. Henderson and his family didn't like Columbus, and Henderson asked his old college coach to explore a trade. Schmid accommodated Henderson's wishes by trading him to New York and chiding Henderson to "remember this favor."

DID THE SOUNDERS REACH out to Schmid to gauge his interest in the Seattle job? It's impossible to believe they didn't. While there was assumption on the Seattle end that Schmid would be interested, and an assumption on Schmid's part that Seattle might be interested in him, business is rarely done best on assumptions.

There's also this: Columbus knew Schmid was in the last year of his deal. If they wanted him to continue as coach they could have made him an offer any time during the 2008 season. By not locking him up they left the door ajar allowing the Sounders to burst through.

An MLS investigation into the matter concluded the Sounders did not officially tamper with Schmid, yet the league still ruled Seattle had to pay Columbus what was called "allocation money" in order to complete the deal. The Sounders sent about $100,000 to Columbus in early December and signed Schmid a few days later.

MLS isn't quite yet the money-making gravy train that is the NFL or MLB, but it's still a professional sports league, and $100,000 to get the coach you want is the dictionary definition of "chump change."

And make no mistake about it: Schmid was the guy the Sounders wanted.

"I remember very early on in my dealings with Sigi feeling like he was the type of person I wanted to do business with," says Hanauer. "For an expansion team, I thought he was the perfect choice. He knew how to build winning cultures and winning teams."

"It's hard to ignore the championships," Henderson said. " Sigi's won at the international level, at the Olympic level, at college and in MLS. You don't win that much unless you're doing things correctly."

Schmid's work in Los Angeles at both UCLA and the Galaxy had drawn the attention of Joe Roth who also liked what he had seen. At the end of the day Henderson says the decision to hire Schmid "was kind of an easy one for us."

The fact that the coach was interested in Seattle defies some common logic at first glance. Why leave a championship team you had just built to coach an expansion franchise? For Schmid it was again about a challenge. He'd had success at UCLA, with the Galaxy and the Crew. Could he now take an expansion team and quickly build it into a contender? He wanted to find out.

Schmid also was intrigued by the Sounders' unique setup. With Hanauer installed as both the owner and GM he figured he could expect good access and quick decisions, something he didn't have in the top-management-heavy Columbus organization.

"I knew the decision making process wasn't going to be a long, drawn-out process. In Columbus it was sometimes months before you'd get an answer on things, which meant a lot of things didn't happen."

It also didn't hurt that the expansion team was on the West Coast, where Schmid had lived almost his entire life. His wife had kept their home in Los Angeles. The idea of being closer to home was appealing. Still, once the Sounders were cleared to officially meet with Schmid there was one more potential hurdle to overcome.

Five years after Tim Leiweke had fired him in Los Angeles despite the fact his team was in first place, Tod Leiweke would be among his bosses in Seattle. It still rankled Schmid that he was booted from his post in his hometown and now he would be signing a contract to work for an organization where he again would answer in part to a Leiweke. But Schmid says any trepidation he felt dissipated when he first met Tod Leiweke, who not only addressed the elephant in the room, but kicked the potentially distracting pachyderm right out.

"He shook my hand," Schmid recalls with a laugh, "and said 'Hi, I'm Tod. I'm the good Leiweke. I never would have fired you in Los Angeles.'"

Truth is, by the time he met Leiweke, Schmid was already convinced Seattle was the place for him due to his past dealings with Hanauer and his relationship with Henderson. He had always liked Seattle when he traveled there, and remembered the glory days of the NASL Sounders and how red-hot the game had been there.

"You could sense the good vibe that existed up here and these were quality people. You could sense that this was something that could be really big."

Schmid was officially introduced to Seattle fans and media as the first head coach in Sounders FC history on December 16, 2008, and just six days later made his first hire as he began assembling a staff. The guy he hired was a guy some fans thought should have been the head coach.

CHAPTER EIGHT

JUNE 1980
SEATTLE, WASHINGTON

℘

"Welcome to the NASL, son!"

S chmid's hiring left some fans feeling a little hollow. He had just won the league championship in Columbus so there was no denying his credentials. But some fans grumbled a bit that the job should have gone to the USL Sounders coach Brian Schmetzer. Why shouldn't he get a chance to show what he could do in the big league?

What those fans knew about Schmetzer was that he had coached the Sounders to two USL championships and a third title-game appearance in his seven-year run as head coach. Obviously he knew what he was doing. When his roots as a player in the old NASL Sounders were factored in it was natural for fans to assume he might be named coach of the MLS team. Not unreasonably they cited a sense of fair play in beating the drum (mostly in internet chat rooms) on behalf of Schmetzer.

When he didn't get the job, it might also have been natural for Schmetzer to burn a little. But he wasn't upset, at least in part due to a conversation he'd had four years earlier.

In January of 2004 Schmetzer attended the MLS player combine in Los Angeles. He had two years under his belt and although his first two Sounders teams won the division he was smart enough to know that there was a lot he didn't know about being a head coach. So he decided to see if he could get some help from a guy who had a reputation as a very good coach, then-LA Galaxy head coach Sigi Schmid.

"I called Sigi up out of the blue and introduced myself and asked him if we could meet. He agreed to have coffee with me. I brought my notepad and we sat for 90 minutes." The kindness of the gesture was not lost on Schmetzer. "He went out of his way to help a USL coach figure things out."

Partially because of that meeting, and because of honest self-assessment, Schmetzer was fine with how things worked out. "There's no question I would have done a good job, but my experience level with the league and how it operates, I was under-qualified for that side of the business. I could have handled the on-field stuff. But the contacts, how the league operates, the cap, Sigi has such a good memory for all that stuff and that information was vital for us to have success."

So in the battle to get a leg up on other expansion teams the Sounders had a built-in advantage: Their new coach already had a positive vibe with his top two lieutenants. His decades-long relationship with Chris Henderson was a huge plus, and Schmetzer's endorsement would help give him credibility with skeptical fans. Those fans knew Schmetzer's Seattle soccer stripes had been earned.

BRIAN SCHMETZER WAS attempting to look like he belonged, but that's a tough act to pull off when you're flat on your back and people are laughing at you.

Like most 17 year olds, he was young, full of optimism, with an unlimited future. In his case the future was right in front of him because he had gotten a job. Not just any job: He was a professional soccer player, signing with the Seattle Sounders of the NASL right after he had graduated from Seattle's Nathan Hale High School.

Schmetzer's first training session with the team was in the Kingdome in June of 1980 and he recalls it being a pretty big deal. The team had signed another Seattle kid, a friend of Schmetzer's named Fred Hamel. "I remember the local media were all there," Schmetzer says. "The Sounders have signed two local lads and everyone's out to watch them train."

Just weeks earlier, Schmetzer had been trying to get a date for the senior prom. Now he was playing professional soccer in America's top league. Schmetzer says at one point during that first training session he got the ball off a pass, when all of a sudden, "I went flying up in the air and landed on my back."

Momentarily winded and a little embarrassed Schmetzer looked up at the lights that formed a ring around the roof. Suddenly those lights were blotted out by the teammate who had sent Schmetzer ass over teakettle. "I looked up and (Sounders center back) Bruce Rioch was standing over me," he recalls. Rioch was nearly twice Schmetzer's age and had logged significantly more miles than the teammate he had just tackled. Coincidentally, when Rioch signed his first pro contract he, too, was 17 (when Schmetzer had yet to celebrate his second birthday).

Everyone else at the session was laughing and Schmetzer laughs now as he remembers Rioch in his English accent saying, "Welcome to the NASL, son!"

This was his on-field welcome to pro soccer. His off-field welcome had taken place just days before when he agreed to terms with the club on a contract ... a contract he didn't sign. "My dad had to sign the contract with me because I was still a minor," he says. "I remember on the drive home he told me, 'You're very lucky to play soccer for a living.'"

Walter Schmetzer wasn't just some dad throwing out random fatherly advice. He had played Third Division soccer in his native Germany before moving to Seattle in 1962. Brian Schmetzer was on the trip, technically, but he doesn't remember anything about it. "My mom was pregnant on the airplane coming over to America," he says. "I was made in Germany but born in the U.S., so I get the best of both worlds."

Schmetzer recalls growing up in a house where soccer was huge. "My dad was pretty passionate about it," Schmetzer says. Passionate enough to help organize a trip for Brian and his teammates to play in a youth tournament that coincided with the 1974 World Cup in Germany. "Our little soccer team had collected glass for four years and recycled it and we raised $12,000 to go to Germany. My dad still had all his family over there." Schmetzer's team played 10 games against German teams and got at least one taste of World Cup passion.

"The most vivid memory I have is, we were kicking the ball around out in the street and all of a sudden this guy opens his window and throws his TV out the window. We're 12 years old and we're all like 'what the hell just happened?' The guy is screaming. We find out later East Germany had beaten West Germany, 1-nil."

It was also about this time that the NASL Sounders arrived in Seattle, and like other kids, Schmetzer was caught up in the excitement the new team created. He followed the Sounders, and remembers pursuing player autographs at the postgame parties the team held at Seattle Center.   Six years later, Schmetzer was playing in the NASL. The contract his dad signed for him didn't pay much ... unless you were 17. "We were getting paid $750 bucks a month, which at the time to me was a fortune. I'm thinking this is the greatest thing ever. I'm thinking I got life pretty good. Then in 1981 the league set a minimum wage scale for players, so my pay jumped to $2,200 a month, so now I'm living high on the hog."

Schmetzer eventually realized that $2,200 a month was fine money, but it didn't really allow for a "high on the hog" lifestyle. Nevertheless he grinded out a 15-year pro career in outdoor and indoor soccer during a time when being an American soccer star put you well out of reach of any bright lights.

Three years after he stopped playing in 1991 some Seattle area soccer people (including Scott Oki and Alan Hinton) revived the Sounders name for use with an expansion team in the new American Professional Soccer League. Schmetzer came out of retirement to join them. The next season, his last as a player, he moved back to the indoor game playing for the Seattle SeaDogs, an expansion franchise in the Continental Indoor Soccer League. After that he spent two years as an assistant to SeaDogs head coach Fernando Clavijo.

A gregarious, likeable guy, Clavijo is Uruguayan by birth, but became a US citizen. He made over 60 appearances for the US Men's National Team and is a member of the US Soccer Hall of Fame. He's at least partly remembered in Seattle for a legendary live interview on KJR Radio after the SeaDogs won the final CISL championship in 1997. Moments after they closed out a 2-nil victory over the Houston Hotshots, Clavijo was asked by broadcasters John Lynch and Jon Horton how it felt to be a champion, and he responded, "I do not have enough words to say. Fuck! My guys deserve everything. They fucking have played great all season."

Lynch and Horton were stunned, but staggered through the rest of the interview. "I remember," Lynch says years later, "hearing the first one and thinking 'did he say that?' By the second one there was no doubt."

When the CISL disbanded later that year Schmetzer found himself out of pro soccer. He began working full time for the construction company he co-owned and coached rec soccer on the side.

AS SCHMETZER'S PRO SOCCER career was ending, Henderson's was just getting started. And like Schmetzer he had gotten a taste of soccer success at a young age. One of the most feted high school players in America, the Everett, Washington, native chose to play college soccer for Schmid at UCLA.

"His work rate was outstanding. He's the only guy I ever had on a recruiting trip who worked out on his own," says Schmid, who claims running is the Henderson family disease. "We were playing a game in the afternoon. His brother Pat was at San Diego

State. He drove up to Los Angeles and the two of them went running and knocking a ball around for about 2 hours."

By that time Schmid had seen a more tangible example of Henderson's willingness to invest work into becoming better. The US National Under-20 team had made it to the semifinals of the Youth World Cup tournament in 1989. The team was short on the left wing so Henderson converted himself from the right to the left side. "That's what the team needed," Schmid says, "so he kept working on his left foot. There are a lot of people out there to this day who think Chris is left-footed."

His work rate can be at least partially credited to the elder sibling. When Chris first started soccer he often ended up with Pat and his friends; good enough at age four that he was able to play with the older kids. "He was always the youngest player on every team he was on," Schmid says. "So I'd say to him 'just get on the wing and run around. Get out of the way and don't bother the big guys.'"

Henderson played on the Bruins' 1990 NCAA championship team, scoring on penalty kicks in the semifinal and championship games to help Schmid win one of his three titles as UCLA coach. That same year (at the age of 19) he had been the youngest player on the USA roster for the World Cup.

By 1991 Henderson was on the US Men's National Team in preparation for the 1994 World Cup. Since they would be the host country, the Yanks would not have to go through the grueling process of qualifying. They would instead put that time to use in a way that would ultimately impact the game in America forever.

The US team was coached by Bora Milutinovic (with Schmid among the assistants), who was hired after taking Mexico to the World Cup quarterfinals in 1986, and Costa Rica through group play and into the knockout round in 1990. His resume created influence and he used that to convince US Soccer to invest in a national training center, a home base for the team that would allow for the kind of dedication to the game necessary to build international success.

By 1993 the idea had become a reality with a sparkling new facility in Mission Viejo, California, where Henderson and dozens of other players would spend the bulk of their time in an intensive education process.

"Bora wanted us together and training every day," Henderson says. "We'd have sessions in the classroom. He used to write on the TV with a dry erase marker. He'd say 'this guy needs to go here and this guy needs to go there.' It wasn't a telestrator. He'd just write on the screen."

The team played approximately 70 games against other national teams in the two years leading up to the World Cup. In between Henderson says, "We lived together, trained together; we went through coaching schools together. It was soccer school every day. Every time we sat down for a meal we were talking about the game. Guys would grab salt and pepper shakers and use them to diagram plays and discuss strategy."

The so-called "soccer school" didn't lead to immediate success in terms of wins and losses. The 1994 US World Cup team (which ultimately didn't include Henderson) had a win, a draw, and a loss in group play before being eliminated by Brazil on July 4th. But the overall impact of the 1994 World Cup on the game in America cannot be accurately calculated, because it's still being measured.

For starters, 10 of Henderson's teammates from those days are executives in today's MLS. Five more are involved in coaching with various age groups of current US National Teams, and another half-dozen are MLS broadcasters.

"It's incredible to go through the list and see the influence they have on the game now," Henderson says. "Bora was an amazing tactician. He changed the whole culture of that generation of players, and now that group is all giving back and it's really cool to see. I learned more in that time than any time in my career."

Henderson's enthusiasm for that period of his life comes despite the fact that just days before the start of the 1994 World Cup he was among the last players cut from the team. It was one in a series of situations that could be used as "what if" fodder for the rest of his career.

He would have played extensively on the 1992 USA team at the Barcelona Olympics, but suffered a knee injury a week before the games opened. Then he was cut two weeks before the opening of the 1994 World Cup. His star-crossed luck continued in the pros: In 1998 he thought he had a deal for the biggest contract of his life to play in the Premier League.

"I had a contract with Nottingham Forest that would have been my best contract ever ... but I was denied my work visa because I didn't have enough national caps that year. There's a rule with the labor union in England. When you are taking a job from an English citizen you have to prove you're special, and one of those rules is you have to have a certain amount of national team caps in that year."

Henderson didn't have the requisite number of appearances, and the Football Association, the governing body of the sport in England, denied him both a visa and his fat new contract. "I was gutted," he says. "It was a chance to have a good career and play in the big league. It was a big letdown."

Henderson picked himself up and went back to MLS (where he had already played two seasons). He would ultimately play 11 seasons in the league with five different franchises. He saw the business from a big-market side (New York) and a small-market side (Kansas City). He also watched as something unthinkable happened when he played in Miami.

"The Miami Fusion was the best team I played for in my pro career," Henderson declares of his one year in South Florida. The Fusion went 16-5-5 on the year and won the MLS Supporters Shield. (The Fusion played just 26 games because season-ending games were cancelled after the 9/11 attacks. On the morning of September 11, Henderson and his teammates were on a bus en route to the Miami airport to fly to a game in New York City when the attacks happened and the busses turned around.)

The Fusion lost in the semifinals of the MLS playoffs to San Jose, but by most definitions the season was a great success.

Then they went out of business.

It didn't exactly come as a shock to Henderson. "We had a feeling that it was coming. I remember when I moved down there, I rented. Things weren't very stable in the league, and the rumors were if they were going to contract it would be Miami and Tampa, so guys were very careful what they did."

Henderson landed back in Colorado, where his career had started. It was during this time that he began pondering his life beyond playing soccer. "I was going into (Rapids general manager) Dan Counce's office asking if could I come in during the off-season to watch what he did. I wanted to see how things worked. I knew this was the direction I wanted to go."

THE YEARS 2006 AND 2007 were big years in Henderson's life. In 2006 with New York he decided to retire at the end of the season. In 2007 he was an assistant coach in Kansas City. In a lucky coincidence, both of those teams were going through ownership changes that resulted in major upgrades in how they did business. In back-to-back years Henderson had a bird's eye view of how to successfully rebuild and rebrand a franchise. "I watched everything and asked a ton of questions. They were going through a lot of the things you'd be doing to build a new franchise, and I saw everything."

In the fall of 2007 Henderson began having discussions about returning to Colorado to become their technical director. If he took the job, Henderson would be reunited with fellow Mission Viejo soccer school attendee Fernando Clavijo, who coached the Rapids (where he presumably had become better at handling live post-match radio interviews). He was one day away from accepting the job when he got a phone call from his younger brother Sean.

Sean Henderson was a third-team All-American for Schmid at UCLA before playing three years in the MLS and two years in Germany. He and Chris had been teammates in Colorado when the franchise started in 1996. He then played five years with the USL Sounders between 1999 and 2004. He was one of the players who had to sit across from Adrian Hanauer when Hanauer took over the club and cut player salaries to stem the flow of red ink in 2002.

His playing days done, Sean Henderson moved to coaching in the Seattle area. Like the rest of the Emerald City soccer community he listened to the rumors of an MLS team coming to Seattle, and after running into Hanauer one day he called his brother.

"I saw Adrian today and he said he might be interested in getting someone up here to help start the team," Chris remembers Sean telling him. "You should call him."

After frustrating near misses with the Olympic team in '92, the World Cup team in '94, and a contract with the Premier League in '98 Henderson had been involved in another close call. But this one worked in his favor. A day or two later and he would have been committed to Colorado. Instead, he had a chance to be a part of the league expanding to his hometown; a move he felt was long overdue.

"I always told Phil Anschutz (one of the co-founders of MLS) we've got to go to Seattle. I'd tell anyone I could because I wanted to go home and play. The timing was never right, but I knew it would be big."

Henderson knew because he was another one of those kids who'd grown up with the NASL Sounders. (There's a chance that 13-year-old Brian Schmetzer once elbowed 9-year-old Adrian Hanauer out of the way to get a player autograph and knocked him into 5-year-old Chris Henderson.) He'd seen the big crowds. He'd even played in front of one of them in 1994, when the US team played Russia in an international friendly at the Kingdome in front of 43,651 fans who roared from start to finish of a game that ended in a 1-1 draw. Veteran soccer announcer JP Dellacamera saluted the crowd as he wrapped up his broadcast calling them "an extra man on the field." Henderson had given the crowd reason to yell with an outstanding performance. His teammate Alexi Lalas headed in the tying goal in the game's 86th minute.

In an interview at the time with John Peoples of the *Seattle Times*, Henderson discussed pro soccer's future in Seattle and his hope that it would someday include him. "It's very important that we have a professional outdoor league that can compete with the world's best," he said then, just 23 years old. "I've heard talk about restarting the Sounders. It would be a dream come true if I could play for a pro team here in Seattle."

His playing career over, Henderson would instead have to be content with helping build the team that the MLS finally awarded to Seattle. He put Colorado on hold and called Hanauer. "We started talking and it went really fast. I came up for a visit and you could see it was going to be a big deal. I could tell the organization was good all the way through."

Henderson liked the challenge the job presented. He'd be helping to start a team from scratch and he'd be doing it in a city whose soccer roots ran true and deep and with which he was intimately connected. He took the job and was introduced to Seattle media in January of 2008.

MEANTIME SCHMETZER had been out of pro soccer since the demise of the SeaDogs in 1997. When his phone rang one day in late 2001 he had no idea he'd be getting back into the sport professionally. He didn't even know who he was talking to. "I'm full on with my construction business when Adrian first called me. I didn't know who the hell he was. He's asking me to meet and I said 'who are you again?'"

They met the next day and Hanauer eventually offered Schmetzer the USL Sounders coaching job. Schmetzer accepted the job and had enjoyed seven successful years when Schmid tapped him as his top assistant coach six days after arriving in Seattle. The two had not spoken at any length since they sat together in a coffee shop in Los Angeles in 2004. Schmetzer made it clear early on that he planned to be a vocal assistant coach. When Schmid asked him to always be honest with him, Schmetzer pointed out that they were both German, stubborn, and possessors of strong opinions. "Honesty," Schmetzer told him, "will not be a problem."

From the start, Schmetzer says the duo had an almost telepathic relationship. They work up scouting and strategy reports on upcoming games based on film, and Schmetzer says it's borderline scary how often the reports are alike, despite the fact they are done independently and without prior conversation.

"He's allowed me the freedom to show the team what I see, and then he fills in what else he wants to tell the group," Schmetzer says, "but the message is usually similar. I'd say 70 to 80 percent of the time our reports mirror one another."

That may not be entirely coincidence. Both coaches owe a lot of their game philosophy to legendary German coach Dettmar Cramer. Cramer has taught the game in over 90 countries and developed a teaching system forty years ago for US Soccer, the foundation of which is still used today to educate current and potential coaches at all levels. At the same time Schmid was studying Cramer's system to get his first coaching license in Los Angeles in the early '70s, Schmetzer's dad was going through the same program to get his coaching license in Seattle. Walter Schmetzer passed the Dettmar Cramer way of doing things on to his son, who now credits the system for some of the unspoken commonality that he regularly has in game preparation with Schmid.

"Either great minds think alike or fools seldom differ," Schmid says with a laugh. "Right away there was a good understanding. Our thought process was similar. I was completely happy with his loyalty and his trust. That might be the common German upbringing, because that's really emphasized to you as a kid — that you've got to be trustworthy and loyal. But sometimes you don't know. He already had a relationship with Adrian and I really didn't. Is that going to be something where he goes around me? I ultimately just felt that wasn't going to happen."

He then concludes with another laugh. "I *did* make sure his contract wasn't longer than mine."

In addition to allowing Schmetzer to do film and scout work for him, Schmid also occasionally lets his top assistant run training. "I've included him on things where you might not include an assistant coach, because he was a head coach for a lot of years."

Schmid's desire for honest feedback and Schmetzer's willingness to give it became the key to their relationship. "We had faith in each other," says Schmid. "I wanted to have open meetings. I need assistant coaches who aren't 'yes men,' but who will challenge me in meetings. And that's been good."

Schmid didn't stop there in assembling a staff with Northwest ties. Tom Dutra was hired as the team's goalkeeper coach. Dutra had played for the Sounders in the '90s and assisted Schmetzer for his final two years as head coach of the team.

Schmid's other two aides were his son Kurt, and Ezra Hendrickson, who he brought from Los Angeles. In addition to coaching, Kurt Schmid was hired to work with Henderson on the team's scouting efforts. It was a job that he had been preparing for since his senior year in high school when he would regularly get to be — in his words a "fly on the wall" — at LA Galaxy training sessions and meetings. With the Sounders he wasn't the only one who was occasionally teased about working for his father.

"Guys joke around and say Sigi is *my* dad," says Hendrickson, who spent eight of his 12 years in MLS playing for Schmid. He was on both of Schmid's title winning teams as well as Galaxy teams that won the CONCACAF and US Open Cups. "We formed a bond. Having been in so many situations with him I know that he knows what he's doing."

As the top assistant, Schmetzer brought another positive to the team, one that might not have been as apparent at first, but became a key to his and the team's success. After playing for the NASL Sounders in the '80s, then helping revive the team in the '90s, and coaching them to two USL titles, he carries an authentic appreciation of Sounders history and as such is a respected voice within the team.

"I have a loyalty to Adrian. I have a loyalty to Sigi. But the underlying thing I feel I have is a loyalty to the club. That's number one. If I see someone doing something that I think is bad for or disrespectful of the club in any way, I'm going to say something and have him stop the behavior."

Hanauer remembers Schmetzer saying in their first meeting that he was willing to do whatever it takes to make the team better, and he says Schmid's top assistant lived up to that promise. "No task or part of the business is beneath him."

That attitude was an extension of the simple statement Schmetzer's father made to him in their car on the way home from signing his first contract in 1980: "You're very lucky to play soccer for a living." From Seattle, to Tulsa, to San Diego, to Tacoma, to St. Louis and back to Seattle, that was something he says he never forgot.

By the time the Sounders soccer staff was settled the team had already signed the player who would become the team's biggest star. On the surface it looked like an easy, obvious deal. In reality it had been quite tricky.

CHAPTER NINE

☙

*"He was so good, people forgot pretty quickly
that he was American."*

K asey Keller and his wife Kristen stood in the middle of their castle in Tonisvorst, Germany, and took inventory. After 15 years living in England, Spain, and Germany, they were facing a crucial transition in their lives, and they were just starting to come to grips with it.

Kasey Keller's soccer career was over.

Keller had played the game since he was a kid and had played it well at the highest levels. He was recognized as one of the greatest American players ever, with 110 appearances on the US Men's National Team. Three times he was named US Soccer athlete of the year, and twice he was named the Honda Player of the Year as the best player on the USMNT.

He had played 364 games in the English Premier League, 61 in Spain's La Liga, and another 78 in Germany's Bundesliga. In all three of those leagues he had been a trailblazer of sorts, the first American born-goalkeeper to earn a starting job.

During their stay in Germany, Kasey and Kristen made their home in an 800-year-old castle named Haus Donk which had been designated a historical monument by the German government. The dwelling included four floors, tight spiral staircases up to bedrooms, and an indoor pool in the basement.

Keller once posted a humorous video tour of his castle/home on the US Men's National Team website. In the video he discusses one of the conditions of his staying there. If he noticed any muskrats swimming in the moat that surrounded the structure he was to immediately contact a man called 'the Jagermeister' (German for hunting master) who would come and exterminate the rodent.

There was a muskrat farm near the castle and as long as the critters were contained they caused no worries. But if they got out of their farm they could potentially do harm to the region's ecosystem. "Vie must kill ze vermin," Keller says he was told by "the Jagermeister."

It was in Haus Donk they now stood, facing the somewhat monumental task of packing up and bidding "abschied" to Germany and Kasey's career.

The 2006-07 German season had ended in disappointment for Keller's club Borussia Mönchengladbach in May. They had been relegated to a lower division following a loss on the final day of the season. Keller's contract with the team was up and he spent much of the summer of 2007 contemplating his future.

"I had plenty of offers, just nothing that I wanted to do," he says. "By now I'm 37, the kids are in school, and teams are looking at you as a stopgap or maybe being a backup, and I had no desire to be a backup. There were also clubs that called me (with a chance to start) but it would have involved taking a little step down and it was in places that I had no desire to move my family."

Among the clubs Kasey met with in the summer of 2007 was a team with no name, no uniforms, no season ticket holders, and no history. But it was definitely a place he and his family would enjoy moving to. While home in Seattle after the German season he had met with Adrian Hanauer, where they first discussed Keller coming home to end his career with the Seattle MLS expansion team slated to begin play in March of 2009 — nearly two years after the end of his final Bundesliga season.

Keller was intrigued, but knew that for an athlete at his age to sit out for over a year was a risky, if not foolish, proposition. Maintaining his fitness, his skills, and his enthusiasm for the game would be impossible over that long a timespan. So while they agreed to meet again when the team would be closer to existence, Keller left the meeting under no illusion that playing for Seattle's expansion MLS team was going to happen.

"At this point it was pretty abstract. The team hadn't been named yet. We agreed to discuss it again in the summer of 2008, but I had no intention of sitting out that long and then playing. I couldn't have imagined doing that. I don't see how I can be retired for what would be a year and a half and *then* come back and be motivated and in any kind of shape ... I didn't want to come in and not be who people thought I was."

In order for Keller to seriously consider a deal in Seattle he needed to find a keeper job in Europe for the upcoming 2007-08 season (which began in early August). But by mid-August nothing had materialized that suited him.

So the Kellers began packing up their house, er, castle, and considered life after soccer. It was going to be good. Keller had earned big money playing in Europe. The couple had a home in Idaho. An adrenaline junkie, Keller would be free to pursue recreational sports like skiing and snowboarding — activities that time, contracts, and common sense had largely kept him from enjoying during his pro career.

Kasey and Kristen had two children (twins Cameron and Chloe) who would turn 10 at the end of August 2007. They had been troupers throughout moves from England to Spain to Germany, but another benefit of retiring would be a chance for the twins to be anchored in one place and grow up closer to their family.

It would have been nice if the timing had worked out better, and he could have finished up helping bring the top level of US soccer to Seattle, but Keller isn't someone who spends a lot of time focusing on regrets. Still, that was a potential disappointment of a magnitude that he would not fully realize until 19 months later.

He knew he had lived a great life as a professional goalkeeper and he had accepted that it was coming to an end. "We had kind of come to the conclusion that I was going to retire."

Then Brian McBride blew out his knee.

McBride was one of several Americans who followed Keller to Europe in the early 1990s. He spent a year with a German second-division team, then came back in 1996 to join MLS during its inaugural season, and spent the next seven years with the Columbus Crew. For more than a decade, McBride and Keller were mainstays and roommates on the US Men's National Team.

In 2004 Fulham bought McBride's rights from the MLS team, and his run with that EPL club was so successful that he was eventually named captain. He became so popular with the fans that a bar inside its home ground (the delightfully named Craven Cottage) was named after him. On August 18th, 2007, Fulham was playing Middlesbrough in an early season EPL match. McBride would score the Cottagers' only goal in the 16th minute of the match. But in the act of scoring the goal, he somehow sustained a dislocated kneecap — recovery would involve surgery and several months off.

Keller called McBride to offer encouragement, and as the conversation was winding down Keller made what he thought was an innocuous comment about Fulham's goalkeeping situation, which he knew to be in shambles due to injuries. "Why," McBride said, pouncing on Keller's question. "Would you come here?"

Keller told him that wasn't exactly what he meant, but McBride was already out of the barn and down the road with the idea. He told Keller he had to go to the team's training ground the next day and he was going to "tell them you're available."

"I got a phone call about 10 a.m. the next day from the goalkeeping coach who is a friend of mine. An hour later I get a call from the head coach. Then I get a call from the club secretary with an offer, and I'm on a flight the next day. I spend two days dealing with physicals. I trained Friday. And I played Saturday."

In five days Keller had gone from accepting his retirement to starting an EPL game. He was back in business. Looking back, the suddenness of his decision makes sense.

"Fulham was in England, where I had permanent residency. I had a green card so there were no immigration issues or work permit stuff. I could come in, sign and play and that made it real easy."

The deal had one more benefit that wasn't lost on Keller: He now had the bridge he felt he needed to get from Europe to Seattle. "I do remember calling Adrian and telling him I've signed with Fulham, and this could be a better stopgap."

KELLER NEVER wanted to be anything other than a pro athlete and as a kid he told anyone who asked that he was going to play professionally in England.

"I look back on the pure blind arrogance of a 15-year-old kid from Olympia, Washington. Who says, 'I'm going to go play in England,' when no American ever had?" he laughs as if the enormity of it is still too hard to fathom. "But I was probably so stupid that I didn't know nobody ever had."

Youthful ignorance aside, Keller planned his journey with his typical meticulousness choosing Portland for college because Clive Charles coached the Pilots. "The whole idea was, if I'm going to be a professional athlete in soccer I need to be in Europe. And who's going to help me get to Europe? This guy. Simple as that. Best decision I ever made in my life."

Charles, who died at age 51 of cancer in 2003, influenced Keller's career far beyond the pitch. He had spent the bulk of his career playing in England and recognized the ability in Keller, but also saw that the brash youngster wasn't always sure how to carry himself. Charles worked to show Keller that to achieve his goals he had to be more than just talented. He had to be disciplined in everything he did.

"I didn't understand at first what a mentor he became," Keller says. "Lots of people have the ability to play pro sports, but don't know how to be a pro athlete. I could easily have been one of those kids. He taught me *how* to be a pro. I learned that from him."

Keller also spent nine years attending Cliff McCrath's summer soccer camps in the Seattle area. McCrath compiled 597 wins in a decorated coaching career primarily at Seattle Pacific University, and his reputation was such that top-notch instructors and players attended his camps. One such instructor was Paul Barron who made over 400 appearances as a goalkeeper in England in a career that spanned 20 years. Keller worked with Barron several times at McCrath's camp and enjoyed the work so much that he stunned both Barron and McCrath one day in 1987.

McCrath had received a phone call from the national soccer team. They wanted Keller to join one of their youth teams for training camp. He told Barron, and the duo excitedly rushed to tell Keller the news. "Tell them I have three more days to train with Paul," was Keller's response. McCrath was floored. Here was a 17-year-old trying to dictate the details of how this deal would go down.

"Kasey," McCrath sputtered, "This is the *US NATIONAL TEAM* calling. You're going to camp." McCrath says it took Barron and him a day to "talk some sense into him" and get him packed up and off to the US team. "But that's Kasey. He's always had his idea of how it works and you're not going to change that."

By this point Keller was establishing a reputation as someone who really might have the skills to reach his stated goal. Sounders sporting director Chris Henderson played with Keller in the 1989 Youth World Cup in Saudi Arabia. Keller was 19 and Henderson 18 at the time.

"At his age, he was ahead of everyone. He didn't drop balls, he was composed, and he had a presence in the back. He was never lacking for confidence and as a goalkeeper you need that. You need to be brave and sure of yourself. I have really good memories of playing with him."

The two Washingtonians helped lead the US to the semifinals in the tournament, which was the farthest a US under-20 team had ever gone. Keller was awarded the Silver Ball as the tournament's second-best player (behind Brazilian star Bismarck).

By 1992 Keller had played in the NCAA Final Four, had been named the top collegiate goalkeeper in the country, and had appeared with the USMNT in the 1990 World Cup. His play earned him a three-week trial with English First Division side Millwall FC.

Millwall is located in a gritty and somewhat dodgy part of East London. Former voice of the Sounders Arlo White comes straight to the point in describing the atmosphere Keller entered in his first English job. "Millwall Football Club ... For goodness sake, it's like going into a war zone. Unbeknownst to him Kasey was mixing with villains and undesirables, but because he was representing the club they were wonderful to him and they accepted him and he earned his chops there."

Keller recalls some colorful experiences during his time with the Lions.

"It's the toughest part of London, no doubt," Keller says. "A friend of mine ran a tire shop/garage in the area where I lived. One day he asks me into his office. He had a gunnysack rolled up on the desk. He told me to look inside and there's a Kalashnikov inside this bag. One of the local gangsters had an old Corvette and was getting something done to it and forgot he had this AK-47 in the trunk of his car. So my friend snuck it into his office."

Keller played in a charity golf tournament and was paired with another nefarious Millwall character. The week before the tourney the guy had been the subject of a media story alleging any number of dastardly deeds. Keller remembers being told before the match "whatever you do, don't ask him about this. And don't ask him about that."

But Keller's demeanor led to a great stint as he turned his three-week trial into four years.

"I never badmouthed Millwall," he says. They treated me and my family and friends great so I'd never talk bad about those guys."

As for his play? "He was so good," White says, "people forgot pretty quickly that he was American."

Eleven years later Keller's season with Fulham in 2007-08 was a mixed bag. He suffered a shoulder injury and missed four months. Upon his return, there were 10 games left in the season and the Cottagers were most likely going to be relegated. But they got hot and won four of their last five matches in what is considered one of the best relegation escapes ever. In three of those four wins Keller had a clean sheet.

As the summer of 2008 approached, he suddenly found himself with more options than he had anticipated. He discussed staying at Fulham, although the club told him that at the age of 38 they saw him strictly as a backup. He had a conversation with Tottenham where he had played from 2001 to 2005.

He also had conversations about returning to the Bundesliga to play for Bayern Munich. Keller says if those conversations had gotten serious, his return to Seattle would have been derailed.

"If the Bayern Munich thing had come through, then I would have never come to Seattle. They were one of the handful of clubs I would have gone to under the premise that I'd be the backup keeper."

No offer was made, Keller believes because Jurgen Klinsmann (who had just been hired as the manager for the legendary German side) couldn't afford politically to bring in a high-profile American.

Keller also was in discussions with Seattle about finishing his career where it began. He wrestled with conflicting emotions as he pondered moving to MLS. On the one hand the desire to bring his family home was strong. But he was irritated at what he felt was a low-ball offer well beneath what he considered his market value.

His career resume dictated he should be paid top dollar, but MLS at the time allowed each team only one highly paid "designated player." Keller knew the Sounders were pursuing other high-profile players with that slot while hoping to sell him on a "hometown-discount" deal, which meant he probably wasn't going to get the money he desired.

"We absolutely wanted to get Kasey, but that was sort of the first deal that I was negotiating in the big leagues," Hanauer says.

"We had a bit of a duel in terms of negotiating a deal. We knew Kasey was worthy of coming over as a designated player, but we weren't prepared to do that."

The club wanted Keller, but it also wanted a big-name field player in his prime, and the only way they could get both was if Keller would sign for less.

In addition to the money, Keller also was apprehensive about the entire MLS vibe. He'd heard stories from other players who had left European leagues to return home and had been shocked in how far the step down could be in terms of how they were treated. Keller had played in the biggest leagues in the world, and he says too often the stories he heard about MLS from friends could be summed up thusly: "Straight-up bush league."

That's what Keller was thinking on May 31, 2008. His season with Fulham had concluded a few weeks earlier and he was on vacation with his family in Greece when the Sounders contacted him and asked him to come to Seattle to attend an international friendly between Brazil and Canada. The entire Sounders organization would be there and it would be a chance for Keller to meet everyone, including new owner Joe Roth. There was one catch, though: Keller would have to pay his own way.

Free agents in European soccer are wined, dined, and courted the way NFL, MLB, and NBA stars are in America. They don't generally pay their own way to visit a team. But the Sounders were making the awkward transition from minor to major league team.

Irritated but intrigued enough by the Seattle situation Keller decided to make the trip on his own dime. There was a huge crowd for the game and as he made his way through traffic to the stadium he had trouble contacting the Sounders. He didn't know where he was supposed to go and he didn't know whom he was supposed to meet. Eventually contact was made and Keller spent the game in a suite with Sounders executives. But the entire incident left him on slow boil. If he was to end his career by coming home (at a discount) he wanted at the very least to be appreciated.

A couple days later he met Gary Wright for coffee and explained the details of his trip. At the time Keller was frustrated enough to consider shelving the whole idea by either retiring or striking up another deal in Europe. But in Wright he found an intelligent and sympathetic ear.

"We wanted you to come here," Wright told him. He was embarrassed that details for Keller's trip had somehow fallen through the cracks and he was determined to salvage what he could on behalf of the organization. He invited Keller to come out to the Seahawks offices later that day and meet with CEO Tod Leiweke.

When Keller arrived at the Hawks headquarters Wright escorted him down a hallway and into an office where Keller was suddenly face-to-face with Seahawks head coach Mike Holmgren. Keller was a lifelong Seahawks fan and admits he was a little overwhelmed by the sudden chance to spend time with a guy he admired.

"I had spent enough time at Gillette Stadium with the national team to see how the Patriots and the Revolution co-existed," he says, "If I'm signing with the Revolution, there was no chance I was going to meet (Patriots head coach) Bill Belichick."

But here he was in Holmgren's office, where he spent 20 minutes visiting. They discussed the Seahawks controversial loss in Super Bowl XL. Keller told Holmgren that he had spent much of that game on the phone with fellow goalkeeper and Seahawks fan Marcus Hahnemann. Keller was in Germany at the time and Hahnemann was playing for Reading in England. They were doing the same thing over the phone that Holmgren was doing on the sidelines: cursing the officials for many key mistakes they made in the game.

Keller then expressed his frustrations about his trip to Holmgren. Dispensing wise advice in his grandfatherly fashion, Holmgren assured Keller this was an anomaly, a mistake that would not be repeated. "I told him that this was a first-class organization," Holmgren says. "What happened to you is not the norm and won't be how things are done."

Holmgren didn't know much about Keller, but when Wright asked him to talk to him as a favor he quickly agreed. An expert in both the anger and self-confidence departments, he says he was taken aback at first by Keller's typically blunt demeanor. "I could tell he was upset about how things had gone," he laughs and says he remembers telling both Leiweke and Wright to "be careful with this guy." Holmgren was concerned that Keller's reaction to his trip might be an indicator of a me-first, team-second kind of guy. "Shows you what I know about soccer."

Keller met with Leiweke after he talked with Holmgren. Leiweke began the process of selling Keller on the positives available if he came home both as a player and after his playing career. The potential deal to bring Keller home was now officially back on track.

"I hadn't made up my mind yet," Keller says, "but those meetings with Mike and Tod really helped."

Keller now had a decision to make. He could take a deal to play with the Sounders, which would allow him to move his family home, but would be for less than what he could make in Europe. Or he could get a deal done in Europe for more money, but know in his heart that he had missed his best chance to get home.

"I'm a professional athlete. I'm one step below a mercenary. There's an idea in MLS that the Americans should come home and take a considerable pay cut just to help the sport for the bigger picture. I almost didn't do the Sounders deal simply because I heartily disagree with that — 100 percent. If it were only about money, I would have never, ever signed the deal. Out of principle."

But there was more at work here. In addition to trying to create a good situation for his family, Keller was thinking ahead. He had no idea how many seasons he had left, but the sand in the top of the hourglass was dwindling. He had to consider what his career would be after playing and whether it would involve working in the game. A transition to a post-playing career in soccer would be easier in Seattle. His decision was reached after two phone conversations.

The first was with his long time friend and teammate on the USMNT Claudio Reyna. He told Keller that if he desired a job in soccer after his playing days ended then he should "find someway to make this deal happen."

The second conversation came with Leiweke who in trying to convince Keller to take "a wage he hadn't seen in years," kept playing on the positives of coming home. "I gave him my word that we are going to do everything we can on this end," Leiweke says. "I told him he could forever look back in satisfaction to being a part of the launch. I told him to come in and be the person we think you are and things will work out."

Hanauer and Roth weren't budging on the money offered, so Keller was left to ponder the intangibles of his decision.

"In the end my decision to come home was an investment in post-playing," he says. "In the end, I hate the feeling that I'm being taken advantage of ... but does that trump your family? No. It doesn't. Other deals I could have made in Europe didn't trump the big picture of coming home to the Sounders."

Once he made that decision to come home he was committed. There was some discussion of setting up a deal that would allow Keller to accomplish both his desire to make what he felt he was worth and his desire to come home. The Sounders wouldn't begin play until March of 2009. It was proposed that Keller could sign with a European team in August of 2008, play the season in Europe, and then join the Sounders early in their first season during the summer transfer window. Keller hated the idea.

"Joe and I both agreed that if I'm going to be in Seattle I wanted to be there from the beginning, because I wanted to have a bit of influence on everything," he says. "I wasn't just coming home to live off my name and get paid. I wanted to be able to instill early on that I'm coming here to play, to train, to lead by example and do things the right way."

So much for any concerns he would place himself above the team. Keller was now a Sounder; committed to the idea of helping build this team into something his hometown could be proud of and would embrace. He also wasn't big on sitting around, so he asked if he could train with the team as they wrapped up their final USL season. His impact was felt immediately, according to Taylor Graham, who was one of a handful of USL Sounders who would end up making the leap with the team to MLS.

"Towards the end of 2008 Kasey started coming out to train with us," Graham says. "You could tell from the first minute he stepped on the pitch even when we were doing small-sided games he was so communicative. He was smart and helped us organize. But that's what you get with his experience. His instincts are spot on."

Keller brought an honest commitment to helping the team without big-timing anyone. All that international experience with the US national team and his success as a pro in Europe might well have turned him into an insufferable presence around a minor-league team. To be sure, Keller is no shrinking violet in the self-confidence department, but he wears his resume not so much with arrogance, but with the cocky assuredness of someone who truly has been there, done that.

Dave Clark is a Seattle soccer writer who started the well-respected "Sounder at Heart" blog in 2008. He sums up Keller perfectly: "He's dismissive of his own fame, but not dismissive of his own talent."

Graham concurs: "The thing I liked about Kasey was he talked about all his experience and playing in multiple World Cups and playing in countless countries at the highest level, but he didn't sit back and puff his chest. He hung out with the USL guys. He knew us. You could joke with him, too. If he was saying too much we could say 'Oh, Kasey, come on!' and he'd laugh at himself."

KELLER SPENT the fall of 2008 and the winter of 2009 establishing himself as the Sounders new leader and making good on his pledge to establish a "right way" to do things in training, in the changing room, and in the community. This was all good, but it would only go so far if Keller couldn't play. He was in the middle of the longest layoff of his career, a nearly 10-month stretch that would come to an end with the start of the MLS season in March. It would be reasonable to have doubts about his play, but Sigi Schmid had none.

Schmid had first worked as a coach with Keller after the Youth World Cup in 1989 and immediately was able to learn something about how goalkeepers should train. At UCLA Schmid worked his goalkeepers with what's known as pressure training. The idea is to fire as many shots as possible at a keeper as fast as you can to fine-tune his skills while also working on his fitness.

"Keller wasn't into that," Schmid recalls. "He was very meticulous in his training and he wanted things done in a certain way. He wanted to make every save clean and finish every save. I had to adjust to him a little bit, so I actually learned from Kasey that the proper training is somewhere in the middle. Work on your fitness, then work on your saves. Make it two separate things."

Now, almost 20 years later, Schmid didn't need much evidence to convince him Keller was still at the top of his game. "Once I saw him train I had no worries about his age," he says. "Sometimes goalkeepers' best ages are from 30 to 35, because now they've got positioning down and they've still got the physical skills."

Actually, by the time opening night rolled around his starting keeper would be 39 years old, but Schmid could lean on his new goalkeeper coach Tom Dutra, who had known Keller since they were kids and had trained him during some of his European off seasons.

"I had a responsibility to Kasey," Dutra says, "to make sure this worked. There was a fear that he was too old, but he was fantastic from the get-go. He said he wanted to do things the right way and he trained as hard as he could. He set a fantastic example."

By the end of 2008, the group that would become the first Sounders FC team was taking shape. It would be a fun twist if the narrative at this point became Keller teaming up with the USL Sounders to make the jump into MLS and challenge for a championship. It would also be unrealistic. To be sure, there would be some USL guys who made the jump, but to be as good as they wanted to be — immediately — Schmid knew the Sounders would have to succeed in four areas of player acquisition.

"You've got to find someone in the draft," he says. "You've got to make sure you find someone in the expansion draft. You've got to do well with your foreign signings, and you've got to discover some guys. If you hit it in three of those areas you'll be pretty good. Hit in two and you're 50-50. Hit all four and you've got a chance for the playoffs right away. I think we hit all four."

Among the players they would find was one that Schmid, Schmetzer, and Hanauer had all discovered in 2008. He was one who, disregarding mileage, had traveled farther to get to Seattle than any of them.

Adrian Hanauer, Joe Roth, MLS Commissioner Don Garber,
Tod Leiweke (L to R) on November 13th, 2007 at the official announcement
of the MLS expanding to Seattle. (Corky Trewin photo)

Tod Leiweke. "He has amazing courage to put himself out on a limb to try
things and make visionary statements that no one has thought of."
(Corky Trewin photo)

120

As Joe Roth addresses the media Gary Wright looks on from his usual location...just out of the spotlight. (Corky Trewin photo)

Adrian Hanauer (center) with Gary Wright (l) and Don Garber (r)
"He was such a huge part of the essence of what the Sounders became."
(Corky Trewin photo)

Drew Carey leads fans on the opening night March to the Match. "We're all
out of the box thinkers. Drew was massively out of the box." (Rod Mar photo)

Fitness Coach David Tenney, assistants Ezra Hendrickson, Tom Dutra, and Brian Schmetzer stand next to Sigi Schmid (L to R) during the national anthem on opening night. (Rod Mar photo)

The Emerald City Supporters.
"They are the passion of the franchise, the secret sauce."
(Rod Mar photo)

Fredy Montero celebrates the team's first win vs New York.
"We knew, we *all* knew this was a guy who's going to do
well in our league." (Rod Mar photo)

Kasey Keller thanks ECS members after the 3-nil win over New York. "None
of us understood the impact he would have." (Rod Mar photo)

Arlo White calls Fredy Montero's game winner vs Chicago in
August of 2010. "Montero...loitering with intent on the far post."
(Laurie Hodges photo)

Joe Roth addresses fans in Occidental Park before a March to the Match.
"He's a great guy to collaborate with because he has an opinion on
everything but he doesn't have to always be right." (Rod Mar photo)

Sporting Director Chris Henderson and Drew Carey joke with
Sigi Schmid before a game. (Corky Trewin photo)

Brad Evans (3) and Nate Jaqua (21) celebrate a
3-nil win over Colorado (Rod Mar photo)

Steve Zakuani in action vs San Jose (Rod Mar photo)

Kasey Keller boots a ball upfield while mean mugging
every one else on the pitch. (Rod Mar photo)

Kasey Keller: "His intensity made me think that if I didn't step my game up I'd be in trouble." (Rod Mar photo)

Freddie Ljungberg advances the ball against Columbus. "The second half of that first year he really put the team on his back." (Rod Mar photo)

Sigi Schmid. "It's hard to ignore all the championships he's won."
(Rod Mar photo)

Ozzie Alonso. "From day one the most influential guy on the team."
(Rod Mar photo)

Brad Evans, Ozzie Alonso, Jhon Kennedy Hurtado, and others celebrate the Sounders third US Open Cup championship in 2011. (Rod Mar photo)

Brad Evans plays a ball during the 2011 playoffs vs Real Salt Lake (Rod Mar photo)

Sigi Schmid, Ezra Hendrickson, Chris Henderson, Gary Wright, and
Adrian Hanauer watch a reserves game vs Portland on a chilly
March afternoon. (Corky Trewin photo)

Clint Dempsey makes his home debut for the Sounders in August of 2013 in a 1 nil win over Portland. "He's the sum of all this stuff that happened before." (Corky Trewin photo)

Sigi Schmid gives the ECS thumbs up after another Sounders win. (Rod Mar photo)

CHAPTER TEN

JUNE 12, 2007
SOMEWHERE ON INTERSTATE 10

ᕳ

"I was incredibly lucky, because I don't think
a lot of people would have stopped to help
me out, but this guy did."

T he Greyhound route from Houston to Miami is as direct as a bus journey covering 1,579 miles and five states can be. Most of the trip takes place on Interstate 10, through Beaumont, Baton Rouge, New Orleans, Biloxi, and Mobile ... and after traveling the length of the Florida panhandle, the driver steers the bus south on Interstate 75 ... through Gainesville and Orlando, down the Florida Turnpike to Fort Pierce ... and onto Interstate 95 for the final stint into Miami.

Under the best of circumstances, it takes 32 hours. By any definition it's a long trip, but from the perspective of a 21-year old making the kind of leap into the unknown that Osvaldo

Alonso had committed himself to, the minutes went by in alternating slow and fast increments, brought on by the mix of anxiety, hope, and sadness that ran through his mind as the bus hurtled down the road. Each minute meant another mile away from the only life he had known, and another mile closer to ... what, exactly?

"I was scared," Alonso remembers. "I was thinking about my family, my life, and how I couldn't go back."

Just 24 hours earlier, Alonso had been in Texas with the Cuban national soccer team for the 2007 CONCACAF Gold Cup tournament. Cuba had played Panama to a 2-2 draw in New Jersey on Sunday, June 10. The next day they flew to Houston to play Honduras, and it was then that Alonso began to seriously put into motion a plan he had long considered.

"The night before I began to think about different opportunities I might have, to defect," he says. "I had thought about it all the time in Cuba, but that night in Houston was when I really thought about the details of how I was going to do it." Alonso began his new life the next afternoon in one of the most symbolic American institutions of the 21st century, a Wal-Mart store.

"Everyone on the team was spread out. Some people were buying things and some were just looking. I saw this as my best opportunity," he says. Decision made, he simply walked out the front door of the store, as quickly as he could without attracting any attention. He thinks he walked about a mile when he stopped a man on the street and asked him if he spoke Spanish. The man nodded but was certainly unaware of the sensational tale he was about to hear.

Alonso quickly explained he was Cuban, had defected about 15 minutes ago, and needed to call a friend in Miami who could help him. The man let Alonso use his cell phone to make the call.

"I was incredibly lucky, because I don't think a lot of people would have stopped to help me out, but this guy did and he was very helpful. After I spoke with my friend (in Miami) the guy gave me a ride to the Greyhound station." Such is the lot of the angels of kindness who sometimes pass quickly through our lives: Alonso never even got the man's name.

Alonso was on his way. He had to change busses twice on the trip and subsisted on vending machine food at rest stops (talk about quickly adopting to American culture). Both times he switched busses, he asked people for help to make sure he was on the right bus. Unlike the sidewalk in Houston, he found no one who spoke Spanish. "I didn't know where I was. I just looked at signs. I was very nervous. I was so thankful to God when I saw the sign that said Miami."

Alonso's decision to leave Cuba had less to do with politics and much more to do with a young man's desire to be the best he could be at the game he loved. "My original motivation was to become a professional football player. Those opportunities weren't available in Cuba. I thought about leaving when I was 18, but it wasn't until I was part of the national team that I really thought about how I could do it."

In Miami he was reunited with his girlfriend, Liang Perez (who had left Cuba three years earlier), as well as friends and a support system that helped him get his new life in order. After trials with MLS sides Chivas and Columbus, Alonso decided the USL would be a better fit in terms of playing time, so he agreed to a deal in 2008 with Charleston.

It was during that 2008 season that he first came to the attention of the Sounders. They played Charleston three times in USL play and in the semifinals of the US Open Cup. Alonso played in every minute of the four matches, impressing the Seattle brass with his aggressive style of play. Hanauer remembers Alonso "ate us alive" in those games, and at the end of the season he was named the USL Rookie of the Year.

MLS had granted the Sounders one so called "USL discovery player" as an expansion team, meaning that from an available pool of USL players they could select one for their roster. Schmetzer and Hanauer both thought Alonso was the right choice. They didn't have to do much of a sell job on their new head coach. Schmid had been the coach at Columbus when Alonso had tried out there in 2008 before going to Charleston and had offered him a developmental contract. When Hanauer and Schmetzer both voiced a desire to sign him, Schmid quickly agreed.

Other players Seattle would sign for that first team also had interesting journeys to Seattle, although none more daring or courageous than Alonso's. There was, however, one journey Sounders leadership would make to sign a player that had elements of courage and daring. In the fall of 2008 Hanauer and Henderson became aware through an agent of a rising star in Colombia named Fredy Montero. After watching video of Montero they decided they wanted to meet him and watch him in person. "We went to Colombia to watch a handful of players," Hanauer says, "but Fredy was our number one target."

The trips to South America (the Sounders made three) were full of adventures. Colombians take their soccer seriously. This is the country, after all, where legendary star Andres Escobar was murdered, reportedly by gangsters upset that his own goal in the 1994 World Cup prevented Colombia from passage to the knockout round.

Hanauer and Henderson didn't have anything quite that harrowing to deal with, although Henderson remembers that on their first trip a car bomb exploded near the hotel where they were staying. "I heard this giant explosion and I thought, 'that didn't sound right.' There were a lot of people injured. It was very scary." Henderson also remembers being less than thrilled with the car ride they took to meet Montero on their second trip to Colombia.

"Some of the driving, the trip through all the coffee plantations and jungles and mountains on these twisty roads in a taxi, this guy is passing cars, there's a cliff on one side and he was driving like a maniac." Henderson says. He remembers spending much of that ride playing a video game on his phone to take his mind off what was happening inches from his car door. When they finally arrived at the home of a board member for Deportivo Cali (Montero's Colombian team) Henderson was struck by Montero's youth.

"They brought Fredy up and he barely spoke English. I couldn't believe how young he seemed. His first question to us was 'if I go to the US, can I get medicine for my acne?' He was a young, naïve person." Brian Schmetzer was a part of this trip, and while struck by Montero's youth, was also keenly aware of his talent.

"It was very evident," Schmetzer says. "His feet were so good and his technique on the ball — what he can make the ball do is tremendous. There are not a lot of guys who can do what he can do."

The trio concurred that Montero was worth pursuing, and Henderson became convinced they would not be alone in going after Montero's services. "He was just dominating. After we saw him in person, every time he'd score I'd say 'Please stop scoring. Quit scoring bicycle kicks.' One game we saw him play in Colombia he dribbled to the right side of the field and chipped the ball over the goalie's head and into the back of the net. Only a player with the quality and touch Fredy has could score a goal like that. He had all these amazing goals, and I was afraid someone was going to sweep him up."

Hanauer worked the phones to Colombia aggressively before the third and final trip, when the Sounders hoped to complete the deal to bring Montero to Seattle. "I don't like rumors," he says. "I like to keep things on the down low. I called the key people and we all agreed to keep the deal quiet until it was done."

When he and Henderson landed in Bogotá they collected their bags and got into a taxi. As they were pulling away from the curb, Hanauer (who speaks Spanish) laughed when he heard the lead story on a news report: "There was a report on the radio about the Seattle contingent who had just landed at the airport and were here to watch Fredy play and sign him to a deal." Hanauer asked the cabbie if he'd heard the story correctly and the driver confirmed it for him. So much for keeping things on the down low.

The third trip proved to be the charm, and Hanauer and Henderson left Colombia with Montero signed up to join the Sounders. "He was excited about the opportunity," Henderson says. "And we knew ... we all knew ... this is a guy who's going to do well in our league."

Montero was just 21, but had experience that belied his youthful appearance and attitude. In an interview with KJR Radio, he was asked about traveling so far from home to play professionally.

"When I was 13, I had to move to another city to play soccer," he said of his deal with Deportivo Cali, a club located 650 miles south of his hometown of Campo de la Cruz. "I am used to being away from my family." His lone concern about the move was one shared by many a new resident to the Emerald City: the climate. "Where I'm from, it's hot and sunny every day. Do I miss that? Sure."

Weather and distance be damned, the Sounders had found themselves a gem who would ultimately develop into one of their first stars. He also paid dividends for them in pursuit of another Colombian player, Jhon Kennedy Hurtado.

"FREDY WAS THE ONE WHO told the Sounders about me," Hurtado says. "We didn't grow up together, but we played against each other all the time. Then we ended up playing together on Cali. When the Sounders were looking at Fredy, he told them they should look at his friend Jhon."

Actually, by the time Montero had encouraged the team to look at his friend, Hurtado was already on their radar. "We needed a center back," Schmetzer remembers. "We were looking at our notes and someone said 'do you remember that guy we saw play when we were watching Fredy?'" Hurtado at the time had his sights set higher than an MLS expansion team. Italian giant AC Milan had been scouting him for months and in January of 2009 offered him a trial. When things didn't work out in Italy, a Greek team showed interest in signing him. However, Hurtado had visa issues and couldn't get himself cleared to play in Greece. In short order he had gone from being so close to a dream job to being back home.

"I was disappointed about not making Milan and not being able to go to Greece. I came home to sort things out. It was a difficult time." It was about this time that the Sounders reached out and offered Hurtado a deal. Emotionally drained from his just completed Italian roller coaster ride Hurtado didn't jump immediately.

"My wife was pregnant and I didn't know what the financial details of a contract with Seattle would be. So I had to talk to my agent and my wife and sort through the details and develop a plan to make it work. I knew other Colombians played in the league and playing in America was appealing to me."

Hurtado had seen a handful of MLS games on TV, and felt his style of play would fit well in the league. He and his wife warmed to the idea and began doing research on Seattle. The first thing they learned? "We saw that it rained all the time," he laughs. "But once we got there and saw the city I loved it."

Hurtado's talent alone merited the Sounders consideration, but it wasn't lost on Henderson that they also could use him as a companion to Montero to help with the move to America. "When his trial with AC Milan didn't work out we wanted to go get him. We thought a little about how he and Fredy can help each other acclimate. They could learn English together."

So the pursuit and signing of one Colombian player led to the acquisition of another. Perhaps the whole thing was preordained. Schmetzer remembers a little detail from his trip to Colombia that might have served as a sign: The group traveled everywhere in a Mitsubishi Montero.

An easier, but no less important part of building the first team was the MLS expansion draft, in which the Sounders had acquired, among others Nate Jaqua from the Houston Dynamo roster, Jeff Parke from the Red Bulls, James Riley from San Jose, and Brad Evans from the league champion Columbus Crew.

An Arizona native who played collegiate soccer at UC Irvine, Evans was the 15th player selected in the 2007 MLS SuperDraft. Pro soccer didn't start out well for Evans in Columbus, as he suffered through an injury-plagued first season in a town that felt utterly foreign to him. "In the beginning Columbus was difficult for me to say the least. It was a little different, a complete culture shock."

Evans figured soccer would help ease the transition to mid-Ohio, but he hadn't planned on a series of hamstring and quad injuries that limited him to four matches in his rookie season and left him dejected and contemplating drastic measures. "I was hanging on by a thread and I couldn't have been more miserable," he says. He gave thought to shelving the whole idea of pro soccer and going back to college. His family intervened and convinced him to go back to Ohio for his second season.

In 2008, finally healthy, he began enjoying himself and his new home. He played in 26 games, started all four playoff games, and helped lead the Crew to their first MLS title. Once his girlfriend (now wife) Becky began warming to the idea of leaving the West Coast for the Midwest, Evans had a total change of heart. "I thought 'this is the real deal' and saw myself having a future in Columbus."

But he also was intelligent enough to do the math on the upcoming expansion draft that would stock the new MLS team in Seattle. He knew Columbus would have to protect certain players due to contract, salary, and/or native country. He realized that he and teammate Eddie Gaven were probably on the fringe and that one would most likely be leaving.

Three days after the Crew won the 2008 MLS title, Evans found himself meeting with the team's general manager Mark McCullers, who told him that while the team wanted to keep him they'd have to leave him unprotected. He thought it a little odd that the team's coach (Schmid) wasn't in the meeting, but at least now he knew where he stood. The draft was the next day, and Evans flew home to Phoenix preparing for the worst (starting over in another new city), and hoping for the best (the chance to stay with a team he liked in a town he had grown to enjoy).

WHEN HE LANDED AND TURNED on his phone, the messages stacked up quickly. He clearly knew why he had so many messages and was disappointed at the thought of leaving the league champions for an expansion team. His mood changed a few days later when he got a call from his old coach — who was about to become his new coach.

"I got a call from Sigi, which is when I first realized this could be something big. When a hugely successful coach leaves a championship team to come to an expansion team he's got to know something is in the works here. He wouldn't do that for shits and giggles. He started to say things about how the organization was going to do things right. He told me not to be discouraged about leaving a championship team. He told me to trust him and that everything was going to be fine. Then he says, 'by the way, we've sold over 10,000 season tickets already.'"

Evans remembers his two-word response. "Holy shit."

He also remembers arriving in Seattle in early 2009. The team was training at the Seahawks facility on Lake Washington and Evans was blown away. "It was amazing, on the water and the sun was out. It was only 30 degrees, but it was brilliant, just first-rate from day one."

Evans also remembers noticing Montero right away. "He was standing on the left side and the ball got played in pretty deep from the right side. Somehow he gets up and barely touches it with his head and it just floated to the far post and in. I thought 'that was a pretty sick goal. He's going be the real deal.'"

He wasn't surprised at how good Montero was because his coach had tipped him off. "When Sigi says 'he's going to be a good player' then he's going to be a good player. He's the best judge of talent."

As an expansion team the Sounders would have the first pick in the MLS SuperDraft and they used it to take a guy who played college soccer in Akron, Ohio, just up the road from where Evans and Schmid had teamed up to win the MLS Cup. It's fair to say Steve Zakuani was a soccer prodigy.

Born in the Congo, his family moved to London when he was just four. He began playing soccer with other neighborhood kids when he was six. He was good enough to attract the attention of Arsenal, which signed him to a contract to train at the club's youth academy when Zakuani was all of nine years old. "They were the best team in England at the time, so when you sign with them it sets you apart from your friends in the park. I come out the next day wearing all this Arsenal gear and it made them realize I had something special going."

Zakuani traveled across Europe with the Arsenal youth team playing similar squads from other big clubs. He was aware enough of his own talent to know he was pretty good and says it was at this point he began to think he could play soccer for a living. It was also at this point that his father Mao began pushing his son to get the most from his talent. With good fatherly intentions the elder Zakuani would spend postgame time analyzing Steve's play.

"From day one he was pushing me harder than I pushed myself. I was nine years old and I still wanted to have fun. He was always telling me to focus on football. After the game the drive home would be 'in the 10th minute you missed this pass and then you missed that ball.' We'd win games and he'd still be upset because I didn't do this or that. Maybe I scored 3 goals, but he was always pushing me."

Zakuani harbors no ill will towards his father. He says at the time he'd protest the critiques, but as an adult says he needed that kind of pushing to reach his potential. Still, it's fair to wonder if it was all too much for a kid to handle. Prodigies can burn out on their first love and that's what happened to Zakuani as a teenager.

First, he was cut by Arsenal. Signed at the age of nine, deemed no longer worthy at the age of 14. "Out of 24 boys they kept the seven biggest ones. It really hit me hard and made me think maybe this won't happen. I had supported Arsenal and I loved Arsenal. I couldn't see myself playing for any other team. My dad wanted me to sign with another team but I told him I needed time to see if I still wanted to do this. I ended up playing for some smaller teams, but it wasn't the same. I'd lost my love for it."

Time he once dedicated to soccer was now spent aimlessly messing around. He was part of a group that stole a motorcycle. When it was his turn to ride it he crashed, severely injuring his knee. It was two years before he could play again and by then he was done (or so he thought) with the game. But a high school coach convinced him that he had the talent to be special and got him back on track. His play at an academy team attracted the attention of the University of Akron and they offered him a scholarship.

"Those 2 years at Akron allowed me to get my fitness back, my strength in my leg back and my confidence back," he says.

They also put him in a position to be selected first by Seattle in the 2009 MLS SuperDraft.

"I had never been anywhere near the place but I was aware of Seattle right before the draft because Sigi used to come to my college games when he coached Columbus. Plus they had signed Kasey and Freddie."

AH, KASEY AND FREDDIE — players famous for being stars in Europe.

Swedish native and long time Arsenal star Freddie Ljungberg had been signed in October as the Sounders' designated player. It was a move that made soccer fans in Seattle (and at least one guy still coaching in Columbus) sit up and take notice.

"He was huge for the franchise from name recognition," Schmid says. "He brought more credibility to the Sounders right away. His signing and Kasey's signing made people think 'these guys are serious with what they're trying to do.' It was a statement signing."

Hanauer and Henderson got an idea of how big the signing was when they took Ljungberg out to dinner in Seattle. His signing had not yet been announced and, in theory, no one knew he was in town. As the trio left a restaurant they were stopped briefly by a man on the street standing before them, stupefied.

"You ... you ... you're *FREDDIE LJUNGBERG!*" the guy finally managed.

Ljungberg brought not only talent and name recognition to Seattle but also a bit of a superstar attitude.

"He trained really hard," Schmid says, "But he had certain beliefs on when he should or shouldn't train. Arsenal used to play so many games, so they had fewer training days. We had fewer games, so we had more training days. That was something that was hard for him to adjust to. He wanted everything to be like it was at Arsenal, but our schedule wasn't the same so it wasn't going to be the same. That was something that was hard for him sometimes to wrap his head around."

Ljungberg also was particular about his diet. He suffered from migraine headaches and any variation from his diet could apparently trigger a reaction. He was particularly careful about wine, cheese, and sauces. His pickiness reached a comical level during a preseason team dinner hosted by Mick McHugh at F.X. McRory's.

A waiter served Ljungberg a piece of salmon that had a side of hollandaise sauce. Ljungberg demanded the sauce be taken away.

"He saw it," McHugh says, "and kept saying 'I can't have that. I can't have that. It's got to be plain salmon.' So I remove the side of sauce, he has a bite and says, 'I think there's salt and pepper on here ... I can't have that. I can't have that.' So I take it back to the kitchen. We broil it and I bring it back. There must have been a little butter on the grill because he picks that flavor up and says 'I can't have that I can't have that.'"

McHugh laughed and says he finally told Ljungberg, "I'm not sure what more I can do for you. I'm trying to take care of you and I want you healthy. You wanna come back and cook it?"

Everyone in the private room including Ljungberg laughed. Maybe he was trying to be funny, or maybe it was just business as usual for a guy who had been a superstar in England. He was used to having things a certain way and having his wishes accommodated.

"He had certain quirks," Schmid laughs as he's reminded of the salmon story. "But then after we played in Columbus one night, he insisted on taking the whole team to McDonalds and getting everyone a Big Mac. He had a Big Mac as well, and I'm thinking 'how does that fit with the no cheese, no wine thing?'"

One of the subtexts of that first team was the relationship between Keller and Ljungberg that hovered somewhere between cordial and antagonistic.

"They were from total opposite ends of the planet," says Schmetzer. "A lot of it had to do with ego. They both had that inherent confidence in their abilities and that was a clash. Keller was down to Earth and kind of a country boy. Ljungberg was a little flashier. They'd sit next to each other on flights, Ljungberg with his headphones on and his hoody pulled over his face and Keller reading the New York Times. I'd get on the plane and see them and I'd laugh."

"Their personalities jostled," is how Arlo White puts it. "I think Freddie's style and personality didn't mesh with Kasey's ideas of what a leader should be. Kasey has that very blue collar, grew up on the egg farm morning-noon-and-night work ethic. Freddie had a more privileged upbringing in Sweden and had that slightly entitled air about him that didn't mesh well with Kasey."

Keller respected Ljungberg as a player, but felt he didn't make the full effort necessary to make his Seattle situation work.

"I played against him a bunch of times when he was at Arsenal. He was a great player. There are a lot of players who came to MLS who thought they could train and play at 75 percent, and their ability would get them through, and that doesn't work. You can tell people about playing games on artificial turf and you can tell people about the travel, but until they experience it they don't get it. Then they can either buy in or not. Freddie didn't buy in."

In retrospect it was inevitable that Keller and Ljungberg would spar a little bit given the natural fissures in their relationship.

Setting it all up was the money. In the era of one designated player per team the Sounders had one gigantic contract to hand out. Keller felt he had earned it with the length and depth of his career. He was annoyed at the attempt by MLS teams to sell American players on coming home at a discount for the betterment of the game so expensive contracts could be bestowed on international stars who otherwise wouldn't give MLS a look.

He had agreed to his deal, which everyone knew was well below what he was worth, and then everyday had to look at Ljungberg, who was making considerably more as the club's designated player. Ljungberg became a daily reminder to Keller that his decision to put his family and his post soccer career first had led to him taking the type of deal to which he was philosophically opposed.

The second reason they weren't ever going to be completely on the same page has more to do attitude and approach. Keller believed success wasn't a given and that to be successful you've got to approach everything with effort and discipline. Do the things you're supposed to do, do them to the best of your ability, and do them that way every time. Whether it's training, a friendly, a big match, or a trip to the grocery store for a carton of milk, Keller is going in with the no-nonsense attitude that consistently permeated his game.

Growing up on a farm certainly helped instill some of that in him, but London native John Bayliss from The George and Dragon pub thinks Keller's first professional stop in blue-collar Millwall permanently forged the way he would conduct his soccer business.

"He obviously adopted some of that 'this is a working man's sport and I don't need no airs and graces,' Bayliss says, 'these people are here paying my wages and they will live and die by the results of this club.' He brought a lot of that to the Sounders."

It got the attention of his new teammates including Zakuani. "I'll never forget my first training session with Seattle and seeing how hard Kasey was working and yelling. If you were on his team in training, you had to get your stuff together. His intensity made me think that if I didn't step my game up I'd be in trouble."

Ljungberg was every bit Keller's equal in the talent department, but he approached his Sounders FC gig a little more casually. When he got too casual it was not only natural for Keller (who had clearly become the team's Alpha Dog) to hold Ljungberg to a high standard, but it was also necessary.

"There were certain things about Ljungberg that irked me a little bit, pissed me off," says Evans. "He was relaxed and sometimes not ready for training to begin. He'd have his shoes untied at the start of a training session." Evans says the policing of such situations almost always fell on Keller.

"None of us had ever been around a big personality like Ljungberg. But Kasey had, so he was the one who had to step in and say 'that's bullshit. That can't happen.' *Now* if someone tried that I'd say 'Hey! Tie your fuckin' shoes pal.' But I was 23 years old. I wasn't telling Ljungberg to tie his shoes. No way."

A third reason Keller and Ljungberg were destined to not end up on each other's holiday greeting card list was built between 2001 and 2005 in England, when Keller played for Tottenham Hotspur and Ljungberg played for their North London neighborhood nemesis Arsenal. The two sides have been playing one another since 1887 with the requisite amount of mutual bile built up by more than a century of athletic competition. Their stadiums are separated by just over four miles.

"It's one of the premier big-time rivalries in London," says current Sounders FC broadcaster Ross Fletcher. "The communities are buttressed up against each other. Players who dare move from one side to the other (less than 20 ever have) are vilified forever. Such is the acrimony between the two sides."

Keller played for Tottenham from 2001 to 2005 during the middle of an eight-year stretch when they never beat Arsenal. On three occasions Ljungberg scored a goal on Keller. So to the more important issues of money and conduct, add professional rivalry to the Keller-Ljungberg stew.

With all that factored in, tension was bound to creep in to the team, and while it clearly did, it just as clearly never boiled over into anything too disruptive — which in the end speaks volumes about Keller and Ljungberg and their professionalism. Sigi Schmid thinks either consciously or subconsciously the two superstars used the tension to create good things.

"There's always going to be a little friction, maybe even a rivalry between stars," he says. "I look at it like they pushed each other. They both end up saying 'I think I'm better than you and I'm worth more than you.' If that's kept in the right context, it can push both to play better and that makes the team better. That can end up being a positive. It can be a negative, but in our first season it was a positive."

Zakuani had a unique perspective on the relationship and echoes Schmid's belief. He was sitting in the stands in the old Arsenal Stadium with his mom when Ljungberg scored a goal against Manchester United in his debut with the Gunners, and remembers being somewhat awestruck by the talented Swede who was, in some ways, his Arsenal teammate.

"I used to watch him eat," Zakuani laughs. "I watched and studied him in games. He was playing on a wing position so when we went to watch games our coaches would tell us to watch the guys at our position. I would watch Freddie and study him and try to implement things from his game into my game."

Ten years later Zakuani was no longer the awestruck kid watching Ljungberg eat. He was a teammate and says his respect for both Ljungberg and Keller grew as he watched them deal with their differences.

"It never escalated. A lot of pressure to do well was on their shoulders and when they came on the pitch they figured it out and it never became a distraction for the team. I think the proof is that we were successful. It wasn't an issue."

SCHMID WAS HAPPY with how the roster looked and felt they had the potential to be good. By this point Schmid's confidence level in the organization was sky high. The guy who felt that at times things moved too slowly in Columbus was impressed with the comparatively rapid nature of decision-making in Seattle

"Early in preseason I remember sitting down with Adrian and Chris and saying 'right now what we have at center back isn't really strong enough to compete in this league', and within a week we had Tyrone Marshall, Patrick Ianni, and Jhon Kennedy Hurtado." Schmid says that week made him realize that his executives were going to be responsive to his needs.

The Sounders had done well in all four of the areas Schmid felt were critical to building an expansion team. They had made some noteworthy discoveries. They had several solid picks through the expansion draft. Zakuani was a great find at the top of the collegiate draft, and they'd found some gems in their foreign signings.

But there was a fifth area that proved fruitful in helping establish the team's future while connecting it to the past. It wouldn't produce a superstar, but it would produce something more valuable. Historic context.

CHAPTER ELEVEN

SEPTEMBER 28, 2007
SEATTLE, WASHINGTON

♂

"I would have been completely fine if things didn't work out ... but I'm so, so grateful that they did."

By 2007 any doubts Adrian Hanauer had about his ability to run a soccer team in the USL had faded. The Sounders had closed out the 2007 USL season with a 4-nil thrashing of Atlanta to win the USL Championship. The title was the second in three years for the Sounders, and it had come in the wake of some big news involving the future of soccer in Seattle.

The night before the championship game, the team gathered at the Triple Door Lounge in downtown Seattle for the USL Championship Banquet. Rumors had been flying about Seattle obtaining an MLS expansion franchise, and several weeks ahead of the official announcement Hanauer decided it was only fair to let his current players in on the news. He confirmed to them that MLS was close to making an announcement on a team for Seattle and that he would be involved with the ownership of the team.

"Guys had a ton of questions," Taylor Graham says. "He didn't have a lot of answers, but the one thing he kept saying was he felt like he had a core group of guys from the USL team that he thought he could take into MLS and have the sort of continuity that you don't get when you're picking players in an expansion draft."

Hanauer was accurate across the board. The 2007 championship team had 11 players who had also played on the 2005 title winning team. Brian Schmetzer had coached them in both seasons. Hanauer's notion that he had a core from which he could build success was more than just idle talk. The group he was looking at had the uncommon closeness and bonding that comes only with championship teams.

"We were a group of guys who loved to play the game and loved to be around each other," says Roger Levesque. "The organization was just one you wanted to be a part of, even though no one was making money. Adrian was losing money on the deal. Everyone had other stuff going on. Most of us coached. Brian had his construction business on the side. But everyone loved to be a part of it and that's why we did it. Everyone was kind of fighting the good fight."

Zach Scott, who like Levesque and Graham played on both USL championship teams, remembers being proud of what had been built and while he may have harbored dreams of bigger things, he was happy.

"All my eggs were in the USL basket," he says. "If the opportunity came to move up to MLS, I would have chased it. But nothing came up and that was OK because we were a really good team. We were on par with MLS teams when we'd play in Open Cup."

One question on everyone's mind once they found out MLS was coming to Seattle in 2009: Where does that leave the status of the Sounders for 2008? Hanauer didn't have an answer right away, but he was tired of losing money in the USL (for that matter he didn't expect to make money in MLS). He also thought shutting down for a year might be a good idea since it would create pent up demand and anticipation for the MLS launch in 2009.

"People were planning to either join another USL team or just give it up," Scott says.

"Nobody was sure and we weren't getting any indication if we were going to have a team. But fortunately they did keep the team around another year."

In the end Hanauer decided keeping the team afloat one more year in 2008 would be judicious for a couple of reasons. The primary reason was that MLS had created a transition rule that allowed the Sounders to take any player they wanted from their USL roster and bring them into MLS. If Hanauer had folded the team those players would have scattered to other teams. Not only would they be gone but their culture of winning that Hanauer hoped to transfer to MLS would be gone.

There was another factor in play for Hanauer. A couple years earlier he had reworked his partnership with the team so he was the majority owner. Now, his partners were not moving with him into the MLS venture, so they wanted out for 2008. That meant any money lost in the final season would come from Hanauer's pocket.

"Adrian accepted the fact that he was going to lose money that last year," says Gary Wright. "To me it made sense to play that USL season, but it wasn't my money. He took the whole loss."

NONE OF THE SIX players who made the jump from the USL became a superstar, but they were solid contributors. They also gave the MLS Sounders an important connection to the loyal fan base that had supported the team in the USL.

Levesque remembers the USL Sounders supporter's group fondly. "They were called the Pod and they were amazing. They were as passionate as any soccer fans in the States at the time. Granted it was much smaller group. But the level of personal relationship was more pronounced because it was smaller. They'd come out to training and bring lunch to us a couple times each year. They'd have scrapbooks with articles from the NASL days. These are true Sounder fans from when the organization first started."

Levesque says he sees the Pod as the foundation of the support the MLS Sounders enjoy now, and clearly it was a desire to continue that support that was the second reason the team existed in 2008. Hanauer ultimately concluded it made more sense to keep the excitement with the fans he had rather than attempt to build an artificial anticipation by taking soccer away for a year.

"I think it was the right move," he says, "Because we were able to keep the players together.

There was some discussion and uncertainty as to whether it would cloud things for the MLS team. We wanted to make sure fans knew that the MLS team was going to be a different team. Turns out our fans were so sophisticated and understood the dynamics so well it didn't matter."

So the Sounders would return in 2008 to defend their title and attempt to put a great ending on their stay in the USL. The season would serve as a yearlong tryout of sorts for anyone hoping to make the jump with the club to MLS. The upside of the situation was obvious: Have a good year and go to the big leagues. The downside wasn't as apparent at first but became noticeable, particularly to Schmetzer.

"It affected me in some coaching decisions and it affected the group from a human nature standpoint. You're thinking to yourself 'am I going to be involved or not?' We had some good players on that team playing hard and showing what they can do. But on the flip side, on your darkest days you're thinking 'what if I'm not involved?' Every mistake you made was magnified."

Tom Dutra was Schmetzer's goalkeeper coach and minces no words on what it was like trying to coach a team in which everyone was essentially on trial. "That year was miserable. As much as I hate Portland I told their guys when they went through it (in 2010) that I wouldn't wish it on anyone."

Schmetzer says he could feel guys putting added pressure on themselves, particularly when they would struggle. All professional athletes have bad games or bad stretches of a season, but when that comes in a season that might be your one chance to grab a seat in the top league performance anxiety is magnified.

Schmetzer was in the same situation as his players on this one. He would eventually be tapped as Sigi Schmid's top assistant coach, but he spent most of 2008 in the dark as to what his future would be. "I was not directly involved with any conversations where Adrian pulled me aside to tell me what was going on. By the end of the season I felt that I'd be involved on some level but there was no direct conversation."

Schmetzer says the early signing by the MLS team of Sebastien LeToux created some issues within the team. LeToux had been the 2007 USL MVP and in May of 2008 became the first player signed by the MLS Sounders, who then loaned him to the USL team for the remainder of the season. Given LeToux's talent level it was probably the right move, but the unintended effect was tension brought on by the fact that there was now one guy on the team who had the security of a deal with MLS.

"Seba turned out to be a success story in many facets of Sounders history, but his signing created a bit of a rub with some of the guys," says Schmetzer. "Having a guy who was already on the MLS team created a gap between the have and the have-nots. Some guys were OK with it, but some weren't."

LeToux didn't purposely cause problems and his performance indicates he didn't go into cruise mode after his deal. He led the team in minutes played and had 14 goals. Still, Schmetzer says, his deal was in the back of everyone's mind all year. "The other guys are hungry and fighting every day. Seba was very dedicated to Seattle and he wanted the team to win, but at the end of the day he was secure and that took its toll on the team a little bit, particularly towards the middle and end of the season."

Zach Scott felt the tension, not only from LeToux having a deal, but also from the overall vibe within the club. Hanauer was (and still is) a hands on general manager, but in 2008 his time was obviously divided between the USL team's final season and preparations for the arrival of MLS to Seattle.

"It was a bit chaotic," Scott says. "They were focusing on the future, but there was still a team playing. It wasn't our best year.

Part of that were all the off-field distractions. But in the end I can see what they were trying to do, because it was a big deal to move up to MLS."

Scott knew Hanauer as well as anyone. Born and raised in Hawaii, he played college soccer at Gonzaga before joining the Sounders in 2002, the year Hanauer took over. He played 154 games over the next seven years and to supplement his income used his accounting skills to help crunch numbers for some of Hanauer's other business interests. As the 2008 season wound down, he harbored no illusions about making the Sounders MLS squad.

"My off-season training was going back to Hawaii and playing for high school clubs. I didn't know how to prepare correctly. I didn't know what the future held. My wife and I had to make the assumption things weren't going to work out. We had two kids. We had to assume that it wasn't going to be a sure thing. All indications were that we would move back to Hawaii and turn the page on that chapter in our lives. There weren't going to be any complaints."

Levesque felt the same way, which for him meant business as usual. He approached soccer with a kind of "What, Me Worry?" attitude going back to the moment he left his home in Maine to go across the country to play soccer and go to school at Stanford. "I took a chance because it was my best chance to play at the highest level. I wasn't on scholarship so it was kind of 'let's go out and see how it goes,' which has been my philosophy every step of the way."

After college Levesque had a few appearances with San Jose of MLS between 2003 and 2005. His MLS career was waylaid somewhat by an ACL injury he suffered in a game with the US National 23-and-under team that prevented him from playing his rookie season. He never was able to get traction with the Earthquakes after that, but still views the injury in a positive light.

"It was definitely a setback and it took me a little longer to recover not only physically but to get myself into a position to think I could play again. At the end of the day it was the best thing that happened in my career. Because that gave me the opportunity to come to Seattle, and who knows if that would have happened if I hadn't been injured?"

He played 144 games with the Sounders over six seasons and cemented his relationship as a fan favorite with a legendary postseason in 2005, when he scored three goals in a win over Portland, and then netted a stoppage-time goal to lift the team past Montreal in the semifinals.

Graham had played college soccer with Levesque at Stanford, and like his college and pro teammate, never took for granted that soccer was a sure thing. "My entire career I've never been the best player. I always tried to keep pushing and get better. I walked on at Stanford and I fought so hard just to make the team. I thought then maybe there was a chance to play professionally."

He was drafted by Kansas City of MLS in 2003 and played 19 games over two seasons before being released. The Sounders signed him and Graham had a sensational year in 2005, playing every minute for the league champions and being named USL Defender of the Year. That season earned him a deal with New York (where he would play alongside Chris Henderson). He made just 15 appearances for the Red Bulls in a season and a half. When he was released in 2007 he returned to the Sounders and helped them to their final USL title.

The 2008 season ended with the Sounders about as average as a team could be: 10 wins, 10 losses, 10 draws. When they lost at Montreal in the first round of the playoffs, everyone was free to focus on the task at hand, attempting to make the new MLS team.

The 15 USL players who showed up for the first day of training were greeted by the welcome sight of Schmetzer and Dutra who were both part of Sigi Schmid's staff. Their hiring had definitely been noticed by the players, and proved that Hanauer had been more than just posturing about maintaining a sense of continuity from the USL to MLS.

Scott says there was some concern among the players as 2008 wound down that Schmetzer might not get a chance with the new team. "It was along the same lines of 'we're going to throw away the Sounders name and go in a different direction to make something new.' Really start over. I'm so happy they didn't do that. Schmetz was a big part of that core of Seattle soccer and what made it successful in the first place."

"No one deserved to be a part of what was going on more than Brian did," adds Levesque. "I didn't realize how big that was going to be in terms of how I think about it now versus how I thought about it then."

Graham was not only happy with the move, but was impressed with how quickly Schmetzer forged a relationship with Schmid. "It wasn't like Brian was coaching the USL guys and Sigi was coaching the MLS guys," he says. "They had a marriage right from the beginning in terms of what we were trying to do and what we were trying to accomplish. And they were consistent to everybody. That was important."

As the team began to take shape it became evident that there would be a core of USL players who would make the MLS team. LeToux, Sanna Nyassi, and Chris Eylander had been signed before workouts began. Graham was signed in late January, but then suffered a broken foot in an exhibition match against the LA Galaxy. The injury, which would cost him much of the upcoming season, went undetected at first, but was finally diagnosed the night before the team was to leave for a preseason trip to Argentina.

Graham figured he was now off the traveling squad, but since he was fluent in Spanish and the team was trying to help Fredy Montero assimilate (as well as getting ready to sign his friend Jhon Kennedy Hurtado) he was asked to accompany them to South America.

"They wanted me to meet Jhon and help with his transition and help with language and culture. I was so desperate to be with the team that I loved doing that."

Levesque and Scott remained unsigned as the start of the season drew near, and both guys found it tougher to maintain their casual approach to accepting whatever might happen.

"As much as I like to think I keep an even keel," Levesque says, "there's that competitive part of you. I never expected to have another shot at MLS. It was a little bit of a rollercoaster. There were definitely good days and bad days."

Scott had already decided this was an all-or-nothing moment for him. He would make the MLS roster, or he would retire and move back to Hawaii.

"Soccer didn't mean that much to me that I would uproot my family and drag them all over. I was ready to pull the plug if it didn't work out."

By the time it finally worked out the start of the season was upon them. Scott and Levesque were offered deals with the team 72 hours before the first game against New York.

"At one of our first practices at the stadium we were walking off the field," Scott says, "and Chris Henderson walked up and said 'we want to offer you a contract. These are the terms.' Basically it was a take it-or-leave-it thing."

Scott was in no mood to leave it. "They could have offered me a bag of peanuts to play and I would have taken it. I had worked so hard to get to that point and I wanted it so bad. I would have been completely fine if things didn't work out, but I'm so, so grateful that they did."

Levesque was of the same mind. "I was happy in Seattle, living a very good life. I didn't want to go anywhere else to pursue an MLS career. It just sort of worked out."

For Dutra, the players and coaches who had a connection to the USL brought an attitude missing in most expansion teams. "It was *massive*. We wanted to make sure this thing went off right. Those guys had so much pride in the USL team and they made sure the new guys knew how important the Sounders were."

Hanauer goes as far as to say the decision to keep that 2007 team together for the 2008 season ended up being one of the biggest ones the organization made. "If you had brought 25 guys from 25 backgrounds into Seattle, some sort of culture would have come out of it," he says. "But because we had a core of six guys who had the same culture and knew the Sounders way, when we added guys they became a larger part of the foundation of that culture. I absolutely think that was one of the key factors to get us off to a good start on the playing side.

"Schmetz was a huge part of that, too."

So was Dutra, who points out that there was someone else with ties to the final USL team who was a big part of helping turn the Sounders history into a winning culture that could be established immediately in MLS: "Kasey Keller was extremely close to those USL guys."

That closeness that developed quickly during the previous fall when Keller had asked to train with the team in their final months in the USL. "If you work hard, you get a huge amount of respect from Kasey," Hanauer says, "and that group of USL guys was a hard-working group."

Graham saw it all from the inside and strongly believes the contributions the USL guys made to the MLS Sounders was to continue a cultural attitude that had led to the dominant success the Sounders had enjoyed between 2002 and 2008. "The mentality of the teams that Adrian and Brian put together was as professional as could be. We joked around that we looked like a men's league team, but we were all so stubbornly competitive and driven and when we trained we worked really hard. Schmetz had to peel us off the field. We all wanted to play for the team and the city we knew and loved.

"We had a group of guys that all believed in the same thing: Work hard. Be friends. Love soccer and life."

CHAPTER TWELVE

ℭ

*"Hold on a second. No one is going
to a strip club."*

S igi Schmid had lost control of his team.

It's not something that happened often with Schmid. Through his years as a head coach at UCLA, with the Galaxy and Crew in MLS, and numerous stints with the US National squads, one thing you could count on from his teams was the kind of serious focus that comes from everyone knowing who was in charge. He didn't yell or lose his temper as much as he did in his younger days, because he didn't have to. As his career unfolded with success after success he achieved that level of respect given to the very best: He commanded it, he didn't have to demand it.

But on this night he had lost control of his team at the end of what had been a great day. Earlier, in their first game ever, the Sounders FC had played a bona fide match against an actual

159

opponent and they had won. On a practice field next to the Home Depot Center the Sounders had picked up a 3-1 exhibition game victory over the LA Galaxy.

A dinner had been planned for that night for the team at The Palm, the legendary West Hollywood steakhouse. Granted it was only one win (and an exhibition win at that) but the dinner had a celebratory feel. Plates of food and bottles of wine were delivered to tables of wide-eyed players who perhaps with the exception of Keller and Ljungberg were not used to having a team dinner held at such a nice restaurant.

"Everyone was blown away," says Brad Evans. "This is crazy. The entire night was memorable. There was lobster, steaks, and wine all on the house. It was 'order whatever you want.' A lot of the guys at the time were making peanuts. Many of the young guys had never been around something like this before. It made us feel like big timers."

The team had just acquired Patrick Ianni in a trade. "In Houston," he says, "we had team meals at the Macaroni Grill. It was nice, but...."

The dinner was the Sounders ownership group's way of establishing to their players that they were proud of them, and they wanted to do things in a first-class way. As dinner wound down Joe Roth stood to address the team.

"I'm not going to just be some owner that sits back and pretends," Taylor Graham remembers Roth saying. "I want to be the best. I want to be a champion and be at the top." Graham says it was easy for guys to take Roth at his word.

"Guys bought in because he said they wanted to be different and they wanted to be great and be the best — and then everything they did was fantastic (including that night's dinner)."

Hanauer and Leiweke spoke to the team as well and echoed Roth's thoughts. This would be a first-class organization and they were prepared to do everything necessary to provide players with a first-class professional experience.

"I remember being a little bit nervous," Leiweke says about addressing the team. "I told them we'd sold this amount of tickets and we think there's this amount of interest. I heard myself saying it out loud and I was thinking 'Wow!' The players were looking at each other and saying 'this is going to be cool!'"

Then Drew Carey got up to speak. His speech was shorter and of a different theme than his fellow owners. "He pulled an Amex Card out of his pocket," Evans remembers, "and said 'Alright guys, strip club on me! We're leaving the coaches behind!'"

That's how Sigi Schmid lost control of his team.

"Guys went nuts," Graham says. "Everyone was yelling 'Yeah!' and pumping fists." The notion of a night in Hollywood bankrolled by the perpetually ready for a good time Carey did not require a team vote. Every player agreed it was a grand plan.

Roth turned to Carey and said, "you're kidding, right?"

"No, I'm not kidding," Carey chirped. "I'll make a call, we'll get a bus, and we'll go to a strip club."

It was up to the coach to regain control and restore sanity. Evans says Schmid was laughing at the chaotic scene as he stood up and put the brakes on the idea.

"He says 'hold on a second. We've got a game tomorrow. No one's going to a strip club.'"

CAREY'S INTEREST IN BEING involved in the ownership group of the team was sincere and legitimate. No Hollywood star looking for a toy; Carey came from a place of true soccer passion. He had become a fan of the sport when he relocated to Los Angeles from Cleveland. He didn't want to forsake his Cleveland roots, so becoming a fan of the Lakers or Dodgers was out. But Cleveland didn't have soccer so he became a fan of the Galaxy.

He also had become interested in photography and was able to get a photographer's pass for a US Men's National Team match in 2005 at Port of Spain, Trinidad and Tobago. He parlayed that assignment into a deal in which he took photos during the 2006 World Cup in Germany. By then he was hooked on soccer and in interviews repeatedly declared it to be his favorite sport.

Carey looked into what it would take to buy an MLS team. Told it was about $20 million dollars, he mulled trying to put a group together. But that idea evaporated when someone pointed out that his team would need a stadium. "I couldn't pull that off," he laughs. "I don't have stadium money."

So Carey told his lawyer that he wanted to explore ways to join an MLS ownership group. As it turns out, his lawyer also did business with Roth and told Carey that Roth was putting together a group to put an expansion team in Seattle.

Carey arranged a lunch with Roth, but due to schedules the meeting was set up six weeks out. It was a long way off, but it did give Carey plenty of time to rehearse his pitch to join the ownership team. "Joe's heard a million movie pitches, and it was almost like pitching a movie. I knew it better be good right off the bat or you're going to lose his interest."

If common sense had overruled soccer passion the lunch meeting might not have ever happened. The lunch coincided with Carey's final day of rehearsal for the TV game show *The Price is Right*. He was the show's new host, following in the footsteps of the legendary Bob Barker. As the rehearsal wound down Carey started goofing around with one of the stage props used in the 'Grocery Game.'

"We had a big wall that spins around to reveal the game," Carey says. "I put my hand in like it was going to crush it and I didn't get my hand out in time and it crushed my wrist. I thought I had fractured my arm."

EMTs were called to the set and after treating Carey suggested he go to the hospital. Carey was in severe pain but was also mindful that it had taken six weeks to get on Roth's schedule. "So instead of going to the hospital, which I honestly should have done, I went to this lunch with Joe."

The mishap made Carey late, which added even more pressure to the situation. "One of Joe's pet peeves is people who are late. He hates it. I show up 15 minutes late but I walk in with ice on my arm and the injury so that's my out."

Ignoring the pain Carey says, "I just shot right into it ... arm in a sling ... covered in ice ... should have been in the hospital ...

and telling him passionately about something I believed in. I think that's what sold him."

Carey told Roth about a show he had hosted for The Travel Channel when he examined the rivalry between Real Madrid and FC Barcelona. It was during that show, on a tour of Barcelona's legendary Camp Nou stadium, that a guide had casually mentioned to Carey that *Barça* fans were able to vote out the team's president if they so desired. Carey's first thought: "I would love to do that with a team in the States."

He and Roth discussed marketing and agreed the sport had not done a good job of marketing itself in the USA. He told Roth about his adventures with the US Men's team. On and on the soccer discussion flowed, and Carey admits he had one conflicting thought (or maybe two if you factor in the whole 'I should be in a hospital right now' thing).

"Here I am in show business and I'd love to be in movies. I'm meeting with Joe Roth the big famous movie producer. So I should have been talking about the movies with him, but all we did for an hour and a half was talk about soccer and marketing."

In classic Hollywood style, at the end of lunch Roth took a napkin and wrote down an offer for Carey "He turns it around and slides it across the table to me. I'm thinking 'how many times has he done this in his life?'"

Carey liked Roth's offer and immediately accepted it with one proviso. "I was adamant the vote thing had to be part of the deal. I wanted to bring that philosophy to sports. I didn't want to be part of a sports ownership group and do the same old thing. I had to have the vote thing. Otherwise I wouldn't care and I wouldn't have done it."

Roth said he'd have to run that idea past the other owners. After doing so he got back to Carey about a week later and they had a deal. Drew Carey was now a professional soccer team owner.

WHEN ROTH TOLD his co-owners about Carey's idea, the team's general manager was among those who loved the idea.

"It resonated with us right away," says Hanauer. "Joe's an out-of-the-box thinker and I like to think of myself as an out-of-the-box thinker. Drew is *massively* out of the box. It's fantastic thinking. Sometimes we get set in our ways."

Leiweke had a bit more pragmatic thought when he heard the plan. "I asked Drew," he says, "If he wanted to be with me when we told other teams about this."

Leiweke actually loved the idea, but he knew there would be flak. He was right. But by now everyone involved was getting used to the idea that they were working for a team that was going to be very different from other sports franchises, and they all found that very satisfying.

"When we made the announcement there were a number of owners and presidents from other sports who thought we were crazy," says Hanauer. "I'm not sure anyone thinks we're crazy anymore. But no one has copied us yet."

Maybe they should. Carey's passion for the fan vote on the status of the general manager is not just some gimmick to attract attention. By the time he met Roth, he had thought through the plan thoroughly and realized that by empowering the fans they would be building in uncommon loyalty.

"It's great because the fans are invested in the team no matter what happens good or bad. If we ever have a bad streak the fans aren't going to turn their back. They're going to rise up and do something about it. People are never going to go 'Fuck this I'm not going to the games anymore.' That's what you *don't* want. I think the vote thing will keep that from happening. Fans will say 'We have to rally together and get rid of this GM and save the team.' That's what they'll do."

Carey says all of the Sounders interactions with fans are influenced by the empowerment this idea created. "Believe me when I tell you that vote is always in the back of our minds. It's there all the time and it's a real thing that we have to consider."

Hanauer concurs. "The whole notion of democracy in sports is a very well-formulated well-structured way of asking for it and forcing it upon us. It's putting our money where our mouths are.

They can affect things in our business and it will evolve and expand over time."

ONCE THE SOUNDERS accepted Carey's idea that fans should be able to vote on the fate of the GM, a structure needed to be put in place to allow for such a thing.

Thus the "Seattle Sounders Football Club Alliance" (known as "the Alliance") was born. Membership was open to all season-ticket holders. Those who didn't want season tickets but were still fans could join by paying a small yearly fee. Alliance members not only get to vote on the fate of the GM every four years, they can petition for a vote at any time. They also get a say in determining some of the club's charitable partners and programs, the right to advise the team on the game day and fan experience at the stadium. They also can attend the team's annual meeting each December.

Since the team's original season ticket drive was so successful the Alliance was made up of tens of thousands of members and needed a governing body. That structure was called the Alliance Council and is presided over by council president Paul Cox. A lifelong fan of all sports, Cox's passion for soccer was such that he had twice attended the legendary derby between Glascow, Scotland sides Celtic and Rangers, which is considered among the fiercest sports rivalries in the world. "It's a real eye-opening experience," he says, "where they've got armed guards and helicopters and mounted police and the whole nine yards."

He occasionally attended USL Sounders games but committed to season tickets (and thus became an Alliance member) when the team jumped to MLS. Within a few games he says he was hooked on idea of doing more and decided to campaign for membership on the Alliance Council. That was attainable by convincing 25 Alliance members to nominate him, as any Alliance member needed. Cox made it, and within a year was taking on an even larger role.

"In 2010 we decided we had to make the council a little more organized," he says. "We needed a structure, a framework for how we were going to operate. Without that we were just a glorified focus group and we wanted to be more than that. We wanted an active role in helping guide the club in areas that affect the fans."

To do that, Cox and his fellow council members decided they needed a constitution and some basic by laws. The Sounders supported the idea and let the group use the conference room at their offices to hold their meetings. Use of the room came with one stipulation from the club.

"They asked us," Cox says, "to please turn the lights out when we were done."

Cox was elected president at one of the first meetings and he and his fellow Alliance Council members drafted and ratified a constitution and charter that defined their role in club business. The Sounders approved the documents and they are now posted on the team's website.

Also posted are the minutes from the group's monthly meetings. They discuss everything from the mundane (approval of past minutes and new members) to the important (jersey and scarf design ideas). In 2013 the team added towers that shoot flames from directly behind the net after goals. The council promptly discussed that the towers partially block some fans views and whether flames after a goal was necessary or appropriate. No matter what is ultimately decided the team pledges they will listen to their most ardent supporters.

"As long as it doesn't affect us financially in a way that is detrimental," says Roth, "We will listen to anything."

"They definitely listen to us," says Cox. "They want to hear from fans about what they can do better and what they're doing well. If someone wants to bitch about something they can talk to them, and the owners take it seriously. Joe in particular has said he wants to hear from people. He comes from an industry where you have to give people what they want. That's how he makes his money. So he wants to hear from the people who are involved."

Fans were obviously going to love the idea of getting to vote on the future of the general manager. The fact that they took the idea so seriously that they wrote documents on how to govern themselves didn't surprise Carey.

"It's just how I thought it would be," he said. "I figured fans would run with it and make the most of it. Everybody got it and I'm so glad they embraced it. It's not like they're running the team, but they have a voice."

It's a voice Carey says that provides the team's management with invaluable feedback. "If something is going on we want to know about it. They're our canary in the coalmine. We can hear way ahead of time any inkling of anything."

IN THE EARLY YEARS the Alliance and the Alliance Council have been made up primarily of hardcore Sounders fans. Hanauer says he'd like to see it grow in depth and width. "Our hope is that over time it gets even bigger so that it is more representative of the overall fan base." Hanauer, by the way, successfully survived his first four-year stint as GM and was given a "vote of retention" by the Alliance in December of 2012, when 96 percent of the more than 13,000 votes were cast in his favor.

Once on the Council you might be selected to represent fans on the Sounders Advisory Board, which consists of representatives from club ownership, the technical staff, corporate partners and members of the soccer community. John Bayliss of The George and Dragon sits on the Advisory Board.

"You go to the meetings, and there are great minds there," he says. "They've got great ideas about what the fans want, what do they want to see and how is their experience. It's an honor to be on that board."

You would think that any team in any league in any sport would borrow this idea from the Sounders, but that hasn't been the case until the the summer of 2013, when one team did.

"The notion of democracy in sports resonated with people," says Peter McLoughlin who in 2010 replaced Leiweke as CEO of Vulcan Sports, making him Paul Allen's representative in the ownership group. "As a result of that, we're creating a

Seahawks council modeled off the Sounders council, because I want to do the same thing with Seahawks fans: Ask them what's on their minds and what we can do better. Their input is important and that makes the fans feel appreciated." (The Seahawks version, however, does not give the fans the power to vote out the GM.)

CAREY IS CLEARLY SERIOUS about empowering fans and his ideas helped create a powerful bond between the Sounders and their fans. But the comedian's playful side has been on display as well. One spring day in 2009 after training when the team came into the locker room, each player found a vase filled with tulips in front of his locker. In the vase was a card. Players thought maybe a local flower shop had sent them a welcome to Seattle type gift. Very nice.

Brad Evans sat down and opened the card and began reading. "It said 'Dear Brad, Welcome to the Sounders. I am so happy to have you on the team. From Drew. PS— YOU'RE my favorite player."

Evans was excited. He was a very young player and wasn't sure how or why Carey had settled on him, but if one of the team's owners wanted to say he was their favorite guy, then he would be more than happy to take it. He walked over to Tyson Wahl's locker.

"Check this out dude. Look at the PS. I'm his favorite player. He shows me his card and at the bottom it says: PS— YOU'RE my favorite player. We go around the whole locker room and every card says PS— YOU'RE my favorite player."

His point was made, comically and literally ... and the players loved it.

His name didn't necessarily buy him cachet with Seattle fans right away. Carey earned his credibility with fans in honest, no-nonsense fashion. His legitimate passion for the game and his approachable personality combined with a willingness to work the bars full of fans around the stadium gave fans something they never got with other teams: a direct connection to ownership.

Occasionally buying drinks for an hour at Fuel didn't hurt him either.

"The ECS dug him because they knew he dug them, so there was this thing," says Leiweke. "He added a lot of credibility to our dealings with them because it wasn't just 'I'm a star of movies and TV shows.' He cared a lot and he had a lot of passion."

Cared a lot and had a lot of passion? No wonder he and the ECS dug each other.

CHAPTER THIRTEEN

AUGUST 2010
SAN SALVADOR, EL SALVADOR

ᘓ

"These guys are like a breakaway Baltic Republic."

Aaron Reed didn't know if he was following the guy with the AK-47 or the guy with the shotgun. But when they stopped, he stopped. When they unlocked a gate for him, he walked through it. And when they paused to relock the gate behind them, he thanked them.

The armed security guards at Estadio Cuscatlán in San Salvador were leading Reed and a small group of fans through the stadium to their seats for the CONCACAF Champions League match between the Seattle Sounders FC and Isidro Metapán. (CONCACAF stands for the Confederation of North, Central American and Caribbean Association Football, and among other things conducts an international tournament for clubs in the northern half of the western hemisphere.)

At the end of each section of the stadium, the guards would unlock the padlock on the gate in the fence separating the sections, open the gate, and let the group through ... and then they'd stop, the guard would lock the gate behind them, and on they'd go. They repeated this exercise through six sections before finally coming to their seats, which weren't even seats.

"They were terraces," Reed says. "It was a level piece of concrete that's six or eight feet wide. Then it goes up six inches. Then there's another piece of concrete." And one other thing: "And there's a moat in between you and the pitch that's about six feet deep and three feet wide."

The two guards who escorted the Seattle fans retreated, locking the gate behind them. A third armed guard appeared. He would stand next to the gate for the entire game.

The group was now locked in a section surrounded by a barbed wire-topped chain link fence. The section they were in was directly behind a goal. They would spend the game standing on concrete with a poor view of the action since they were so low. They had traveled over 3,000 miles to attend this match, and they were going to view it from the worst seats in the stadium.

And they couldn't be happier.

Meet the Emerald City Supporters.

MORE SO THAN most sports, soccer crowds can be divided into two general groups:

There are people who follow the team with varying degrees of passion. They know rosters, stats, and strategy. They attend games, buy concessions and merchandise, take their kids (if applicable) and root for the home team. They don't necessarily live and die with each result, but they care about their club. Like any other sport we would call these people "fans."

Then there are people for whom knowing the roster and strategy and attending the games and rooting for the team simply isn't enough. Perhaps it's the tribal nature of the sport that brings out this behavior, but for some people anything less than a 100-percent buy-in is considered unacceptable, if not downright callow.

These people differentiate themselves from average fans by singing, chanting, dancing, waving flags, and cheering in an effort so thoroughly organized that the best of these groups become more than fans at a game, they become part of the show. It's something like a student section at a college football or basketball game; but these folks never lost their enthusiasm for organized cheering. These soccer fans organize themselves into "supporter groups," and the first and largest of those groups in Seattle are known as the Emerald City Supporters.

Whether home or away, support groups traditionally sit in seats behind the goal in what's called "The Curve" or in its Italian origin, "Curva." In most stadiums these seats (or in the case of Reed and his group in San Salvador, concrete platforms) offer little in the way of view, even less in terms of amenities, and zero protection from the elements.

The location does allow for a better atmosphere for the kind of organized chaos that groups like ECS create. Since seats in The Curve are usually the cheapest in the stadium, and because they are traditionally General Admission, they are available and affordable to anyone who wants to join. The only caveat is that you're expected to participate in the singing and cheering throughout the match, and you probably won't be as comfortable as those sitting in more posh seats elsewhere in the stadium.

Reed remembers that on the sweltering August night when his group arrived at the Estadio Cuscatlan, the ticket salesman tried his best to show the hardy wayfarers from the Pacific Northwest hospitality.

"For a 10 dollar ticket," he began, "You can sit right here in the middle about half way up. The best seats in the house!"

Reed thanked him but on behalf of the group, declined the generous offer, and asked to be taken to The Curve. The ticket salesman looked at Reed and shrugged his shoulders.

"OK, Gringo," he said in a tone that mixed mild surprise with 'have it your way.' He motioned that they should follow the armed guards to the terraces.

"Supporters are interested in *not* being with the suite holders or in the so-called best seats in the house," Reed explains. "They want to be as far away from that stuff as possible. You want the cheap seats. It's part of the culture. It's the punk rock aesthetic of the whole thing."

The Sounders organization is similar to most North American sports franchises in that most of the key people are not all that into the punk rock aesthetic of anything. But long before they would play an MLS game, the Sounders had to develop a plan to work with the already established ECS. This led to some uneasy moments and tough discussions that happened within both organizations and between the Sounders and the ECS regarding how the supporters group would integrate with the overall fan experience so critical to the success of the team.

From the ECS standpoint, the leaders quickly realized they needed to present a united and professional front. This wasn't some group of soccer hooligans looking to create trouble. This was an organized group of passionate fans who wanted to sing, dance, cheer, and chant in support of a team they were already in love with. They wanted to do things on their terms, but they approached the Sounders organization with respect and a willingness to listen and compromise where needed. They sought reciprocation from the team.

From the Sounders standpoint the prospect of having a group of hundreds, if not thousands of fans who wanted to support the team at the highest level, but wanted to do so under their own set of rules created a nervousness best explained by Leiweke one spring afternoon prior to a match in 2009. "These guys are like a breakaway Baltic Republic."

The team wanted the ECS to integrate with 'Sound Wave,' the Drew Carey-inspired Sounders marching band. To that, the ECS said "no."

The team wanted them to clean up some of the bawdier, less-family friendly parts of their songs and chants. To that, the ECS said "hell, no."

The team wanted them to sit in assigned seats in section 113 on the side of the field. The ECS asked to be in The Curve and wanted those seats to be General Admission and not assigned.

The ECS wanted to march to the beat of their own drummer, and much like Mikhail Gorbachev ultimately concluded that there was nothing the Soviet Union could do to prevent the Baltic States of Lithuania, Estonia, and Latvia from leaving the crumbling Soviet empire, the Sounders would eventually conclude that the Emerald City Supporters were a living, breathing, functioning ... *thing* ... that had to be treated properly. And if treated properly, this thing could ultimately help them. A lot.

Engaging them was not only the right thing to do, but the proper one as well, because while the ECS may have behaved like a breakaway Baltic Republic in that they didn't want to be governed or told what to do, unlike Lithuania, Latvia, and Estonia they weren't interested in breaking away from anything. Indeed they sought to play an important and continuing role in the Sounders success as the franchise moved up to MLS.

THE ECS had preceded MLS in Seattle. A small group of passionate fans led by David Falk had for several seasons made up a supporters group called "the Pod" for the minor league Sounders. As time passed some of the younger adults in that group wanted to take the support a little closer to the edge (the Pod was considered a family friendly group).

Sean McConnell was among that group. He had moved to Seattle from Clarkston, Washington in 1990. In the furthest southeast corner of the state in about as rural a setting imaginable, McConnell grew up a soccer fan. He played in youth leagues and then for Clarkston High School. His coach was a native of Turkey, and McConnell's first exposure to the European side of the sport came by watching videotapes of games made back in Turkey by friends of the coach. After high school he moved to Seattle and when the Sounders were reborn as an APSL (American Professional Soccer League) club in 1994 he began attending matches. By 2004 he had emerged as one of the new leaders of the Pod.

At an off-season meeting in the winter between the 2004 and 2005 seasons the idea of a new name for the group was discussed. McConnell and fellow supporter Eric Gilbertson had noticed a banner someone had been bringing to events. The banner said "Emerald City Supporters."

"Eric and I thought it was an all-encompassing name," McConnell says. "It's Seattle without saying Seattle. People could attach to it."

The Sounders FC of MLS fame was still four years away from playing its first match when the Pod officially became the "Emerald City Supporters." Typical of their grassroots way of doing business, this huge decision came in a meeting held at tables pushed together at the Burgermaster in Kenmore.

One of the traditions the ECS started around then was the March to the Match. It was an idea borrowed from clubs in Europe and South America. Before games, fans meet at various watering holes getting primed for the match. At a predetermined time they march from the pubs to the stadium, making their presence felt with songs and chants.

In Europe and South American hundreds, if not thousands of fans join the marches. The ECS March had somewhat humbler beginnings.

"Eric and I were sitting at Fuel," McConnell remembers. "This was in 2006 and we said 'we all leave at the same time to go to games, so why don't we head down Occidental carrying our flags and sing a couple songs?' There were five to 15 of us at first."

But the small numbers didn't deter the ECS from continuing the March before every home game the USL Sounders played. Traditions, after all, have to start somewhere. This tradition would end up being an important one in terms of connecting the ECS to the Sounders as the move to MLS approached.

The team and the supporters had several meetings in that winter between the last USL season and the first MLS season. It was at those meetings that the Sounders began to realize they had an organized group of diehard fans ready to back the team but not ready to follow a bunch of rules. The ECS began to realize that the MLS Sounders would be a bigger entity than they'd been used to dealing with, and so they might have to compromise or at least negotiate on some issues.

"The early meetings were very awkward," ECS co-president Greg Mockos says. "Like a first date." First date awkwardness is generally remedied with some kind of ice breaking moment. That moment for the Sounders and ECS came when the supporters invited the club to be part of the March.

"We dropped an idea to the front office that the March would be an interesting tradition for them to take on. Drew Carey loved the idea," Mockos says. "We told them 'this is something we do on a small scale and we think it can be huge for you guys. And they're like 'yeah we like this.'"

The March to the Match was an immediate hit with fans. What had begun with "five to 15 guys" a few years earlier began drawing hundreds on a regular basis and over a thousand fans for big games. It eventually got so big that the Sounders did what professional sports teams do: They figured out a way to make money on it. The team sold a title sponsorship deal to Budweiser so the March became "The Budweiser March to the Match."

The ECS hated the idea.

"The March is *OUR* tradition," Mockos says, "which *we* allow the Sounders to *borrow*."

The group met with the Sounders and asked them to not allow the March to be sponsored. The ECS worries about things like this. There's a kind of purity to it ... and it's at the core of what they do.

"When you look at something that's built naturally and organically and grassroots style," says McConnell, former president of ECS, "people buy into that so much quicker than they'll buy into something that a corporation fabricated and put in their face."

American sports franchises don't typically dam up potentially lucrative revenue streams. The idea of fans complaining that selling a sponsorship to something would ruin the "purity" of the event would be laughed at openly. Most sports executives wouldn't even be polite enough to let you leave the room. They'd go *"Shark Tank"* on you and laugh right in your face.

But when the ECS contacted the Sounders to voice their opposition to the Budweiser deal something different happened: Team management listened to their most passionate fans. The March, after all, was not only their idea but also their tradition. They had invited the Sounders to join in the fun. In an amazing decision, forced to choose between more money coming in and doing what's right by the fans, the Sounders chose their fans.

The "Budweiser March to the Match" banners went away.

Leiweke, who quickly came to admire the ECS, used the pregame event to leverage belief out of skeptical potential sponsors and business partners. "I'd tell people who didn't understand the power of the Sounders," he says, "to get to the game an hour early."

Leiweke then took them to the corner of Occidental Avenue and King Street just outside F.X. McRory's. As the March began, Leiweke's sales pitch to potential customers was a simple "watch this."

What they'd see was a huge group of fans carrying flags, banners, and signs. Singing, chanting, and dancing, the supporters have an uproariously good time snaking down Occidental towards the stadium. Since the ECS agreed (at the Sounders request) not to light flares in the stadium they get that out of their system during the March.

Reed points out that they use marine flares instead of road flares because road flares drip and last for 20 minutes. Marine flares spit smoke and last for about three minutes. Washington state law requires boaters to have a pack of four marine flares on any water-going vessel.

"The flares are good for 18 months, so in theory most boaters buy four flares every year and a half," Reed laughs. "At the height of Sounders season I'm walking into the marine store and buying 40 flares a shot."

SIGI SCHMID vividly remembers the first time he sat in The Curve, because it was the first Bundesliga game he ever saw. It was 1964 at Mungersdorfer Stadium in Cologne, West Germany.

The FC Koln Billy Goats were playing Offenbacher Kickers, and Schmid attended the game with his dad, his uncle, and his cousin. While the elder Schmid brothers sat in the stands, 11-year old Sigi and his cousin were given cheap tickets and told to go stand in The Curve.

"I couldn't see shit. There were flags flying in front of me. I remember something warm on the back of my leg, so I think someone probably pissed on me. I didn't turn around, so I'm not sure," Schmid recalls with a laugh. "I had the greatest time of my life. I thought it was fantastic to be in there with the fans."

Schmid's forays into supporter's sections aren't confined to his youth. In 2007 he and his son Kurt were traveling in Germany, and wanted to see Canadian star Kevin McKenna play for FC Koln. The Billy Goats were playing at Mainz and the only seats available were in the visiting team's supporter section. Father and son watched McKenna and attempted to scout other players while dodging flags, banners, and various warm liquids.

After the press conference on the day he was hired, Schmid attended a reception at F.X. McRory's where ECS members boisterously presented him with a scarf. Schmid has come to admire the loyalty and organization of the supporters in Seattle. When he coached in Columbus he dealt with rival support groups that argued and fought with each other before he and several players convinced them at a meeting that by joining together they could do far more good for the team. That was something he didn't need to do in Seattle.

The Sounders and ECS continued to build mutual respect and confront head-on any issues that came up. The team had the good fortune of having access to people like Matt Johnson, who understood supporter culture and its importance to the growth of the franchise.

Johnson is a Seattle native who doesn't remember a time when he didn't play soccer. As he matured, his youthful enjoyment of the game grew into a full-on passion for the sport, which he slaked in part by traveling with his brother to the semifinals and finals of the 1994 World Cup in Los Angeles. On their flight home they proposed that they would make a habit of experiencing the World Cup. They haven't missed it since.

After several years as a Seattle radio producer, Johnson joined the Seahawks media relations department in 2005. As producer of the team's radio broadcasts, he was in on the early meetings the Sounders had regarding the ECS, and helped form the team's philosophy.

"ECS were a vital integral part," he says. "Our thought was to get them involved and engage them ... ask them what they want. What do they need for their fan experience to be what they want it to be? It wasn't 'let's show 'em who's boss,' it was 'give them the respect. They've been doing this for years.'"

His international soccer travel as a fan gave him the experience to envision what the March to the Match could be. He didn't need it explained ... he already got it.

"It's one of the most brilliant European things," he says. "In any part of Europe, you're at the pub and it's like 'let's drink up ... let's go.' It's that unity, that thing of doing it together."

The ECS also found a voice willing to listen to them and respect them in Gary Wright. Like Johnson he had traveled to Europe many times and had been exposed to the culture and traditions of the sport, which for some European clubs go back more than a century. He saw the value of ECS, and his willingness to engage them did not go unnoticed by the group's leaders.

"Gary was never condescending," Reed says. "He treated supporters like they were peers. He didn't pat us on the head and give us a lollypop and tell us to have a nice day. He wanted to know what we were interested in, what we were trying to do. Whether he was going to help us or not was almost immaterial. He just wanted to know. He was a smart businessman, too."

"He had a complete open mindedness to listen to us," Mockos says. "I never felt judged by Gary. We're a risky thing to work with, but the positives..." his voice trails off before he concludes: "Successful businessmen are willing to take risks. I credit his listening to us and hearing our side of the story, enabling us. Enabling us was the biggest choice they made."

The risks the ECS posed had more to do with the reputation of other similar groups around the world, where on occasion enthusiastic support devolves into the hooliganism and violence that has been known to mar the sport in Europe and South America. It's worth noting that the terms "supporters" and "hooligans" have come to mean two distinctly different things within the soccer culture worldwide.

Supporters are intent on supporting their team and upholding traditions. Hooligans are, well, hooligans. They're looking for a fight and use big soccer matches as an excuse to start one. To differentiate themselves, supporters always wear the colors of their club. Hooligans usually don't wear the colors of their team, so they can blend in with the other team's fans and create mayhem.

Given that hundreds of matches are played every day without a problem in leagues all over the world, actual incidents of hooliganism or fan violence are rare. They are almost unheard of in MLS. But in the summer of 2008 there was a brawl in Columbus involving supporters of the MLS Crew and fans of the English side West Ham United during an international friendly between the two clubs.

West Ham fans have earned a reputation for inciting violence, a reputation glamorized by the 2005 movie *"Green Street Hooligans."* The brawl involved about a hundred fans after West Ham supporters went into the Columbus supporters section. Police and security quickly contained the fight and only one fan was arrested, but the incident certainly got the attention of the Sounders who wanted to preclude anything like that *ever* happening at their games.

In the ECS they found a willing partner. ECS wanted to borrow the good things from supporter groups around the world without incorporating the bad things. That meant no smoke bombs in the stadium or violence of any kind. It meant singing, waving flags, and chanting was in. It meant women were welcome — that's a major difference between American supporters groups and their counterparts around the world, which are almost always 100 percent male.

Reed credits Wright with understanding that clubs in England had overreacted to fan violence within supporters groups in the 1980s. Several ugly incidents led to teams taking measures to curb the antisocial behavior. Seats replaced general admission sections and ticket prices were increased. This led to a pricing out of the troublemakers, but also of many legitimate working-class supporters who couldn't or wouldn't pay the higher prices.

"They yanked the leash really hard," Reed says. "I think Gary recognized that they had gone too far. He saw room for a middle ground, which is easy to see now, but I'm not sure how easy it was to see in 2009."

As McConnell sees it, the Sounders began to realize that the positives of ECS were going to outweigh the negatives.

"At one point they're like 'oh, gosh. This is going to be hard to control,'" he says. "But they also saw that we could appeal to people that they would never be able to appeal to: The alternative music punk rock kind of crowd that aren't into sports. People who say 'screw those big professional leagues, it's all about money.' They still watch them on TV, but getting them to come out and spend money to go to a game is another thing. But because there's like-minded people in ECS, fellow counter-culturists, they're comfortable doing so. If the entire stadium were full of soccer moms they'd *never* come out."

The ECS was more than just a place for counter-culturists. Young professionals who may or may not have even been into soccer saw the Sounders and ECS as a cool way to socialize and have fun.

The ECS game day mantra was pretty simple. Arrive early, march to the match, sing, cheer, chant, and wave flags. And do it for the entire match. They instantly became part of the show at Sounders games and that paid big dividends not only for the team, but for them as well.

"We only had 400 members (on opening night) and not all of them were in the supporters section," Mockos remembers. "But we showed enough of a good time that the initial crowds who came to the first three or four home games actually converted themselves and all of a sudden games became a huge recruiting tool for us."

That was all more than just a happy coincidence. McConnell and the ECS hierarchy had concerns about whether they could set the tone for supporters inside the stadium. They made that one of their top early priorities.

"That was something we talked about a lot for that first game; coming in there and leading that stadium. I wasn't expecting everyone to sing the songs right away, but we wanted to set the tone. I think the fact that our section was in there pretty early that first game, and the fact that we were standing not sitting ... I think a lot of people looked at each other and said 'OK ... we're standing.' The amount of noise and vocal atmosphere we brought, people were like 'Oh, this is what this beast is all about!'"

Reed remembers the feeling as the ECS instantly become part of the show. "In those first games you had the rest of the stadium with one eye on the game the other eye on this thing they'd never seen before."

Adds Mockos, "Those first days were very delicate. Other groups could have drowned us out. Another group could have emerged, maybe not as well organized or with the same vision. We had expressed the vision that the whole Brougham end would be supporters, but there were times we were worried about being drowned out."

John Rizzardini says another worry for the Sounders was that if the team targeted the ECS too much in terms of early marketing efforts, the casual fan might feel detached from the group and unwilling to engage with the team. That was another worry that evaporated as the ECS emerged.

"They established the atmosphere in the stadium and everyone followed their lead," Rizzardini says, "It was brilliant and it led to everyone else figuring out their chants."

Indeed, the ECS is part inside joke and part all-inclusive. At the kickoff of each game the group belts out the 1969 Perry Como song *"Seattle"* which includes the lyric "the bluest skies you've ever seen are in Seattle." The song is delivered in its entirety and done with enthusiasm and completely without irony on the nights of early or late season games where not only is the sky not blue but it is often hurling some horrible combination of moisture at you.

The group also delivers a version of the Woody Guthrie tune *"Roll On, Columbia,"* which is the official folk song of the State of Washington. The ECS sing the song (about the river that bisects the state before forming about half the border between Washington and Oregon) to commemorate Colombia native Fredy Montero's scoring of the first goal in Sounders history.

In addition to those and other songs, the ECS has developed at least two things that involve the entire stadium to help set the tone at matches. The first is a simple call and response chant: the ECS members shouting *"Seattle"* and the rest of the stadium answering a second later with *"Sounders."* The other is the so-called "Boom-Boom-Clap" cheer, which starts with a member of ECS hitting a giant bass drum twice. That's quickly followed by a handclap from everyone else in the stadium. For people who don't know the words to *"Seattle"* or *"Roll on Columbia,"* these two simple things allow them to feel as if they are part of the ECS.

The ECS also produced a Tifo for the Sounders opening night MLS game against New York that helped establish their reputation. The giant, painted sign was unfurled to reveal a drawing of the Space Needle with the line "Tonight Our History Becomes Legend."

Reed laughs as he remembers the reaction from many fans. "It looked like the kind of thing the club had put together and most people didn't realize that it was homemade because they didn't know soccer support groups had the culture of doing that on their own. They don't really realize that people actually will get a sewing group together to make that."

You need more than a sewing group to make the gigantic banners that have become common at big games in Seattle. It takes money (in the case of the opening night Tifo $4,000 that was raised by "passing the hat" according to Mockos) and a location big enough to create the banner. The opening night Tifo was painted in the basement party room of a fraternity house at the University of Washington. Mockos remembers "it took forever" to get the first one done.

"But we've gotten better at it. We know where to buy stuff and how to order in big quantities. We hammered away at the guy who manages production of the Tifos that he has to plan better. As a consequence, when you plan you save money."

They may have found a way to save money in the overall production end of the Tifos, but they've challenged themselves to get bigger and better along the way. The "Decades of Dominance" Tifo for a 2011 game against Portland was made up of nine different sections and took two minutes just to unfurl. Cost? $12,000. A Tifo saluting Sigi Schmid before the 2012 Portland match cost $20,000.

YouTube videos of these displays have been viewed thousands of times. The ECS informs the Sounders when they are doing a display. The Tifos are so big and costly and their display so enormous and professionally done that it's jaw dropping to realize that this is done completely by the supporters, independent of the team.

For a game day when a Tifo is being displayed, a group of about 10 ECS members will arrive at the stadium about four hours before kickoff. Depending on the style and size of the Tifo, there might be as many as 10 different banners that have to be moved into place. The banners weigh close to 150 pounds each when painted and are stored in the convention hall behind the stadium.

From there they are lugged, pushed, dragged, and pulled into position. If cards or some other media is being used as part of the display, they are placed under seats in the section. It's an incredible amount of work that goes into creating and setting up something that will be displayed for perhaps two minutes.

Stadium officials allow the use of rigging within the stadium to help display Tifos. They also provide the group with carts and access to a freight elevator to move the giant banners. But the creation and execution of the display is done entirely by the ECS.

Why does the group decline to seek — or even accept help from the team for such an undertaking?

"It's a purity thing," says McConnell.

Asked where that idea comes from Mockos says, "It doesn't come from anywhere. I just want it to be 100 percent mine."

Consider it the difference between fans' passion and corporate advertising — never the twain shall meet. It's not a message from the team and its owners; a Tifo is a message from the supporters. Period.

What if the Sounders insisted on being involved with the display?

"That's a deal breaker," Mockos declares.

Ultimately the awkwardness between the team and the ECS faded into the background. After all, they are meant for each other. The team appreciated how the ECS presented and conducted themselves in meetings. The ECS appreciated how the team successfully navigated its way into MLS.

"The buildup to the first game from late 2008 to 2009," Mockos says, "That wasn't random. The way they signed Keller, Ljungberg, announced the logo, the jerseys, the scarf Seattle campaign. They did an extraordinarily good job in marketing."

Once the games started the Sounders were impressed with how organized the ECS was and how they were willing to police themselves in terms of fan behavior within The Curve. Idiocy wasn't allowed and the ECS insured that by creating a system of leaders who communicated with stadium officials and each other throughout games.

"We have no tolerance for that," Reed says. "We've built this for ourselves and that's how we sell the give and take. We have accountability. We have responsibility. If something happens in our section, half the time the ushers will come to one of our leaders to solve the problem. When we're at road games we introduce ourselves to security right away.

"We're not willing to let any selfish individual put the group in jeopardy."

The security system was just one part of the ECS hierarchy that impressed the Sounders. The group has committees that handle fundraising (for Tifos), travel to away games, recruiting of new members, and elected co-presidents that oversee everything. Built and governed differently, the ECS nevertheless was just as solid an organization as were the Sounders.

Ultimately the team and the ECS brought out the best in one another. The Sounders gave the ECS a winning big league organization to support. "Back in the USL days there was like 16 of them," Hanauer says. "They wanted to have the voice of thousands but they weren't a big enough fan group to have the juice. But as MLS came and their numbers grew it was clear that we needed to pay attention to them and their needs. It was in our best interest because they were our best path to a fantastic atmosphere."

The ECS meanwhile gave Sounders games a unique look and feel right from the start.

"They were the passion of the franchise," says Leiweke. "The secret sauce. We always thought they were critical, but then they really became the centerpiece. When we listened to them and took their suggestions and expanded on them, it was powerful. I'm not sure how successful it would have been without the ECS. They were what differentiated us from all the other teams. The authenticity of our fan base made us different."

That fact is not lost on the Sounders players. "The environment is different at our games compared to other games," says Zach Scott, "To get people who have pages and pages of chants and songs and they're drunk off their asses and love soccer and hanging out ... that's cool and it gets you going."

"We in Seattle are the experts in supporter culture," Mockos says. "There is no question about it. At the beginning the Sounders had questions. 'Are you guys the best to lead this atmosphere and run this atmosphere?'

"Yes. Yes we are."

Chapter Fourteen

July 14, 2011
Seattle, Washington

♪

"So, the club looked after your Dad?"

Sir Alex Ferguson might be the best example of soccer royalty the sport has to offer. He played for 17 seasons in Scotland, scoring 171 goals. He began his managerial career in 1974 and took over the direction of legendary Manchester United in 1986. His success rate there is the envy of any coach in any sport, as the Red Devils won 60 percent of more than 1,500 matches played on his watch and filled up trophy case after trophy case. They were big when he arrived, but since then they've become a worldwide soccer colossus with supporters in every corner of the globe. His retirement in 2013 was one of the year's biggest stories in sports.

Like anyone who has presided over such an empire for nearly three decades, Ferguson could be excused for having moments when he thinks he's heard it all about Manchester United. But on a July afternoon in 2011 Ferguson listened intently at the yarn being spun to him by a gentleman he had just met named Arlo White.

Ferguson was in Seattle for an international friendly between Manchester United and Sounders FC. As always when he and his club traveled it was with the surrounding hype and noise fitting of a giant rock band. White was the broadcast voice of the Sounders and was to serve as the moderator for a press conference welcoming Ferguson and his club to Seattle. As such, he was able to spend a few minutes visiting with Ferguson before the formal questions started. He used that time to pass along his thanks for a gesture of kindness Man U had made many years earlier.

On an autumn day in 1984 in Leicester, England, 11-year-old Arlo and his younger brother Mark were abruptly removed from school and taken home.

"We got home and were told that dad had an accident at work," White recalls. "We panicked straight away in that situation wondering about the severity. Dad was a printer and he worked on a big Heidelberg machine. He was brilliant at his job, very highly skilled, and he knew all the tricks. He'd make that machine purr."

But on this day, Mel White was careless for just a second. He reached too far into the press and his arm got stuck in the rollers of the enormous machine.

In the first moments after the accident, drastic measures were considered. Mel White's brother Roger was contacted and hurried to the shop. "Uncle Roger had to sign a form saying if we can't get him out we'll have to sever his arm," White says. Meanwhile a search was underway for a company engineer who might be able to dismantle the machine.

"Two engineers from the company were in England, but nobody knew where they were," White says. "So everyone was frantically calling every printer within 10 miles, 20 miles, 50 miles, 100 miles. They finally find these guys and they're in Sheffield about 70 miles north of Leicester. They were able to come down and take the machine to pieces and eventually they were able to lift the machine up. Dad's arm was plastered against the roller like a Tom and Jerry cartoon. He had a full hand reconstruction and went through enormous amounts of rehab."

For a long time the family had no income. White's fellow workers helped with what the English call a whip-round to raise money to buy Christmas presents and help fill the family's basic needs. Another group stepped forward as well.

Mel White had been working on a program for an upcoming Manchester United match when he suffered his injury. Ken Ramsden was the Man U secretary at the time and sent the family a letter encouraging them to let the club know if they needed anything. They also sent food for the family and gifts for White's young sons: Man U soccer boots and playing kits as well as a signed soccer ball.

White made a full recovery and a story that could have been much worse actually had a happy ending. The family never forgot the kind gesture Manchester United made, and now halfway around the world, the Sounders announcer shared a bond and a word of thanks with the Man U icon.

The story had taken place before Ferguson began his run with Man U, but he was nonetheless delighted to hear that the club had done things the right way. "So," he said, "The Club looked after your dad?" Thrilled at the chance to say thanks all these years later White smiled back at Ferguson. "Yes, Sir Alex, you did."

"It's one of the most wonderful moments I've had," White says in a voice tinged with emotion. "To have the opportunity to pass on my and my dad's gratitude to Manchester United and to do it to MISTER Manchester United in Seattle was a fantastic experience."

The fact that Arlo White was standing in a room with Mr. Manchester United at a hotel in Seattle was another great example of the serendipity that repeatedly kissed the Sounders story. If things had worked out differently for a Seattle broadcasting icon White might not have been there.

"I'M AN ASTERISK, A FOOTNOTE," Kevin Calabro laughs when asked about his year as the original voice of the Sounders.

"People will say 'didn't that guy, the Sonic guy, didn't he do the Sounders for one year?'"

In a life full of mostly great times, 2008 was a decidedly ugly year for Calabro. The entire city of Seattle was impacted when the NBA Supersonics were sold and moved to Oklahoma City that summer. But no one felt the Sonics departure as personally as Calabro did.

For 21 years he had been the wildly popular voice of the team. No cookie cutter, he peppered games with sensational off-the-cuff comments and riffs influenced by music, movies, and pop culture. His signature phrases, things like "Get on the magic carpet, and RIDE," and "Flyin' chickens in the barnyard," and "Get on up for the down stroke" became part of the Seattle basketball fan's lexicon. You were as likely to hear someone yell them in the crowd as you were to hear Calabro use them in a broadcast.

But Calabro was more than just stylish flare. A student and historian of the game, he was also a solid announcer who used pacing, timing, and rhythm to consistently produce memorable broadcasts. Calabro made bad games sound good and good games sound great. His talent combined with a gracious and approachable personality turned him into a rock star in the city. It helped that the Sonics were usually good during his tenure, too, making the playoffs 13 times in 21 seasons.

Calabro cemented his reputation with Seattle fans with a decision to not seek nor accept an offer from Oklahoma City. Long before the deal to move the team was finalized Calabro told KJR Radio "I'm a Seattle guy and I'm staying in Seattle."

That comment got the attention of Tod Leiweke, who like most of Seattle felt helpless as he watched the team leave. In what was more of a symbolic gesture than anything else Leiweke, acting as Paul Allen's rep in the owner's meetings (Allen owns the Portland Trailblazers) cast one of two votes against moving the Sonics. (Dallas Mavericks owner Mark Cuban also voted no.) He admired Calabro's decision on behalf of the community. The Sounders needed an announcer for the games and the guy they would hire would play the crucial role of connecting the team to the fans.

"Kevin was an obvious choice because when the Sonics left it broke a lot of hearts," Leiweke says shaking his head in wonder at the stand Calabro made. "Here was the guy as synonymous as anyone with the team and it was the ultimate nobility: 'I love the Sonics, but I'm not going to Oklahoma City. I'm staying in Seattle because this is my home.' I was really enthusiastic about talking to him about working for us."

The Sounders reached out to Calabro shortly after the taillights of the moving vans faded en route to Oklahoma City. They found a guy who, despite not having soccer in his background, was willing to listen.

"The NBA or ESPN hadn't reached out to offer me anything," Calabro says. "I didn't know what direction to go at that point. I'm not the kind to sit on the sideline and wait to see what happens next. I felt like I've got 21 years of equity built up in the market...I might as well use it. They said 'we'd like you to give it a try' and it resonated with me."

Calabro was hired in August of 2008 and his immediate role was to act as the face of the team at press conferences. In that role he shined, giving this new team cachet with the average guy on the street who might not know soccer but certainly knew Calabro. He also attracted at least some basketball fans that had been suddenly orphaned by the NBA, their leap onto the Sounders FC bandwagon made easier by his involvement.

"I've got name and notoriety in the market, which is what I think Tod wanted," he says. "I thought I could help get them off the ground. I think another part of their plan was to take some of the disenfranchised Sonics fans and pull them over and make them soccer fans — and I think to a degree that worked as well."

As the season approached Calabro threw himself into preparation for game broadcasts, but all the hard work he invested couldn't make up for the simple fact that he had not grown up in the sport. His exposure had mainly come from watching his kids play the game, and while the basics were simple and obvious enough to grasp, he struggled to get to a knowledge point he felt necessary to do the kind of broadcast he had always done with the Sonics.

"I thought I could get up to speed on soccer, and it was absolutely more difficult than I thought it would be. It has its own pace and tempo and nuances and language. The nuances of the game were something I just couldn't grasp. I think the only way you latch on to the nuances or subtleties of the game is by playing or coaching at a young level."

Savvy fans noticed early that Calabro was playing from behind in the nuance and subtlety departments, and they made their feelings known.

"We end up putting the games on KING-TV," Leiweke says. "They were the number one station in town and we had huge audiences. A lot of the people watching knew more about the game than Kevin. He was learning on the job."

Attempting to learn on the job was made more challenging by relentlessly negative feedback Calabro was getting from a percentage of the team's fans who (not without a valid point) wanted someone who knew the sport as the voice of their team.

More so than most, soccer fans are quick to bristle when they sense someone who doesn't possess their knowledge or appreciation of the beautiful game. On the one hand soccer fans want to see the sport grow, but having a *basketball guy* as the Sounders' announcer felt like a slight to many.

"The fans killed me, which I was not used to. I came out of the experience kind of beat up. It was a good experience, but from a broadcasting standpoint it was a total disaster," he says with a hearty laugh, much more indicative of self-awareness than self-pity or anger. "It won't be on my resume nor will I ever attempt to ever to do soccer again."

By the end of the first season Calabro knew the job wasn't for him. On the bright side, he had been hired by ESPN to work NBA games, so he was back to his first love. He had without question helped establish the Sounders in the community, and in a perverse way his lack of knowledge of the game led to feedback that gave the team an honest indication of the depth and passion of their fan base.

He also wishes he had been able to translate into the broadcast the fun he found in the Sounders. "It was a fun team to follow and I enjoyed working with the athletes. It was just disappointing that I wasn't able to articulate that into the game broadcast. Real disappointing."

"Sounder at Heart" blogger Dave Clark heard the slings and arrows thrown Calabro's way by fans and while acknowledging their point, is quick to credit Calabro for being a part of the bigger picture of the successful launch of the team into MLS.

"A lot of soccer fans discount this," Clark says, "but getting that first over-the-air TV deal and getting Kevin was huge. Just being associated with someone like him helped the Sounders connect to the general sports fan. It certainly wasn't his finest performance, but the effort he put in to try to make it work and to grow this Seattle thing was an important and often overlooked aspect of the story."

Still, it was obvious to everyone by the end of that first season that the Sounders needed an announcer who knew the sport, and the team had a pretty good idea who that guy might be. He had been standing right next to Calabro when the team debuted on opening night with a win over New York.

IN MANY WAYS ARLO White is a British version of Kevin Calabro. They have remarkably similar personalities and talent levels. At a young age they both had the gift of gab and a desire to entertain using sports, but Calabro grew up in basketball-mad Indiana and his early "broadcast" experience involved goofing around with his friends at a basketball court. Meanwhile in the soccer-drenched world of England, White's first experiences talking about the sport came alongside his grandfather.

"My brother and I would spend lots of time with my grandparents when my parents traveled. We loved being there. We were treated like Harry and William. My grandfather was a soccer nut and on Sunday morning I'd take him a cup of coffee and the newspapers with all the soccer reports in there. He had a hi-fi system with a tape player in it with a record function and a microphone, and I'd do mock announcing of games and grandpa would be the analyst."

White's brother Mark was the best man at his wedding and as a surprise to the groom dug up one of the tapes from when Arlo was six years old. It was played at the wedding to much merriment.

"I'm commentating on a fictitious Leicester City/Derby County match in which LC won 4 goals to nil and played superbly," he laughs. "So there was a love of radio, a love of soccer and a desire to broadcast that was in me by about the age of six. I can remember as a kid going to bed with a little transistor radio and listening to the BBC's Bryon Butler and Peter Jones from places like Old Trafford (Man U's home) and Highbury (where Arsenal played) and Anfield (Liverpool) and it sounded so exotic. I remember thinking even then: I want to do that."

White's passion for soccer and broadcasting blossomed to the point as a teenager he bought a portable tape recorder to take with him to Leicester City matches where he and his buddies would commentate on games. He admits the tapes lacked in the professionalism area.

"Leicester City was awful at the time so it often descended into comedy and high farce," he says and laughs that even when the Foxes were able to muster a goal "all you'd hear was the tape machine hitting the ground and all of us celebrating."

But attending games in the mid-1980s was becoming less enjoyable in England because it was becoming too dangerous for spectators.

"It wasn't a particularly good time to go and watch games," White recalls. "The atmosphere was aggressive, feral; it was right in the middle of the hooligan era. You'd get pushed around on the terraces and there was always a chance you'd get into a fight. You had to duck coins being thrown. You were herded into these areas in the stadiums like cattle with fences all around you. There were chants with swearing, predictions of riots. 'We're going to kick your head in after the game!' You had to really love the game to go through all that."

White attended fewer games and he began filling some of his newfound spare time with, of all things, a game infinitesimally more violent than soccer and for that matter more violent than the wildest of hooligans on their best day: American football.

In 1982 a new TV network launched in London called Channel 4. The network was the first in Great Britain to show National Football League games. The NFL was making its first tentative steps towards expansion of its brand overseas and for the first time the average person in England was exposed to the best made-for-TV sport ever.

"Suddenly on the TV screen you've got these wonderful stadiums," White says. "This razzamatazz, this glamorous sport with these gladiators with helmets on. It seduced a lot of people at the time, including me."

White became fascinated with the NFL. He listened to games broadcast on the Armed Forces Radio Network late on Sunday nights. The only problem was the AFRN broadcast originated in Germany, so the games faded in and out. "It seemed at every key moment in the game the signal would disappear and be replaced by Belgian folk music. Sometimes you'd have to wait days to get the final score. You had to be really dedicated."

White was nothing if not dedicated to his new passion. He scoured the papers daily to find news and attempt to locate final scores of games from the previous week. And his emerging love was about to get a kickstart that would serve as the first few steps on the path he'd take from Leicester to Seattle.

White's Aunt Kathleen lived in Chicago, and when she and her American husband visited England, White was fascinated to be able to talk directly to someone who had knowledge of the NFL. White plied his Uncle Bill with questions about the games, the teams, and the news of American football. Their connection was genuine and enjoyable enough for Bill and Kathleen that they invited 13-year-old Arlo to come visit them in Chicago.

"The experience was life changing. I remember being picked up at O'Hare Airport and it was an attack on my senses. I remember being on the Dan Ryan Expressway just wide-eyed. When I saw downtown Chicago come into view, my jaw hit the ground. I didn't blink for five minutes. I couldn't take my eye off it, this splendor, and this enormous downtown area. From that moment there was a love affair with the United States and a desire to spend more time there, and perhaps one day live there."

Life marched on for White and while he burned with desire to be a sports commentator, he had no idea how to go about making that dream come true. He knew no one in the business and therefore had no clue or guidance on how to get a job. So he got a sales job, but admits he often pulled off the road to listen to soccer or cricket on the radio, which was "not very good for the selling part of the sales job."

He also by now had met his wife-to-be and she would serve as the final impetus to get him into the broadcasting business. "I'm obsessed with being a radio broadcaster," he laughs, "and Lizi says, 'I think you could do it but I'm kind of tired of hearing about it. Either do something about it or let's move on.'"

White quit his sales job and got a meeting with the local BBC station. In the universally understood language of the broadcast business, he was told they had no money to pay him but he was welcome to show off his skills providing in-game reports on a match that weekend between Bedlington Terriers and Mickleover Sports.

With the home team (Bedlington) leading 4-nil the lights at the stadium went out with 20 minutes left to play. The game was rescheduled, and this time with the home team trailing 2-nil the lights again mysteriously went out. White had inadvertently stumbled onto a big story.

"The Football Association after a short investigation determined skullduggery from the home team led to the lights being turned off the second time so now they're being told they have to play the game a third time ... but this time in Mickleover."

In a few weeks White had gone from selling plastics to covering a story that had generated a significant amount of interest. He performed flawlessly and began covering games as a freelancer. When a job opened up with BBC Radio 5 Live White wanted to apply, but realized he had failed to get tapes of any of the reports he had done.

Somewhat chagrined he went to the station on a Saturday afternoon and explained that he needed to somehow recreate his reports. The guy who helped him was a young chap named Ross Fletcher. Those tapes got him the job, and White and Fletcher became friends. (Their friendship would impact Seattle soccer fans years later.)

White had great success at the BBC covering all sports, including the NFL. He was the network's play-by-play man five times for their coverage of the Super Bowl. It was at the Super Bowl in 2008 that he first met Brian O'Connell, a Seahawks broadcast executive. At his core White was still that 13-year-old boy staring at the Chicago skyline and wondering if he could ever live in the USA. O'Connell told him the new MLS team in Seattle might have opportunities for him and the duo agreed to stay in touch.

"From that moment on," White says, "I followed everything that was going on in Seattle. From the announcement of the franchise by MLS, to the kits, to the crest, to Sigi, to the name all being announced. I followed the whole story all the way through. Then it transpired that Kevin had been given the job, which was a smart move on their part. I'd researched the history and I knew that the Sonics were gone and that Kevin was beloved in Seattle and it seemed to me that it was a very smart move."

When Calabro accepted the Sounders offer in the summer of 2008 it was with the understanding that he wanted to occasionally be able to miss MLS games if he was hired to do an NBA game. He also had a vacation scheduled for the summer of 2009, which would cause him to miss a game. The team would need a back-up announcer. O'Connell reached out to White and invited him to Seattle to do a mock broadcast of the Sounders opening night game so the team could audition him.

So on opening night while Calabro was originating a broadcast for Seattle, White was standing in the next booth over (with SPU coaching legend Cliff McCrath as his analyst) doing a mock/audition broadcast to be Calabro's pinch-hitter.

For White that first trip to Seattle sealed the deal. He had been impressed that the team had treated him so well considering he was only here on an audition. "They put me up at a very nice hotel," he remembers. "I knew they meant business."

AFTER THE GAME, WHITE made the rounds and met Tod Leiwcke, Gary Wright, Drew Carey, and Kasey Keller, among others. The entire experience left him happily spinning in a swirling eddy of his own thoughts.

"I came away from that night and my whole outlook on my career had changed," White says. "My outlook on the next 10 years of my life had changed. I remember sitting at the bar at the hotel after the game with a glass of wine. From that moment I wanted to be the voice of the Seattle Sounders. I was obsessing about it. This was going to be my future; I really genuinely at that moment believed it."

White also met Calabro that night after the game. Calabro recalls with a laugh thinking to himself "why don't they just hire this guy?"

They would do that after the first season as Calabro transitioned back to the NBA. White became an instant fan favorite who served as a conduit between the young team and its growing fan base. He combined a lifelong love and knowledge of the game with an honestly acquired understanding and appreciation for American culture and wrapped it all up in a delightful and easy-to-listen-to English accent.

White began appearing on KJR Radio each week, ostensibly to discuss soccer. The conversation often evolved (devolved?) into music, pop culture, and the quirky differences in the ways Brits and Americans looked at things. He referred to July 4th as "Tactical Retreat Day" and laughed at the fact that he was being compensated for his time with gift certificates to a bar, which allowed him to actually drink his KJR paycheck.

Seattle fans loved him. His Twitter account grew by huge numbers on a weekly basis. He would ask his followers for restaurant and bar recommendations and often laid his soccer soul bare with pointed commentary about his beloved Leicester City FC. His soccer commentary during games was as colorful as Calabro's basketball calls. He once described Fredy Montero's position on a game winner in stoppage time as "loitering with intent by the far post." Michael Fucito didn't just score an extra-time game winner versus Kansas City he "thrashed a rifle shot into the net." Kasey Keller didn't just make saves; he "smothered the danger."

"His arrival pushed things to a whole new level," says Leiweke, "Because fans were now ready to learn some of the subtleties of the game. He called such a beautiful game. I remember getting chills listening to him. I wondered if having a guy with a British clip would work, but the fact is Arlo knew how to call a brilliant game. He was as beautiful in soccer as Kevin was in the NBA."

If there was a problem with White it was that he was too good. After his second season he was snapped up by NBC to be the network's primary MLS announcer and to handle coverage of the sport at the 2012 London Olympic Games. When he first realized that the NBC job was likely his, White thought of the guy who had been helpful to him on that Saturday afternoon years ago in England, and who had become a close friend.

"Whenever he was back we'd talk for a couple of hours down at our local pub and he would inspire me about what MLS had to offer," Fletcher said. "Before Arlo came to the US, I didn't have much of an interest, but then it was like 'what's this all about? Why not get a slice of this pie?' I thought if I could get the chance to be there, it would be great."

Fletcher spent a month in Vancouver covering the 2010 Winter Olympic Games and began exploring the possibilities of working with the expansion Whitecaps, who were slated to join MLS in 2011. But Fletcher was still available when White first informed him via email that the job in Seattle was about to open up. "I know you're keen on MLS," White wrote. "Would you mind if I put your name forward to the Sounders?"

Mind? Fletcher jumped at the opportunity and his hiring allowed the Sounders to continue a British connection in their broadcast. "Having discussions with the club and with Arlo, I was really confident that it would be a success. This wasn't a shot in the dark. I had quite a bit of knowledge about what I was getting myself into."

Meanwhile White went on to get himself into something that would bring his story full circle. In the spring of 2013 NBC obtained the American TV rights for the Premier League in a deal that would allow the Peacock and various subsidiary networks to show every game played in the league on American TV. Their choice as lead announcer was obvious and with the acceptance of the offer White and his family would move home to England.

His last trip to Seattle for MLS announcing duties came in early June of 2013. Several dozen Sounders employees and players attended a farewell party for him at Kasey Keller's home. During his stint as a national announcer for MLS he had done his professional best to keep his love of the Sounders in check. A friend pointed out to him "with your return to England, that will no longer be necessary."

White smiled, officially a Sounder 'til he dies.

CHAPTER FIFTEEN

MARCH 19, 2009
SEATTLE WASHINGTON

♪

"Nothing's going to stop us today. We are turned on and it's go time."

T he last day of winter in 2009 was a cool, gray, drizzly day — while not exactly beautiful, it fell squarely into the "we'll take it" category for Seattle residents weary of dealing with a Mother Nature who spent much of the season acting as if she had a vendetta against the city.

Seattle had ground to halt in December when back-to-back heavy, wet snowstorms were followed by freezing rain, windstorms, and then record rainfall in January that caused massive flooding. So while temperatures in the mid-40s with constant mist did not make for a perfect opening night for MLS in Seattle, the fact that it wasn't snowing, flooding, or hang-on-to-your-hat windy could be viewed as a victory.

Sportstalk radio that day was dominated with action and analysis of the first day of the NCAA basketball tournament, and thousands of fans made the journey to Portland, where both the University of Washington and Gonzaga were playing (and winning) first-round games.

The forecast in Seattle was still bright for the Sounders. The players, staff, and fans all knew that 30,000 fans were expected for the team's first-ever MLS game. But like any forecast, it's one thing to read it on a piece of paper. It's impossible to know what it's going to be like until you actually experience it.

Taylor Graham got an early indication that things were going to be different when he stopped for lunch at a sandwich shop, and he suddenly realized the guy in front of him was wearing a Sounders FC jersey. His pulse quickened a bit. He had enjoyed his time with the USL Sounders but didn't recall seeing fans wearing jerseys around town. He idly turned around to check out the line behind him and saw another Sounders FC kit on the person directly behind him. Graham was floored.

"I asked them if they were going to the game that night and they both said yes," Graham says. The trio talked soccer and Sounders while waiting for the line to move. Neither guy recognized Graham, who was struck by the level of excitement the conversation generated. "We hadn't played a game yet, but they both had already bought in and loved it."

Four blocks from the stadium and a few hours before kickoff Fuel was already packed with Sounders fans and members of the Emerald City Supporters. Mike Morris had two thoughts as he scrambled to keep up with a crowd ready for a little pregame fortification: "I thought it felt like a huge Seahawks playoff game. Absolutely packed with a line out the door. And I remember thinking 'Is this just for opening day, or will it always be like this?'" Morris admits he thought he was looking at the anomaly of an opening night crowd. "I remember thinking it would wear off."

Adrian Hanauer spent most of the afternoon of March 19 in a constant battle with himself to stay calm. "I remember the nerves," he says. "Massive nerves." Hanauer says what most helped soothe his jangled insides was the sight of fans arriving.

He says that even years later he typically will find himself wondering on game night if anyone is going to come. "I had a sense of relief when people started showing up at the stadium."

Tod Leiweke remembers feeling "fear in my belly." He had been the one who had convinced Paul Allen, Joe Roth, and Adrian Hanauer that this was a grand idea that couldn't possibly fail. Now, as kickoff approached he wondered and worried about everything a CEO wonders and worries about from game presentation, to the concessions, to whether or not the men's and women's rooms were clean. He also had a nervous owner on his hands.

"It was magical," Roth says. "But it was frightening, too, because it was the first time we'd see what we actually had."

KASEY KELLER WAS UPTIGHT, TOO. "I was massively nervous. Part of it was coming home. It was the expectation on this franchise and I wanted it to be successful from the start. I just wanted the sport to work here. I felt we had a good grasp within the mainstream media in Seattle and I wanted that to continue. I wanted people to like it because I was coming back for the long haul. I wasn't coming back to move somewhere else. So my view was to get this thing kicked off in the right way."

Unlike Hanauer, Keller could directly impact the game, and he dealt with his nerves by reminding himself that to *not* be nervous before a big match would be unusual. "I've always been a big proponent of good, strong nervous energy. Anyone who tells me they're not nervous for a game … that's absolute bullshit. They're not ready to play and they don't care. If you're going to go out there and have any pride in your own ability you should be nervous."

He adds, "but it was more so than usual."

Chris Henderson, who together with Keller had played in some big games on some big stages was struck by the enormity of it all. "There were so many emotions, primarily the disbelief that this was happening in our hometown. The energy in the stadium was beyond expectations."

Henderson had been in all the meetings where the word "expansion" was verboten. He had played in 317 MLS games and had a healthy respect for the talent in the league. He felt the organization had put together a pretty good team and he is basically an optimist by nature, but admitted having a little doubt. Friends around the league wishing him luck and meaning well cautioned him to lower expectations.

"People kept saying to me that we'd be lucky to win or draw half our games," he says. "I would smile at them and think to myself 'I'm not going to have a job if that's the case.'"

Hanauer continued to calm himself as he watched fans file into the stadium. As they did, the teams left the pitch after warm-ups while several pregame ceremonies took place.

The Seattle soccer community presented Fred Mendoza with a crystal soccer ball. Any lingering hard feelings over Mendoza's decision years earlier to endorse turf over grass in the stadium were set aside. It was Mendoza, after all, who persistently reminded anyone who would listen that the election to build the stadium had passed because of soccer fans and they had been promised a team for their effort. It had taken a lot longer than anyone thought, but on this night the promise would be fulfilled. The ball presented to Mendoza was inscribed "*to Fred Mendoza. Keeper of promises and maker of dreams.*"

Also honored before the game was the man who had finally made Mendoza's dream a reality, MLS Commissioner Don Garber, who was presented with the first-ever Sounders Golden Scarf by then-Washington Governor Chris Gregoire.

Thankfully, the pregame festivities did *not* include the release of several dozen white doves, a plan that had been called off after a trial run with the birds had gone somewhat awry. A week earlier the Sounders had what amounted to a dress rehearsal before their final exhibition game against Colorado. With the stadium closed to the public, MLS and ESPN officials could see how it looked and sounded on TV, and stadium and game officials could do a dry runthrough of their jobs without the pressure of people in the stands.

The Sounders also decided to test out some of the festivities planned for opening night; one of which would be directly borrowed from something done before NFL games in the stadium.

A few years earlier Leiweke had hit on the idea of having a giant hawk come swooping out of the team tunnel just before the Seahawks come onto the field for their games. The bird's flight lasts less than 10 seconds, but the moment is undeniably cool for fans and helps add to the excitement before kickoff. Leiweke wanted something similar for the Sounders and that meant more work for John Rizzardini.

"Tod has these great ideas and then I've got to go make them work," he says in a tone bordering on exasperation. "The hawk that flies out of the Seahawks tunnel before games was Tod's idea but became my project. It took me two years to get that one done."

The idea they settled on for the Sounders was to have a flock of white doves come out of the tunnel just ahead of the team's arrival on the pitch. The feeling was that the dove was a symbol of peace, and that soccer is the world's game, so by doing this before game the Sounders would be promoting the nice thought of peace on Earth. The team found a guy in the area who owned white homing doves that could be used for every game, because after they were released they would find their way home.

The dress rehearsal was set to include a trial run with the doves. Although there were no fans allowed in the stadium, there were a few hundred people on the pitch. A kid's game was planned as part of the opening night festivities and leaving nothing to chance the Sounders had invited the two teams down for the dress rehearsal. So as a couple youth soccer teams cheered on by their families had a nice little kick around, Rizzardini climbed up into the stands to get a feel for how the spectacle of several dozen doves being released would look. He gave a signal and the doves were released from their cage. At this point Kasey Keller picks up the narrative.

"They release the birds," Keller says, "and they're flying out of the tunnel. Now, there are a couple of hawks that live up in the rafters of the stadium. These doves get about 30 yards off the surface and the two hawks come bombing down at them. A hawk hits one of them; another one gets away and goes ripping back the other way towards the south end and smashes into the window of a suite. It was like Bam! Bam! Bam!"

Rizzardini was horrified. "Remember," he says with an embarrassed laugh, "There's a youth game going on between kids and their families are watching from the sidelines. The one dove flies right into a suite window and goes down. The hawk comes around and sees the dove flat on the ground. It's still alive but the hawk picks it up and starts flying around with the bird in his talons. He was kind of like 'Look what I have!' I could hear the screams of all these parents and kids saying 'Oh my God!' The hawk finally drops it right near where I was. I ran over and it was dead."

Leiweke wasn't at the stadium. When his phone rang and he saw who it was he expected to hear a glowing report. Instead Rizzardini give him the painful blow-by-blow description of the fiasco that had just played out. "Imagine," Rizzardini remembers telling Leiweke, "If this had happened in front of 32,000 people."

Keller says he thinks the dove release should have remained a staple of Sounders pregame. "They could have painted the birds different colors and let people bet which one would survive."

Rizzardini and Leiweke thought otherwise. "That," Rizzardini concludes with a laugh, "Is how the Golden Scarf was born."

OPENING NIGHT CEREMONIES concluded, the teams returned to the pitch (without the accompaniment of doves) and were greeted with a thunderous ovation. "We walked out and there was a deafening roar," says Zach Scott. "It was surreal. To go from 2,000 people at USL games to that; I was shell-shocked."

Like Scott, Roger Levesque was a veteran of the USL days. He always appreciated the loyalty of those crowds, but says of MLS opening night, "Walking out of the tunnel, I was in awe. My entire body was vibrating with energy."

"It equaled the feeling I had in China in 2008," says Patrick Ianni who represented the USA at the 2008 Olympic Games. "My surprise and awe factor was like it was at the Opening Ceremonies. It really set the tone. It blew me out of the water. It blew every one of us out of the water."

Up in the press box, Kevin Calabro drew an Olympics comparison as well. "It was fantastic," he says. "It was one of the most memorable things. It reminded me of the opening ceremonies at the Sydney Olympic Games. It had the same feel. It felt like you were a part of great sports history. The reception of the crowd ... large, loud, it was apparent right away that this was going to be very special."

Calabro also thought about the magnitude of the evening in the context of a very difficult year in Seattle sports. "The Sonics were gone, the Mariners were horrible, and the Huskies were winless, and within the framework of all that you see *this* going on. It was obvious to me they were mining some gold here."

In November of the previous year Brad Evans played a key role in helping Columbus to the MLS title. Now, four months later, he was nearly overwhelmed as he came out of the tunnel to start his first game in Seattle.

"I'd never had chills or wanted to cry walking out on the field before. I almost did. I had no idea what we were getting into. We went out early and saw some rumblings in the crowd. Then we go back in, come out and all of a sudden there's 30,000 people there. They're all standing and cheering. None of us had ever experienced anything like that."

Successful coaches become that way due at least in part to an uncanny ability to plan for and anticipate every possible variable around a game. But Sigi Schmid admits all the planning he did for what opening night might be like was for naught. "You anticipated it because of everything you were hearing," he says. "You sort of expected it to be big, but when it happened it still seemed so unexpected. My dad was there and my wife told me he was in tears during the National Anthem. And he's not an emotional guy. That left an impression."

Fritz Schmid wasn't the only member of his family having trouble with his emotions. His son thought back on the night three-and-a-half years earlier when he had first met Hanauer, the night Schmid told Hanauer to remember him when his dream of an MLS team came true. "I thought a lot about Adrian and how he must be feeling because I knew how hard he had worked to get professional soccer in the city. I had tears in my eyes when we walked out. There was all that expectation and to actually see it as a reality … you hoped for it, and you thought it was going to happen, but until you saw it you weren't 100 percent sure."

Schmid's pregame message to players that night had been fairly simple. "He had a lot of confidence in the team," Graham says. "He told us to have fun, to reward the fans for the support, and to reward ourselves for all the hard work we've done to get here."

Local soccer writer Dave Clark took a long look around the stadium. Clark had been a passionate advocate for the sport for years. He was one of the guys likely to be found with a pint in his hand in the early morning hours watching a big match at The George and Dragon. Now, after years of watching the Sounders toil away on the minor league fringe of the Seattle sports scene he tried to soak in what he saw.

"I stood slack-jawed and thought 'these are people like me,'" Clark says. "Finally. I had been used to being the soccer dork. Now I was sharing soccer dorkdom with 30,000 other people."

Just before kickoff Joe Roth turned to Leiweke. "This is the real thing," Roth said. "We could get blown out 5-nothing after all this great hype and build up. We've never played. Maybe we'll never score a goal. I'm petrified."

KICKOFF NOT ONLY elicited a roar from the crowd but also brought into focus a fact that had been easy to overlook (and fed into Roth's nervousness) in all the pregame excitement: The MLS runners-up from 2008, the New York Red Bulls, were the opening night opponents. Like any good veteran visiting team, they were feeding off the energy of the crowd and, being the better team, figured to pretty quickly bring the Sounders FC balloon right back down to Earth.

In the third minute the Red Bulls and veteran midfielder Sinisa Ubiparipovic got their first taste of the Sounders being more than just an opening night expansion team pushover, courtesy of Evans.

"Ubiparipovic took a heavy touch. I remember coming through and I was like 'fuck it' — and I smashed him right through his foot. I got the ball first. I cleared it all the way through. He went down holding his ankle and I was just so amped and pumped up. I couldn't hear the crowd.

"There was just something inside that made me feel like nothing's going to stop us today. We are turned on and it's go time!"

It went from go time to goal time eight minutes later. At the 10:58 mark of the first half the Sounders past connected with their future. Sebastien LeToux, who had scored 24 goals in two years with the USL Sounders, played a ball out of traffic in front of the net. Fredy Montero was to his right and completely unmarked. Montero actually waved at LeToux who with a quick punch of his right foot delivered a pass that Montero drilled just to the left of defender Kevin Goldthwaite and just to the right of goalkeeper Danny Cepero.

(In the press box Sounders website writer Matt Gaschk noted that the goal came in the 11th minute. Every other media account of the goal listed it as being scored in the 12th minute. Without question the goal hit the back of the net at the 10:58 mark and thus Gaschk was correct. He got all the validation he needed for his original notation in 2013 when the ECS began singing *"Roll on, Colombia"* in the 11th minute of games instead of the 12th.)

"I remember the noise that greeted Fredy Montero's first goal," says Arlo White. "That guttural roar. I had no idea the crowd would be that big, that fervent, that passionate, that loud, that noisy, and that colorful."

It wasn't just the crowd. "There's a picture of the bench after Fredy's goal," says assistant coach Tom Dutra, "And you would have thought we'd just won the World Cup."

Aaron Reed was standing in the middle of the deliriously happy Emerald City Supporters section where Montero's goal had triggered a huge celebration. Amid the lovely drunken chaos he remembers having a somewhat sobering realization.

"I thought, 'Now it's real, now we're here, and now we've got to win this game.' It was one thing to be there and it was another thing to be ahead. New York was one of the top teams in the league, we were just supposed to show up and suddenly it was like 'Man! We might beat these guys.'"

Upstairs in the owner's box Roth was experiencing a mixture of pleasure and pain. He was thrilled with Montero's goal, but had subsequently been on the receiving end of wicked high five from Leiweke. "I thought I had a broken hand," Roth says.

About ten minutes later ESPN commentators JP Dellacamera and John Harkes began a conversation about team co-owner Drew Carey's idea that allowed for a vote on whether Hanauer could keep his job as GM. As the conversation continued Evans took a pass from Montero and blasted the ball into the net to double the Sounders margin. "They're not going to fire him now," Harkes said as the crowd again exploded and the broadcast cut to shot of a beaming Carey holding a scarf above his head.

"I couldn't believe it." Carey says. "I was in shock. It was like going through a rip in space time, where everything was turned around. Seeing soccer stuff in this famous football stadium. The place is packed. People are screaming for soccer. Everything was just crazy."

With a two-goal lead Seattle was in position to dominate the match. Part of the reason they were able to do so was the effort turned in by defender Jhon Kennedy Hurtado that was noteworthy for both its thoroughness and against whom it came.

"I was marking Juan Pablo Angel, who is a legend in Colombia," says Hurtado, who was nine years old when Angel began his career as a prolific goal scorer at Colombian powerhouse Atletico Nacional. "For me to be marking him in that game and in that environment was a big deal."

Hurtado says that in the moment he was able to set aside both Angel's legend and their shared heritage. "It was funny, during the game it didn't mean anything that he was Colombian. He was just another forward. I only worried about winning the duels within the match."

As the half went on Rizzardini made his way to a perch on the stadium's unoccupied third deck. Eighteen months of meeting, planning, and hoping were summed up in front of him. He stood alone in the upper part of the stadium and allowed himself to be satisfied and amazed.

"It was one of the finer moments of my career. To start this from scratch and determine what we wanted to be. We discussed everything. What does it sound like? What does it look like? What food are we selling? Who's there? So opening day, it all feels pretty good, but I still didn't know what was going to happen. I remember walking out onto the deck on the third level and just looking out at the supporters groups chanting and everyone else standing and there's all this pageantry. It's rare in any business to plan something out, walk in, and have it actually happen."

At halftime Rizzardini made his way to Leiweke's suite. "We made eye contact and had the same reaction," he says. "We both had a look of 'what the heck have we done?' It was a good feeling. It was a great moment."

By the time the second half started, Kasey Keller's pregame nerves (which had been nagging at him for months) were gone. "I wasn't having to make a lot of saves and that's when I knew we were going to be all right. I knew we were going to able to compete. There was nothing there that scared me. I could tell right then we were going to be able to compete in this league."

Steve Zakuani checked into his first-ever MLS game in the 60th minute. "What I remember," he says, "is that you couldn't hear the guy five yards from you. It was that loud. It was something unseen to that point in this country."

Keller was a little more active in the second half particularly during a flurry of activity around the 69th minute. In the 71st minute he punched a shot over the goal post and then barked instructions to his teammates. Four minutes later Montero stole the ball and was able to go one-on-one with Cepero before putting the finishing touch on a 3-nil win with his second goal.

A few minutes later Schmid cemented his connection with Seattle's USL fans with a classy nod to history in the game's 90th minute when he subbed in fan favorite Roger Levesque.

"Just before I came on," Levesque says, "Sigi pulled me aside and said 'I wanted to get you on for all your hard work through the years and your dedication to the organization. Good luck.' It was pretty cool. He said he felt like it was something he wanted to do."

At about the same time Hanauer finally allowed himself to relax. "The clock hit 90 and we're ahead 3-nothing and I know we're going to win. I thought about my father (Jerry Hanauer passed away a few months before the opener) and my childhood and the original Sounders. It was such a moment."

SHORTLY AFTER THE GAME ENDED Hanauer and Schmid met on the field. "Sigi found me and gave me a giant hug and whispered in my ear 'this is all because of you. I'm here because of you. None of this could have happened without everything you've put into this game and this city. Be really proud.'"

Hanauer then lost a battle with his own emotions as tears welled up in his eyes.

Leiweke, too, was emotional. Within weeks of his arrival to fix a broken NFL team in 2003 both Hanauer and Mendoza had cornered him about fulfilling the promise made to fans to bring soccer to Seattle. It had taken almost six years, but Leiweke had stayed true to his word and the fans, when the sport finally arrived, had delivered the goods on a memorable opening night.

"I remember having tears in my eyes," says Leiweke, who in the weeks leading up to the opener continually asked everyone if they really thought the crowd was going to be that big. "I remember vowing that I'll never count the fans out again. The bond that pulled everyone together was a desire to be a little bit different and make a statement to the rest of the world; it was an amazing feeling."

Angel approached Hurtado at the game's conclusion. The Colombian legend congratulated his young nemesis. "He wished me luck on my adventure in MLS and the United States," Hurtado says.

"I can still picture the look on Sigi's face when he came into the locker room," says Zach Scott, who played the entire match a little over a week after learning he had made the team. "He was so content with our performance."

Everyone involved remembers a very happy locker room scene after the game but nothing over the top. It was a great night and a great win, but it was, after all, the first game of a long season.

White left the building that night feeling like he was back home in England. "I remember it felt like a genuinely authentic soccer town. It was so brilliantly choreographed. It was better in some respects than a lot of atmospheres in Europe. That atmosphere and the experience on opening night would not have been out of place in any other league in the world."

Ezra Hendrickson spent 14 years as a professional player, 12 of them in MLS before joining Schmid's staff as an assistant. He had played in the all of the biggest markets MLS has to offer: New York, Los Angeles, DC, and Dallas. He says his first night as a coach was among the most memorable of his life.

"I had never witnessed anything like it. I remember walking off the pitch and thinking to myself, 'Wow. Maybe soccer has finally arrived in America.'"

Dutra didn't have quite the visionary attitude about the win as his fellow assistant. He preferred to think of the night more locally than globally. "I remember telling (his wife) Molli," he says laughing, "That if we could just win 5 or 6 games it might be a good year."

CHAPTER SIXTEEN

SUMMER 2013
SEATTLE, WASHINGTON

℘

"We talked as if we weren't an expansion team.
We didn't want that in the vernacular."

The Sounders won the six games Tom Dutra thought they needed for a successful first year, and they did it before the halfway point of the season. Any discussion on how and why the launch of the Sounders ended up working so well has to start with the very simple point that they were *good*.

"To this day, I don't know what would have happened if they had come out like an expansion team," says Aaron Reed of the Emerald City Supporters. "If they'd come out and gotten drilled in that first game ... which they should have by all accounts. The Red Bulls were coming off an appearance in MLS Cup and they were one of the best teams in the league. If they'd shown up and lost 4-to-1 no one would have been surprised. But what would have happened to attendance?"

That will always remain a question unanswered. Kasey Keller started the 2009 season by guarding the Sounders goal like a man who acted as if a shot on goal was an affront to his dignity and a threat to his manhood. Keller set an MLS record by playing the first 457 minutes of the season without giving up a goal.

He led that first Sounders team to the US Open Cup title and the MLS playoffs. He would repeat each of those accomplishments in 2010 and 2011. His high level of play and the fact that he maintained it for three seasons was one of the great and most pleasant surprises of the Sounders MLS story.

"I'd be lying if I said I thought he'd come in and be the best goal keeper in the league for three years straight," Hanauer says. "I expected the great hands, holding everything, good positional play, and leadership. But there were saves that no 39-year old should be making. And he was making them. It just absolutely blew me away."

Keller also became one of the team's primary ambassadors to the community. He rarely said no to a media request, which was something that Schmid in particular appreciated.

"Because he is such a big name he drew the attention," Schmid says, "Kasey drew all the pressure because he was coming home. That allowed our younger guys to toil in a little innocence and not be noticed, but get the job done."

In retrospect Hanauer says he hopes Keller's front-end salary sacrifice will ultimately be worth it for him in his post-playing career, which was the reason Keller was willing to take the deal. "That would certainly make me a little happier," Hanauer says, making it clear he recognizes that Keller deserved a more lucrative deal. "I don't think anyone realized how important he was going to be during the three years he played. None of us understood the impact he would have."

Keller saved his best for last with a legendary performance against San Jose in the final home game of his professional career. On October 15, 2011, 64,510 fans jammed the stadium to say goodbye to the hometown guy who had proven, Thomas Wolfe be damned, you *can* go home again. In the 65th minute Keller gave those fans what amounted to a going away present. In 12 seconds he managed to stop a barrage of four San Jose shots, the performance immortalized by a sensational call from Arlo White who — without hyperbole — concluded the frantic sequence by exclaiming "This is absolutely astonishing! You will not see better goalkeeping anywhere in the world!"

Obviously, it took a full team to create the success that the Sounders enjoyed in the final three years of Keller's professional career. But he was without question the team's bell cow in those early days.

"He was absolutely perfect for a new franchise," White says. "You need heroes, icons, someone about whom you can say '*he's our guy.*' He was so thorough and professional and at that stage of his career he could have taken the entire stadium and put it on his shoulders and taken them wherever they wanted to go. He was that good at what he did. Kasey represented everything that was great about Seattle and Washington."

Keller got help from Fredy Montero who parlayed his hot opening night start into a team-leading 12 goals along with seven assists in 2009. He stayed for three more seasons with the club and regularly left observers both amateur and seasoned speechless with his spectacular play.

"He has some of the qualities of Carlos Ruiz," says assistant coach Ezra Hendrickson referring to the former MLS MVP who was his teammate with the Galaxy. "When it's around the box and he gets his foot on it, he's going to finish it. He scores the goals where you're sitting on the bench going, 'how the hell did he do that?'"

Montero left the Sounders in 2013 to join a club in Portugal.

Ozzie Alonso ended up playing a huge role in the team's success, not only with his play on the field but with his leadership and a willingness to mentor Montero. "Ozzie from day one was the most influential guy on the team, and they became best buddies," Brian Schmetzer says. "So you've got the ultra-talented guy (Montero) who's scoring goals everywhere and then you've got the heart of the team in Ozzie and they're inseparable. That was the start of something special."

Freddie Ljungberg was good when he played, and although he missed 8 games with a variety of ailments and injuries, he managed to lead the team with nine assists the first year. He seemed to get better as the season wore on and was named MLS player of the month in October and was also named to the league's Best XI team at the end of the season.

"That 2009 second half of the season Ljungberg really turned it on," says Brad Evans. "He carried the team on his back. The next year everything became a battle for him. But that first year he was a special player."

Ljungberg dealt with more physical ailments in 2010 before being traded to Chicago and eventually retiring. His time in Seattle was certainly influenced by his confrontation with the end of his career.

"Once his body started to go," says Dutra, "he began taking out his frustrations on others."

Keller gives credit to the team's management for the thought they gave to putting the initial team together and in hiring the right coach.

"If you're going to have to form a team on a salary cap, you have to have a really good grasp of what players can do a job for you with lower incomes. Your stars, that's no problem. But can you put a squad together of guys who are making MLS money and bring it all together? You need someone who has a good grounding of where everybody is in this league and knowledge of those players."

THAT SOMEBODY FOR THE Sounders was actually three somebodies: Hanauer, Schmid, and Henderson. The top three soccer guys in the organization each brought a different perspective to any discussion involving the on-field product, and those perspectives (and the three men's personalities) combined into a formidable executive team evaluating players.

"One of the great things about the organization," says Hanauer, "is that it's really functional working as a team."

Hanauer's experience and unique title of owner/GM helped foster that attitude. He had less soccer experience than either his head coach or his sporting director, but his successful years running the USL Sounders on a tight budget had given him the ability to spot a diamond in the rough and the understanding of why those guys were important. It also established a discipline in him to attend training and to be more involved than most GMs, something the players noticed.

"When your owner/GM is out there every day at training it makes you feel good and confident," says Evans. "I'm not trying to kill Mark McCullers (the GM at Columbus) but I saw him maybe four times at practice in two years. Adrian also comes to every single game."

Evans says it's not just Hanauer's attendance, but the knowledge derived from that attendance that makes him valuable.

"An owner who's involved and sees what goes on in the locker room and outside on the training field is going to realize when a player is an important piece to the team. What he does on the field, and how he acts in the locker room, and how he interacts with media. That's all huge and it really benefits the players."

Henderson brought a player's eye to the table. He had been the all-time MLS leader in minutes played (most of them for good teams) when he retired after the 2006 season. He had played in five different organizations and developed a philosophy of how a successful team should be put together.

"You need a good balance between guys who hate to lose and guys who love to win. That mix is good," he said. "You need guys whose emotions are all over the place and you need other guys who are calm. I think that balance really works well."

Henderson also knew the unique demands the league placed on players and kept that idea in mind as the team was being built. "You need to have a solid base of proven American players in order to do well in this league," says Zach Scott. "Guys who know the league, how the travel works and how physical it is, and that's exactly what they did."

By the time Schmid arrived in Seattle, his nearly 30 years of experience at UCLA, with various US national teams, and with the Galaxy and the Crew, the $100,000 "allocation fee" the Sounders paid Columbus became the best investment in this story.

"He's done it, he's lived it, he's breathed it," says Ross Fletcher. "He's a walking history book of US Soccer. If anything significant has happened, he's been there. And he's always found a winning recipe wherever he's been. Some people may be just born winners. They have it, it's one of those intangibles you can't put on a stat sheet in any sport."

Matt Gaschk is the lead writer for the team's website and as such spends as much time observing the head coach as anyone. He's come to the conclusion that Schimd's success starts with one very simple thing.

"Anywhere we go in the country he'll run into a player he coached or the high school coach of a player he coached and he remembers those people. That's an underrated quality. Sigi remembers names, why he knows that person, little stories about that person. That takes you a long way in gaining the trust of a player or an assistant coach or ownership."

This trait is confirmed by a story Schmid himself tells. He first met legendary Serbian goalkeeper Milutin Soskic in 1993 when Soskic joined the US Men's team as an assistant coach. Schmid told Soskic that as a kid he had attended a Bundesliga game in which Soskic played. Soskic at first didn't believe the story until Schmid started listing minute details of the match, which had been played nearly three decades earlier.

Kevin Calabro has covered the NBA for nearly three decades and in his one year as the voice of the Sounders recognized traits in Schmid that he had seen in successful pro hoops guys like Pat Riley, Phil Jackson, and Gregg Popovich. "All the good coaches have a great book in their heads about opponent players, opponent coaches, tendencies, conditions, stadiums, fans ... all that stuff that sometimes we don't consider that goes into a game and can affect a game."

Another story Schmid likes to tell illustrates how well he interacted with Hanauer. Early on the Sounders had a player who Schmid wanted to cut because he was convinced the guy couldn't play. Hanauer argued with his head coach that cutting the player would be a mistake because he felt the player still had some value in the league.

A few days later Hanauer was able to work out a trade for the player that netted the Sounders some cash. Eventually the player was cut by his new team, causing Schmid to walk into Hanauer's office and proclaim, "See? We were both right. He had value ... but he can't play."

One of the reasons Schmid wanted to leave Columbus was frustration with the lack of access he had to ownership. To access ownership in Seattle, he merely walked out of his office and into Hanauer's, which was right next door. If Hanauer wasn't in, Henderson was in the next office over.

THE EASE WITH WHICH the top three executives got along helped the team establish what players often cite as a reason for the success of the organization.

"Part of what makes Seattle special to me is that they've created a family atmosphere," says Ozzie Alonso. "It's an environment that allows me to make my life here good both on the field and in the community."

It sounds a tad cliché, and it's a characteristic that every team in every league boasts about. In many cases the idea of creating a "family atmosphere" within a sports team is nothing more than words. The Sounders back up the words with several long-term relationships within their organization that lead to the things most important in a family dynamic: love and trust.

Start with Schmid and Henderson whose relationship goes back almost 25 years. Schmid recruited Henderson to UCLA and helped develop him into national team player. Years later it was Henderson recruiting Schmid to come to Seattle and help start the Sounders franchise.

Schmid has known Keller for almost as long since working with him as part of the national team in 1989. His goalkeeper coach, Tom Dutra went back to high school days with Keller, when, Dutra says, the joke was that Keller had "extra muscles in his butt cheeks to get to some of the saves he made."

Evans played for Schmid and won a championship with him in Columbus. Evans and Patrick Ianni both played for Schmid on the US under-20 team in 2005, and Ianni had first met Schmid as a 7-year old when his brother Tayt played for Schmid at UCLA. Defender Tyrone Marshall and midfielder Peter Vagenas had played for Schmid in Los Angeles.

Taylor Graham had known Schmid since his senior year at Stanford. "The summer before my last year in college, two team-mates and I went and trained with the LA Galaxy. Sigi invited us down for a week. It was 2002 and it was a big deal because they were training at the Rose Bowl. So when I was with New York in 2006 and 2007, whenever we played Columbus I would always say hello and ask him about other Stanford guys. We had a little rapport."

Schmid's staff reflected a family attitude as well since it included his son Kurt. And Ezra Hendrickson spent 10 of his 14 years as a professional playing for Schmid.

Schmid had done business with Hanauer dating to 2002 and had known him since 2005. He had known his top assistant Brian Schmetzer since the day in 2004 when Schmetzer cold-called him in Los Angeles to ask for coaching advice.

Coming from that side of things, Hanauer and Schmetzer went back to 2002 when as one of his first decisions as owner and GM Hanauer hired Schmetzer to coach the Sounders. The duo had long relationships with guys like Graham, Scott, Levesque, and LeToux that further cemented the idea that despite being an expansion team the Sounders were created with a family-style structure already in place.

That's led to a remarkable stability that helped fuel success. Five years into existence the organization had seen minimal turnover. Schmid's staff was the same through 2013 as it was on opening night.

"It's kind of a simple thing that a lot of teams don't follow," says Schmid's son Kurt.

ANOTHER KEY WAS the timing of Seattle's entrance into the league. When the league awarded two franchises (Real Salt Lake and Chivas) in 2004 the fee was $5 million per franchise.

Just three years later the Sounders FC group paid six times that amount, yet Hanauer maintains they got lucky.

"The 30 million we spent in 2007 was better than the 5 million we would have spent in 2004," he says. "I don't think there was enough momentum in the league yet to have made it successful in Seattle. You only get one chance to launch. I think if we had started in 2005 today we'd be sitting with about 8,000 season ticket holders and struggling to get 15,000 people to a game."

Hanauer's reasoning is mainly based on the fact that the Seahawks would not have been involved with the 2004 expansion team. Their involvement in 2007 changed everything about how the team was built.

"Left to my own devices from my USL experience," he says, "if I had bought the MLS team myself in 2004, I would have cranked up a supercharged version of the USL structure, whereas Tod approached it from the perspective of a slightly downsized version of the NFL. From day one Tod said 'we're going to treat this thing like it deserves to be treated, like a top-level professional team in this country.'"

Two things happened to MLS between 2004 and 2007 that validate Hanauer's point that the later expansion while more costly, had more value. First, in 2006, the league reached a seven-year TV deal with ESPN. Then, in early 2007 it was announced that the LA Galaxy had reached a deal with superstar David Beckham. In addition, five teams opened new stadiums between 2004 and when the Sounders first played an MLS game.

The MLS that the Sounders joined in March of 2009 looked very different than it had five years earlier. The 2004 expansion would have, if MLS Commissioner Don Garber had had his way, also included the Sounders building their own stadium.

"In retrospect I am thankful we didn't get the franchise and try to get a stadium built in the suburbs," Hanauer says. "It would have been a disaster. Today if one of those communities handed me a stadium with no investment on our end, I wouldn't take it because I'm such a believer now in the power of a centrally located facility. Clearly the downtown stadium model is what has been successful."

THE SOUNDERS ALSO HAD a legitimate connection with the Seahawks. Leiweke and Wright (among others) coordinated the daily interaction between the established NFL team and its new MLS partner. But the original idea, the idea that the Seahawks would lend their expertise to this venture, had to be approved by Paul Allen. And that was not a given.

It had taken his organization several years to get the Seahawks on the right track after he had purchased them in 1997. During that same time, his other sports property (the NBA's Portland Trailblazers) was going through many similar problems. By 2007 both franchises were doing better top to bottom, and Allen could have very reasonably said, "no thanks" to adding another team to his company, even if it wasn't costing him money. His trust in his executives, particularly Leiweke, was a key step in making the Seahawks involvement in the Sounders work so successfully.

But Allen also wanted to help close the deal for soccer fans, without whose help a new stadium might not have been built in Seattle. Bert Kolde is Allen's longtime business partner and advisor, and has been on the Seahawks Board of Directors since 1997. He was with Allen the day Fred Mendoza proposed getting the soccer community involved in the stadium project.

"It was great to deliver the final step of this vision and promise," Kolde says. "But none of us knew it was going to be as successful as it was. Think about 2008: It was like a nuclear winter economically. It was really a tough time and this franchise opens up to sellouts. I couldn't believe it. I was just blown away. This community really embraced it."

Leiweke's vision to have the team truly involved, not just on the surface, was also big. For years the models for an NFL/MLS cooperative franchise had been in New England — and in that case the whole thing felt like an arranged marriage that hadn't worked

Sigi Schmid noticed the difference in Seattle on his first visit. "When they showed me around the Seahawks offices, you could already see some soccer stuff in there as they were preparing," he says. "It was obvious this isn't the same as the Revolution and the Patriots, where they're distinctly different organizations that happen to have the same owner. These people are involved in it, their energy is good and the philosophy of the club was good. That was a key element."

The Seahawks involvement was as important for what they brought to the table as what they didn't bring. While giving the Sounders a ticketing, marketing, and media backbone they otherwise wouldn't have had, the Seahawks were also willing to loosen their ties a bit when the situation called for it.

"John Rizzardini kept telling us in meetings that we were going to have to be willing to be a little edgy," says Gary Wright.

The NFL strategy on business is pretty rigid and given the success the league has had, that can't be faulted. But rather than force an NFL management style onto soccer, the Seahawks approached the Sounders with a willingness to think differently. There may be no better example of this than a decision made in May of 2010.

Leiweke was standing in a horse barn on a Sunday morning with his daughter Tori at her riding lesson when he got a call from Hanauer. The Sounders had been drilled the day before 4-nil at home by Los Angeles. Hanauer was so irritated by the thoroughness of the ass kicking his team had received that he wanted to take action.

"I hope you're OK with this, because I've already decided to do it," he told Leiweke. Hanauer's plan? Refunds for the 32,000 fans who had attended the match. Not a coupon for a hot dog or a soft drink. *Refunds*.

The piles of waste covering the barnyard floor could accurately sum up Leiweke's initial reaction. But rather than blurt that out, he settled for an equally erudite response.

"Huh?"

Leiweke told Hanauer he wanted to think about the plan for a minute. And then asked Hanauer if he had run the idea by Roth. When Hanauer responded in the affirmative, Leiweke knew the horse, so to speak, was out of the barn.

"I thought things had been crazy, anyway," Leiweke says. "We got so much initial blowback, I heard directly from several other teams — all of whom said it was the stupidest idea they had ever heard."

Leiweke's phone wasn't the only one ringing. Roth says he typically does not have much interaction with other team owners outside of official league business. But when he helped hatch this plan he heard from several of his colleagues all delivering variations of the same three word message: "ARE YOU NUTS?"

Leiweke saw and had to deal with some of the flaws in the plan, but ultimately believed it came to encapsulate who the Sounders were and what made them different.

"It was a knee jerk reaction and it wasn't terribly well thought out, but I loved it because it was this visceral feeling that didn't come from any marketing guy. It came from Adrian. He was proving himself to be such a huge part of the essence of what the Sounders became. He was a thoughtful business guy who really understood the brand."

Hanauer also knew he was playing a big card, but he did so confident in the knowledge that the organization could pull it off ... if only once.

"Success gives you confidence and the ability to take more risks. If you're a healthy business you can afford to take risks. We could have just given everyone a hot dog. We did agree on the idea that every time we get beat badly we can't give people their money back."

The ticket refund is the most dramatic example of another huge reason for the Sounders success. In almost every way they forged interactions with their fans that were different from anything that had been seen in American professional sports.

The Alliance (and Alliance Council) not only gave fans a chance to vote on whether the general manager got to keep his job, but a true voice in a variety of issues relating to how the team is run. Team management got its first taste of how loud their fans' collective voice would be when the fans so thoroughly overwhelmed the ballot box during the "name the team" vote. Rather than dismiss that as an anomaly, they recognized they already had that thing that old teams always strive for, and expansion teams never have: A passionate, engaged, and loyal fan base. They thus empowered them with the ability to weigh in on other decisions.

The decision to work with rather than dismiss the Emerald City Supporters was also one that required a vision that's absent in many pro sports teams. The willingness to really listen to fans also led to the authentic soccer game day atmosphere at Sounders games. The Seahawks, left to their own devices, might have put together a flashier and louder game presentation, but they again listened to the soccer side of the discussion. Soccer fans like their game presentation with lots of ceremony in pregame, but minimal intrusions during the game — sort of the MLS version of a Cubs game at Wrigley Field. Trained to think in the bombastic assault-the-senses world of the NFL, the Seahawks drew back and put together more of a soccer-purists' game-day experience.

"They did the best job at making the games an event, an experience, something people would want to go to," Schmid says.

Part of that was intelligent management of the stadium. Hanauer remembered the bad atmosphere created by thousands of empty seats when the NASL Sounders moved to the Kingdome in 1976. The MLS version of the team paid for tarps to cover unused seats, which served two purposes. The tarps looked better than empty seats, and the team could adjust their stadium capacity from season to season and even game to game when necessary.

ALL OF THIS TAKEN TOGETHER, the good team, the local star, the smart coach, the engaged management, combined to make the team good and the game experience great, which gave the fans the best gift of all.

Validation.

For years, being a soccer fan had been a somewhat lonely proposition. Oh, sure, there were like-minded souls at the so called "soccer" bars, and there were always games being played at area rec fields. But to the masses, people who liked the sport were easy to dismiss. About once a year two teams from overseas, playing something called an "International Friendly" would sell a bunch of tickets, but that was it. Sounders games drew small crowds, and for many Seattle sports fans, soccer could be summed up thusly: "*So what.*"

That changed on opening night. Suddenly there were 30,000, then 35,000, then 40,000 people coming to *every game*. There were fan organizations and alliances to join, and there was pregame and postgame socializing to do where the subject of soccer wasn't laughed at, but embraced.

It was like a neighborhood bar band breaking into the big time. Overnight there was a huge community to whom soccer and its quirky nuances didn't have to be explained. These people, people just like you, *got it.* Almost overnight, the guy at the office stopped laughing at your soccer obsession ... you could laugh at him when he wondered what all the excitement was about.

This huge tribe of fans that suddenly had a place to regularly gather for matches realized that the beautiful game they enjoyed had suddenly become cool. That pent-up emotion came pouring out on opening night and hasn't slowed since.

"Soccer at the top level wasn't in Seattle for so long," Henderson says, alluding to 25 years between the demise of the NASL and the arrival of MLS, "the fans were just waiting and saying 'C'mon! Everyone else is getting these teams, why can't we get one here? Show us some respect and we'll show you guys.' They wanted to show the rest of the country how to cheer and support a team and create an atmosphere."

To hear a lot of longtime Seattle fans tell it, that atmosphere, first evident in the NASL Sounders days, never ceased to exist. Seattle musician Jason Finn (drummer of the Presidents of the United States of America) explains the team's success simply: Soccer is ingrained in the DNA of Seattle. "I wouldn't have predicted any of it, but it was so obvious once it happened. You know, no one ever questions, 'How do you get all those people at Lambeau Field?' They'd be like 'what are you talking about? That's what we DO here!' It was just a matter of providing the outlet."

The entire operation also benefited from the worst story in Seattle sports history; the departure of the NBA Sonics to Oklahoma City in the summer of 2008. Kasey Keller thinks that affected the Sounders in two ways. "The Sonics leaving created two voids," he says. "The void in the fans wanting to find something because they felt slighted. There are enough people who were basketball fans who also had played soccer and they wanted to get behind something. You also have the void in the media. We've just lost something big that we talked and wrote about so let's give MLS a chance. There's no way we would have gotten so much media attention if the Sonics had still been here."

IT'S APPROPRIATE THAT technology had a big role in this story, given Seattle's standing as one of the cities where creating technology advancements is part of the daily routine. The emerging presence of social media and the ability to stay connected no matter where you are allowed for the flow of information quickly from team to fan, fan to fan, and fan to team.

Remember, Hanauer was in France on a business trip when he logged onto a USL Sounders message board and saw the anger building as fans learned the team likely was not going to be named Sounders. From the other side of the world he convinced his fellow executives that a write-in choice had to be placed on the ballot.

That anger was real and was being stoked through fan communication, which would have been much more difficult just a few years earlier.

"The fans are the reason they were called Sounders," says ECS co-president Greg Mockos. "Keith Hodo (another ECS co-president) was really a big part in corralling people to vote Sounders as a write in via the Internet. Honestly, if we hadn't had the Internet and social media, I struggle to envision how MLS would be alive today in Seattle."

Emerging tech and the savviness to use it helped the ECS develop a website that gives them the power to inform and govern their huge membership body. Fans of the sport who for years were used to crumbs of information from mainstream media now could start their own blog or website in a manner of minutes and begin sharing and trading information.

It's difficult to remember that just a few years ago none of these communication devices existed in a form accessible to the masses. The fact that they did by 2009 became a big part of the story of the Sounders FC.

The Sounders also used technology to create a new way of ticketing for their fans. If you preferred to stand during games, there were ticket sections with others who like to stand. Same thing if you'd rather sit. If you were a fan of an overseas team you could be linked with others who shared a passion for your club, but also wanted to support the Sounders.

"That was a collaborative idea," Wright says. "There were a lot of us sitting around discussing that when you go to The George and Dragon to watch a game, the Arsenal guys are all sitting together and the Liverpool guys are all sitting together. We want those guys to be Sounders fans, too. How do you do that? Give them an opportunity to sit together."

Rather than put the onus on fans to organize, the Sounders did it for them through their website, which allowed for the creation of these little communities within the stadium of like-minded fans. Again, technology that just a few years earlier didn't exist.

ROTH OFFERED TWO substantial contributions to the management of the team beyond his financial wherewithal. He had spent his entire adult life in the movie business. He understood that soccer was show business and he brought that attitude to everything the Sounders did.

"He has an expectation of *Alice in Wonderland*," says Keller, "not *Gigli*. He made them both. But he made a lot more *Alice in Wonderlands*. He had no intention of it failing."

Leiweke: "Joe's background was 'We've got a movie, and it's got to open on a certain day, let's go!' He didn't screw around on stuff. He has no time for the dumb details that can trip people up."

The second big thing Roth brought was the perspective granted by his location. The business of making movies requires him to spend most of his time in Hollywood. Yet he and Hanauer talk every day and Hanauer soon realized that the physical distance

Roth had from Seattle and the Sounders often gave him clarity not available to those seeing the picture up close.

"He has the ability to distill down complicated issues and turn them into simple decisions. When you're involved day-to-day, everything starts to look a little gray. It's often not as clear what's right or wrong. I'm able to use him in good counsel that way. Sometimes I'm overcomplicating something and he'll say, 'No, *here's* the clear path.'"

Roth's more dramatic show business style is nicely balanced by Hanauer's conservative business nature. "Adrian studies the game," says Kevin Calabro. "He knows the game and knows how the pieces fit. He's very patient and he keeps his cards close to the vest. He doesn't need the limelight ... he's not that kind of guy."

Roth and Hanauer both admit to having the emotions of ardent fans, but the sense to know that cannot overwhelm their roles as club owners.

"I've been involved in the game for over 50 years," Roth says. "I get frustrated when I see things that should have been done differently, and I find myself saying 'I should be the coach!' Then I say, 'who's kidding who here?'"

Roth showed his passion and his sense of humor to Schmid in May of 2013. The Sounders played back-to-back weekends in Los Angeles, against the Galaxy and then Chivas. Roth had invited a bunch of his friends to the Galaxy match, only to watch in embarrassment as the Sounders lost 4-nil. (Again with the damned Galaxy!)

The next weekend, as he sat in his office preparing to face Chivas, Schmid looked up and saw Roth walking in. Schmid figured his owner might light him up, and braced himself.

"Listen man, this is nothing," Roth said. "I produced *'Gigli,'* and I survived that."

Schmid laughed. "He told us that movie had set people's careers back years but that he had recovered, and so would we."

The Sounders easily defeated Chivas that night.

"It's easy to be a cheerleader in success," Roth says. "The trick to being a good leader, I think, is to be a cheerleader in failure. I know how badly he must have felt."

Hanauer says maintaining a division between the two roles — fan and owner — means "we both have to measure ourselves a little bit in terms of dealing with wins and losses."

But measured only to a degree. "I think that's so important, Calabro says. "Your owners have got to love the game. They've gotta have their emotions invested in it as much as their wallet."

IN THE END, PERHAPS the best explanation as to why this all worked so well is that everyone involved in the launch treated it as if it were a soccer game.

The "beautiful game" is, in the most basic of ways, incredibly simple but also difficult to explain. To the casual fan or the uninitiated, it can end up looking like 22 guys running around chasing, kicking, and blocking a ball. The final score might be 2-nil and much of the stadium will discuss the two guys who scored, plus the goalkeeper who gave up the two goals. Simple.

But like any sport, soccer has a dizzying amount of intricacies and variables to be considered in any match. Wingers might be pushing too far into the center. Midfielders can lose concentration and possession. The team that wins usually does so because everyone involved did their job while working with other players to help them in the effort to do theirs.

What can make that more difficult than other sports is that the game is constantly in motion and formations that were drawn up in perfect symmetry in the meeting room begin instantly shape-shifting at kickoff. The pace and form that the game takes never stops changing until the final whistle. The key to success in soccer is in the recognition of when help is necessary and when it's not in the constantly changing environment.

In that regard soccer is a lot like business, and the success of the Sounders can be attributed largely to the various people involved in recognizing and accenting their strengths while staying out of the way where they weren't needed.

The Seahawks added the muscle and heft of their marketing, ticketing, and management departments, but quickly realized they were dealing with an almost entirely different fan base than football. Crossover on season-ticket sales between Seahawks fans and Sounders fans hovers in single-digit percentages. Early on, the Seahawks executives realized that, and formulated plans to market specifically to soccer fans.

Hanauer's willingness to adjust the way he worked cannot be overstated. From 2002 to 2008 he made or was involved in every key decision of the Sounders organization. Suddenly his dream of getting the team into MLS was upon him, but it required a change in how he thought. From his agreeing to accept Roth as a majority partner to his willingness to let go of things that had been in his charge with the USL Sounders, he recognized what was needed from his changing and emerging role.

"That was a difficult thing for me because in the USL world, everyone had to run in multiple lanes. But once we did this (the deal with the Seahawks) we had great people in every aspect of it. But it was a little tough to let go of all that stuff."

At the same time, Hanauer became an instant and very valuable resource to everyone from the Seahawks organization, trying to bring their knowledge to a new team and a new sport. Taylor Graham retired from playing in 2011 and joined the team's front office as manager of business operations, and has watched Hanauer develop into a valuable in-house consultant.

"Because of his involvement with the USL team, he knows every little piece of the organization," Graham says. "He knows the ticket sales component and the advertising component because he had to do that back in the day. He knows the subtleties of the entire business. It's very rare that you have an owner who can sit down with anybody in the organization and instantly understand a challenge they're facing because he had to do something similar at one point."

Roth, Hanauer, and Schmid also agreed — no, *insisted* — early on to lift their expectations above that of a typical expansion team. One way they did that was to simply not use that phrase. Ever.

"We were cautiously optimistic," says Hanauer. "We talked as if we weren't an expansion team. We didn't want that in the vernacular. At our opening press conference I had said, 'We're not going to be an expansion team — it's not something we have any intention of experiencing.' But the reality is most teams say that and most teams end up being expansion teams."

They all bought in to the ideas brought to the table by Drew Carey, recognizing instantly that this was not just a celebrity with money who wanted a fun hobby, but a passionate advocate of the game and particularly of the fan experience.

They all took advantage of the unique situation presented them by the presence of lifelong sports executive and recently converted soccer fan Gary Wright whose influence continued to be felt over the first few years of the team's existence.

"When I first got here people kept asking 'have you met Gary Wright yet?'" says Ross Fletcher. "I had met him in December (during his job interview) but I had no idea *who* Gary Wright was. Later I remember walking into his office and the memorabilia of soccer from Europe and South America and beyond ... it's almost a cathedral. This is a really switched-on guy who's leading the organization."

Wright also was able to form a valuable executive-level alliance with Hanauer that helped bridge gaps that existed between the Seahawks and Sounders. "It was really nice that when Adrian or I brought up a soccer thing," Wright says, "we weren't just talking in the wind. We had someone to back each other up."

Ultimately the launch of the Sounders into MLS was such a huge success because in Wright's words "everyone respected everyone's expertise."

"It worked so well," Leiweke says, "because everyone stayed in their lane. There's nothing I've ever done that will ever be any greater. There was something good happening every day. When it hit with the force with which it hit, it was the coolest thing any of us had ever been through. It was lovely. It's how life should be."

Wright says, "The whole thing was like a big cosmic boom. Everything came together. Every single thing you would want just kind of happened."

"It's still shocking to me," says Hanauer, "that I'm involved in this thing that's become this massive success."

Maybe, just like so much of soccer, there is no easy explanation.

"For whatever reason it worked," says Brad Evans. "Maybe one day I'll get it. It's obviously a combination of everything. But I know one thing: If I got traded tomorrow, the first thing I'd do is say 'look ... here's what they're doing over *there* and you guys have to up your game.'"

CHAPTER SEVENTEEN

JULY 24, 2013
MOUNT RAINIER NATIONAL PARK

⌐℘

"This can't be only about the sport. There's something greater going on here... some form of people connecting with each other."

F ive years in and the only main character in the Sounders story that had departed Seattle was Leiweke, who left in 2010 to become the CEO of the Tampa Bay Lightning of the NHL. Hockey was Leiweke's first love and his new deal came with a percentage of team ownership.

"Somebody comes to you and says 'You're going to be part owner of a team,' that's pretty cool," he says. "I had grown up playing hockey. Everything they needed in Tampa I felt like I was a perfect fit."

He still returns to the Northwest when his schedule permits, and in July of 2013 that schedule included a trip to the top of

Mount Rainier. Leiweke twice had summited the 14,411-foot sentinel of Puget Sound. He was attempting to make it a third time and would do so on this occasion with his friend Adrian Hanauer.

Climbing "The Mountain" is so alluring because it is so visible and accessible, covered in snow and ice year-round, and requires "only" basic mountaineering skills. Annually, about 10,000 people set out for the summit, but for various reasons (weather, injuries, health issues, etc.) only about half of them reach the top ... and in the past 40 years, 70 climbers have died trying.

In addition to being in great shape, climbers need to carry an uncommon mental focus and stamina. Hanauer had the physical tools to get the job done, but as his trip drew near, his concentration was admittedly at sea level. This endeavor was his second-biggest project of the week.

Eight days before his ascent, he got a phone call from Roth. The Sounders had dropped three of their past four games and had been sputtering for much of the first half of the MLS season. Roth was concerned, not so much about the losses as about an overall feeling he had. He told Hanauer he felt like the organization was perhaps taking things for granted.

"Even though we're getting more and more tickets sold, I started feeling like we were losing our mojo," Roth says. "I just had a feeling. I couldn't prove it to you. It's not my job to prove it to you. It's my job to do something about it."

Hanauer agreed with Roth. "The first five years felt like a startup," he says. "We had that buzz. It was growing. Over time every successful company goes from a startup to something more mature. We talked about infusing that startup dust back into the business."

The explanation for what Roth and Hanauer were both feeling could be boiled down simply: for all their successes there was still one big whale the Sounders were chasing.

"I POINT OUT TO ADRIAN from time to time," Peter McLoughlin says, "Not to forget what the organization has accomplished. We've won three US Open Cups, we lead the league in attendance and TV ratings, and we've made the playoffs every year. That's a remarkable achievement and that doesn't just happen."

The Sounders first season in 2009 was such a massive success that *Street and Smith's Sports Business Journal* and the *Sports Business Daily* honored them as the North American Professional Sports Team of the Year.

They won the Lamar Hunt U.S. Open Cup that year and each of the next two, becoming the first team in 42 years to win the tournament (which is open to all US teams) three years running. In 2010 they beat Columbus for the title in Seattle in front of 31,311, the largest crowd in the tournament's 97-year history. They beat Chicago in the final the next year and drew 35,615.

They not only have led MLS in attendance every year of their existence, they set league attendance records each year. By 2012 they had backed off on the number of international friendly matches they played, having by then hosted the biggest names in the sport — Chelsea, FC Barcelona, Boca Juniors, Celtic, Chivas de Guadalajara, and Manchester United. The matches drew huge crowds and kept Seattle fans in the mix of the international game.

The Sounders stumbled coming out of the gate in 2010 but followed up a lackluster 4-7-3 start with a blazing second half in which they went 10-3-3. Schmid's teams always got better as the season progressed

Keller was named to three MLS All Star teams and to the MLS Best XI team after the 2011 season, joining Freddie Ljungberg (2009) and Ozzie Alonso (2012) as Best XI recipients.

By the end of 2011 they had stacked up plenty of success, but they still had not won in the playoffs (losing in the first round to Houston in 2009, LA in 2010, and Real Salt Lake in 2011). They started 2012 with a risky move, trading Mike Fucito and Lamar Neagle to Montreal in exchange for Eddie Johnson. The trade wasn't popular among all fans, many of whom saw Johnson as not being worth the risk after what could be charitably described as an up-and-down run with various European clubs. But Johnson ignited the Sounders and reignited his own career with an outstanding 2012 season in which he was named an All

Star and MLS Comeback Player of the Year. (The fact that they were able to reacquire Neagle a few months later made the deal that much sweeter for Sounders fans.) Also in 2012 they had to find someone to replace the retired Keller. They did that with a tall Austrian named Michael Gspurning who more than capably filled Keller's massive boots. That 2012 team became the first to enjoy postseason success, defeating Real Salt Lake in the Western Conference semifinals before losing to the Galaxy in the Western Conference championship.

Consistent success on the pitch and at the gate created an atmosphere in which players thrived, and where maintaining and improving your position became a never-ending goal.

"If you're a player and you show up and there's 40,000 people there cheering you on, it's inevitable that you're going to bring your best," says assistant coach Ezra Hendrickson. "You're getting treated like they treat some of the top clubs in Europe, so you want to give your all because you want to be a part of it for as long as you can. Guys are always fighting to get into the 18 and the 11."

Players and agents from around the world were taking notice of the situation in Seattle as well. In pursuit of new talent for the team, Chris Henderson spent huge chunks of time on the road and noticed the Sounders profile changing.

"Each year I go to scouting conferences, and clubs and agents all want to meet with us. They all know who we are. We want to be a global brand, a team that's recognized in our play and our front office globally. Our brand has grown each year."

Henderson says he spent two years working on a deal to bring Obafemi Martins to Seattle early in the 2013 season. Martins had played with Inter Milan in Italy and Newcastle in England, and Henderson says the Nigerian forward and his agents were very aware of the Sounders.

"They said 'we want a deal in MLS. We have emerging markets we're looking at and we think MLS is going to be big.' That wouldn't have happened five years ago. But now they see MLS as the next league. They like the stability and the way it's run."

It all added up to a franchise that had redefined the definition of the traditional timeline of how good an expansion team could expect to be. The Sounders consistently won games, acquired stars, developed stars, and always seemed to be rewriting attendance record books.

And yet...

In July of 2013 the Sounders sat in an unfamiliar place: the bottom half of the Western Conference MLS standings. That position underscored two things that nagged at Roth, Hanauer, and Sounders fans. For all their success they had never won (nor had they even played for) the MLS Cup. And they had never won the MLS Supporter's Shield (awarded to the team with the best regular-season record).

So that lack of mojo that Roth felt and Hanauer understood was rooted in the undeniable bottom line of any business that chooses to hang a big scoreboard up at one end of the stadium: You're judged by winning. Not just games, but championships.

That pursuit was aided by the success they had achieved, the things McLoughlin reminded them about. It was sometimes difficult for Roth and Hanauer to see in the midst of the weekly ups and downs of a season. But it was something that Henderson surely appreciated as he continually scoured leagues around the world for talent.

"Seattle is always a team players and agents know because of our ownership. They see Paul Allen and Joe Roth... that gets us in discussions."

They were all about to have a very big discussion.

FOR YEARS, ROTH AND HANAUER had carried a running conversation about improving the team. Whenever they were talking about ways to get better, Roth would always say the same thing: "We need to get a great American star like Clint Dempsey. How much would he cost?"

Hanauer's response never changed. "Joe, he's not coming. He's a star at Fulham."

Hanauer was correct. In just over six seasons in the Premier League, Dempsey made 184 appearances and scored 50 goals for the Cottagers, and in 2011-12 finished fourth in voting for the title of Footballer of the Year in English football. He rose to such a consistently top-tier level that his name was entered into the continually evolving discussion about who, exactly, was the best American player ever. By 2013 he had become the captain of the US Men's National Team.

He joined Fulham in the spring of 2007 and first came to prominence in August of that year when he cracked the team's lineup after a serious knee injury to Brian McBride.

(As McBride recovered from the injury, he would get a phone call from his friend Kasey Keller, who was in Germany pondering retirement. But you already know that story.)

Roth was undaunted by Hanauer's accurate, realistic, and consistent answer. Time and again he would persist: Let's go get Clint Dempsey. "My idea was to get a great American player, the greatest America has ever produced, who's a top goal scorer in the Premier League. A tough guy who isn't going to take a year or two to adjust."

Sure, wouldn't that be nice?

TWO DAYS AFTER THE "MOJO" conversation, Roth got a call from league commissioner Don Garber. "Of all things, he says to me," Roth relates, "'would you be interested in Clint Dempsey?'"

Roth could have been excused for laughing, but immediately responded, *"Let's go!"*

At the same time, Hanauer received a similar call from MLS executive VP Todd Durbin, and he could scarcely believe what he was hearing. After six and a half seasons in England (the final one with Tottenham) Dempsey wanted to return to America and to the league that had launched his pro career in 2004 with New England.

Dempsey's agent Lyle Yorks had contacted MLS with the news his client was open to a deal that would allow him to return home. Although originally from Texas, Seattle was on the short list of places he would consider, but he would not come easy or cheap. The deal would be for three years and ultimately would land between $30 million and $35 million — right up there with the Beckham deal among the richest in MLS history.

So five days later as Hanauer drove along Washington State Highway 706 (aka, the Road to Paradise) to rendezvous with his fellow Mount Rainier climbers, he was trying to cram in as much business as he could before he lost his cell phone signal. He was on the phone with Yorks trying to hammer out specifics of the deal.

"It was a pretty significant conversation going back and forth," Hanauer says. "We had just gotten through the details we needed to get through, and I lost my cell signal for the next 48 hours."

Everyone involved in the negotiation knew that Hanauer would be unavailable for two days, so it wasn't as if he was jeopardizing the deal by going through with the climb (for which he had been in training for months). Nevertheless....

"As I went up the mountain I knew this thing was brewing and maybe had some hope of coming to fruition, so there was certainly some level of anxiety being out of contact for 48 hours."

His anxiety would be soothed somewhat by the presence of Leiweke, who Hanauer knew he could trust even though the now-hockey exec hadn't been part of the Sounders organization for three years. He looked forward to filling Leiweke in on the details of the proposed deal. But before that happened, Hanauer was given a nice little reminder about how popular the Sounders had become. He got to the mountain town of Ashford and met up with other climbers, including Leiweke, for an orientation class.

"There was a couple in our orientation class from Boise, Idaho, and they were Sounders season ticket holders," Hanauer says. Richard Hernon and Shelley Jacks were thrilled to be alongside a true insider and they peppered Hanauer with questions about the team and any plans the Sounders might have to make a big signing during the current international transfer window.

It's funny to think about the poker player Hanauer maintaining a straight face making small talk with fans about the future of the Sounders and potential big-time signings while the voice inside of him could have screamed, *"WE'RE WORKING ON A 35 MILLION DOLLAR DEAL TO BRING CLINT DEMPSEY TO SEATTLE!"*

Early on the morning of July 25 Hanauer successfully reached the summit of Mount Rainier. Later that day he was able to reconnect with Roth, Yorks, and league officials regarding Dempsey. The deal picked up steam the following week at the MLS All Star game and on Saturday, August 3, Dempsey was in Seattle, a member of Sounders FC. His introduction before the Sounders played Dallas that night elicited a huge ovation from a sold-out Seattle crowd that couldn't quite believe what they were seeing. Five years after they had paid $30 million for the entire franchise, the Sounders were laying a bet of similar proportions on the best American player in the game.

The Sounders were in position to make that offer because going back to the time they met in Denver in 2007 Roth and Hanauer had done so many things right.

Their partnership with the Seahawks had been genuine, shepherded first by Leiweke and then by his replacement Peter McLoughlin. They had listened to their fans. *All* teams claim they listen to their fans. The Sounders *did it.* They had been smart enough to cut Drew Carey into the deal. His ideas about fan empowerment and democracy in sports sounded radical and maybe even corny at first. But they worked.

Going back to the tough deal they made with Keller they had been aggressive with player signings. Some worked (Johnson, Martins) and some didn't (Blaise Nkufo) but there was no argument that they kept trying to make the team better while at the same time maintaining a philosophy of being able to sustain financial success.

"Franchises run the risk of having people involved in key positions who are first and foremost concerned with keeping their jobs," Hanauer says. "That can lead to the wrong balance between today and the future. We want to be a top team consistently year after year. I want to win now and three years and five years from now. We're always looking out at least three years."

Schmid's coaching style meshed perfectly with that kind of philosophy and his steady hand had played no small part in the team's unparalleled on-pitch success for an expansion team. All of it added up to a franchise that consistently won games, was well coached, and continued to draw record crowds — which afforded them the ability to get into the conversation to acquire the player Joe Roth had always wanted. His Hollywood roots allowed him to see clearly what Dempsey could mean to his team.

"If you have a star connected to the right story, you are way ahead of the game. That's exactly what this is."

While money was a huge factor in the deal, there was another key component that influenced Dempsey's decision. In June of 2013 he spent five days in Seattle with the US Men's National Team for a World Cup qualifying match with Panama. In front of a typically wild Seattle crowd, the USA prevailed 2-nil. The crowd at the stadium had impressed Dempsey with their passion and knowledge. But there was something else at work here.

Three nights before the US-Panama game, Dempsey had wandered around downtown Seattle. The Sounders were playing Vancouver that night and a crowd of over 50,000 was expected. Fans milled in and out of bars and restaurants in their rave green Sounders jerseys. Soccer talk filled the air on a warm Seattle night. When the game started, Dempsey was amazed at the number of places he walked by that were showing the match on TV.

"It wasn't just one restaurant or one bar," Dempsey says, "it was multiple bars and restaurants and multiple TVs as you walked down the street. I kept thinking 'Wow … they really love the game here.'"

It was just another night in soccer-mad Seattle. But for Dempsey, it was a stunning revelation of a culture he had never seen in America. After arriving in Seattle once the deal was finalized, he said that night had a huge impact on his decision.

"It reminded me of being in London, to see that type of interest in the game. I would describe it as playing in a city with a

European atmosphere at games, but being able to live in America at the same time."

For a guy who had been living out of the country for a while and was pining to come back it seemed like the perfect fit.

"Being able to come play here after experiencing what it was like to play in that World Cup qualifier was a no brainer because I knew it was a great atmosphere with a lot of passion. To come to an American city with 40,000 fans at the game is incredible. That's not something everybody gets to experience. That's more than when I was playing at Fulham."

So, a franchise that had been built on the fundamental theory that you should listen to your fans, engage them in every way possible, and allow your most passionate supporters to occasionally color outside the lines, now could look at those same fans with gratitude. The culture they created (along with a few million bucks) had helped seal one of the biggest deals in MLS history.

That culture featured an ever-growing base of proud followers who loved the sport, loved the Sounders, and didn't much care anymore if you didn't "get" soccer. Yeah, if you didn't get soccer that was too bad for you: You don't know what you're missing. They were everywhere in their Sounders jerseys; on the streets, in restaurants and bars, even climbing Mount Rainier.

The week after the Dempsey signing Hanauer received an email from his new friends from Boise, who had climbed Mount Rainier with him.

Had we any idea you were thinking about Clint Dempsey, we would not have let you do anything so dangerous as cross the street, much less go climbing. LOL. Nicely done. Congrats on bringing a lot of excitement and fun to Seattle.

— Shelley and Rich

"CLINT DEMPSEY IS THE SUM of all this stuff that happened before," Roth says. "If we were getting 10,000 people a game and losing money I wouldn't even have gotten the phone call. To me Clint is Step Two. You can encapsulate everything that's happened up to now. And I have a feeling that he takes us to the next chapter, whatever that is. It feels like a second opening to me. We're injecting a piece into this that's big enough to suggest that there's another wave of people coming."

Hanauer called it "giving ourselves a little more rocket fuel. This seemed like a really good way to do that. To reinvigorate the fan base and the people who work in the organization and the team itself."

For Roth, the big picture is massive, and not unlike the big screen. "I'm interested in cultural phenomenon," he says. "Every once in a while you think you're just making a movie and it turns out to be this huge success. You don't know that when you're making it. It's the same kind of thing that happened here.

"The right people were involved in the launch, it was a city that was very connected, and then it became much bigger than just a soccer game. It became much more about…you could call THIS a social network. This is not just a Saturday evening phenomenon.

"You can't be in a situation where 18 teams in the league get between 12 and 20,000 people at games and you take a market that's not even a big market and you're getting 40,000. This can't be only about the sport. There's something greater going on here, some form of people connecting with each other. You can't predict that going in, but that's the result of getting things right.

"That's the stuff I love about the job that I do. It doesn't happen very often. When it does, you feel great."

Sounders fans know the feeling.

Extra Time

March 19, 2009
Mercer Island, Washington

℘

"He's big! He's tall! He's a...."

As Kasey Keller crossed Lake Washington and exited the I-90 floating bridge onto Mercer Island he was beginning to process in his mind just exactly what this night had meant to him.

For the better part of eight months he had agonized over what opening night for the Sounders jump into MLS might be like. Soccer players aren't used to waiting around to play games, and the extended layoff between when he signed with Seattle in August of 2008 and the opening game the following March was the longest such period of his career. Given all that time, his mind ceaselessly wandered ... and wondered.

"Everyday I'm thinking, 'What if this doesn't go right?' As a goalkeeper your stress usually starts at the end of training the day before the match. But the stress for that first game really

251

started in August when I signed. I didn't want the naysayers to have a footing. I wanted people to like it."

By his own admission in his first match with the Sounders Keller wasn't particularly busy, which is a good thing for a goal-keeper. The Red Bulls had gotten off just eight shots and only two of those were on goal. As the game ended, there was Keller grinning ear-to-ear, high fiving Zach Scott before grabbing the game ball and gleefully punting it into the stands. The 32,000 fans roared in appreciation, and that roar (as well as Tool) was still ringing in his ears as he drove home.

He thought of all the great games he'd played in England, in Spain, and in Germany. Days and nights representing the US Men's National Team in various tournaments in various cities. His best performances for most of his career had happened on the other side of the world, often out of media reach for the American based soccer fan. Before this night he had never been able to perform in this kind of a setting in front of the people he most cared about.

He had fallen in love with the game during his life and like any other kind of love it was an emotion he wanted to share with the people closest to him. In this case those people were the Seattle soccer community. That was the reason he'd put so much into this night and why the success of this game meant so much to him.

As he made the final turn onto his street Keller smiled remembering the delightfully obscene serenade he'd received from the ECS near the end of the game. "He's big! He's tall! He's a motherfucking wall! Kasey Kellerrrrrr! Kasey Kellerrrrrr!"

THE KIDS WERE ASLEEP by the time he got home, leaving Keller and his wife Kristen some time to visit and reflect on this emotional night and the monumental journey they had taken together. Their odyssey had taken them around the world; a nearly two-decade trip that began when they were full of the kind of youthful naivety that precludes worrying about what happens if things don't work out.

Keller treated himself to a fried egg sandwich and a glass (maybe two) of Lagavulin 16. As the scotch warmed its way through his body he began a series of "what if?" discussions with Kristen.

What if he had retired in August of 2007? What if the offer from Bayern Munich had come through and he had stayed in Germany? What if he had decided he would not accept the Sounders low-ball offer in the summer of 2008? Or what if he had taken the offer but decided to play in Europe for the 2008 season and join the Sounders in the summer of 2009?

They were all moot points now. The most successful soccer player in Washington state history had been deeply involved in perhaps the most important night in Seattle soccer history.

He took another sip of scotch, looked at Kristen and without realizing it spoke for the crowd, the fans, the front office, the soccer community, everyone who had been involved in the long effort to bring MLS to Seattle.

"I couldn't have imagined not being on the field for that."

(end)

ACKNOWLEDGEMENTS

C learly a book like this would not be possible without the cooperation of the Seattle Sounders FC. That they, as an organization, were willing to cooperate with me without exerting any editorial control over the book says a lot about them and means the world to me.

I would specifically like to thank Adrian Hanauer. From the day I sprang this idea on him in October of 2012 through numerous phone, email, and text exchanges he remained available and willing to help.

Gary Wright was also a resource that can only be described as whatever is above and beyond valuable. Thanks to him not only for all the great information and for helping smooth the path along the way.

Speaking of that many thanks also to Suzanne Lavender of the Seahawks and Sounders for cheerfully handling numerous phone calls, numerous emails, and at least one near meltdown.

The next time Jeff Garza says no to one of my requests will be the first. Thanks Jeff. Also thanks to Mike Ferris.

Thanks to Tod and Tara Leiweke for the hospitality and kindness on my Florida visit. And for enduring all 200 laps of the Great American Race with me.

Thanks to all who shared time, history, stories, and beers with me along the way. Specifically thanks to Aaron Reed who was my constant conduit to fans and maintained an enthusiasm for the project that helped me. He also...and there's no delicate way to put this...looks terrific in a blue dress.

Thanks in that same vein to Dave Clark, Jason Finn, Steve Manning, Matt Johnson, Matt Gaschk, and Cliff McCrath for sharing their stories and helping me grasp the history of this team, town, and sport.

Thanks to Rod Mar and Corky Trewin for the great photos. The great cover photo is Rod's work. Thanks also to Laurie Hodges for her photo of Arlo White. Thanks to Grant Wahl for — paraphrasing the late, great, Ronnie Van Zant here — "telling it the way it is. Nothing but true."

Thanks also to Ed Wyatt who convinced me, back in 1993, that it was a big deal to meet a guy named Kasey Keller.

I would thank Don Borst for being all the things a great editor needs to be, but that sounds boring. So I'll thank him instead for being my friend and for among many other things joining Rob and me on the greatest day in Indiana football history. Take that Ducks!

Finally (in the saving the best for last department) thanks to Renee who was, as always, right beside me for every step of the journey.

Made in the USA
Charleston, SC
22 February 2014